LEADING AND MANAGING
PEOPLE IN EDUCATION

Leading and Managing People in Education

Tony Bush
and
David Middlewood

SAGE Publications
London • Thousand Oaks • New Delhi

First published 2005

SAGE Publications Limited
1 Oliver's Yard
55 City Road
London EC1Y 1SP

SAGE Publications Inc
2455 Teller Road
Thousand Oaks, California 91320

SAGE Publications India Pvt Ltd
B-42, Panchsheel Enclave
Post Box 4109
New Delhi 110 017

Library of Congress Control Number: 2004096885

A catalogue record for this book is available from the
British Library

ISBN 0 7619 4407 9
ISBN 0 7619 4408 7 (pbk)

Typeset by Dorwyn Ltd, Wells, Somerset
Printed in Great Britain by T.J. International, Padstow,
Cornwall

Contents

Preface   vii
Notes on Authors   xi

Part I Leading and Managing People: Setting the Scene   1

1 The Context for Leadership and Management in Education   3
2 Leading and Managing People for Performance   16
3 The Importance of Support Staff in Schools and Colleges   31

Part II Key Concepts Underpinning Educational Leadership   45

4 Organisational Cultures   47
5 Organisational Structures and Roles   61
6 Staff Motivation and Job Satisfaction   76
7 Leading and Managing for Equal Opportunities   92
8 Leading and Managing through Teams   107

Part III Leading and Managing Key Processes   123

 9 Staff Recruitment and Selection   125
10 Induction and Retention   141
11 Mentoring and Coaching   157
12 Performance Appraisal and Review   172
13 Staff and Organisational Learning   189

Author index   205
Subject index   209

Preface

This is the second version of this highly successful book. Since it was first published in 1997, there have been many changes in education and, specifically, in the leadership and management of people. These changes include new research and literature, and developments in policy and practice in many countries. This new volume gives much more attention to international research and practice, as educational leadership has become a field of global significance during the past eight years.

People are the most important resource in any organisation. They provide the knowledge, skill and energy which are essential ingredients of success. Even given the contemporary importance of information and communications technology, what differentiates effective and less effective organisations are the quality and commitment of the people employed there. In countries where even basic resources are barely adequate, the opportunities for an effective education may depend even more upon the attitude and commitment of the people in them.

Education provides a unique leadership and management challenge because it is geared to the development of human potential. Schools and colleges should be 'people centred' because children and young people are at the heart of their 'business'. Just as good teachers value the children and students for whom they are responsible, so institutional leaders should value all staff who work in the school or college. Consideration for adults is just as important as care for children if schools are to be genuine learning organisations.

One major change since the previous edition is the increasing, and relentless, focus on performance. This emphasis is reflected in the book, notably in Chapters 2 and 12. Schools in England, for example, are increasingly data driven and are expected to achieve nationally imposed targets in public examinations and tests. In the eyes of the government, and increasingly amongst parents and the media, performance in narrowly defined tests, particularly of literacy and numeracy, is becoming the be-all and end-all of education, to the detriment of other legitimate purposes of schooling such as personal development, pupil and student welfare, and the provision of opportunities for music, drama and sport.

This focus on 'performance' might be to the detriment of the people who work in education and we pose this dilemma in stark form in Chapter 2. The authors' view is that valuing and developing people provides the best prospect of enhanced and sustainable performance because staff who feel recognition from leaders and managers are likely to be motivated to teach and to support to the best of their ability. A sense of belonging provides the best prospect of good performance.

We have stressed the importance of valuing all staff and this has become increasingly important with the Workforce Remodelling programme in England. Roles and role relationships are changing in a significant way as support staff are taking on jobs previously undertaken by teachers. By September 2005, teachers will have 10 per cent of the teaching day safeguarded for planning, preparation and assessment, a vital step forward for English primary teachers, but already the norm in secondary schools. In many other countries, for example China and the Seychelles, there is already significant non-contact time. The growing significance of paraprofessionals in schools and colleges is reflected in the provision of one chapter specifically on support staff as well as by including appropriate issues in many other chapters.

Like the previous edition, this book comprises chapters prepared specifically for this volume and thus includes the most recent research and literature on each theme. The first edition was an edited volume but the chapters in this version have all been prepared by the authors.

The first part of the book, 'Leading and Managing People: Setting the Scene', comprises three overview chapters. The opening chapter, 'The context for leadership and management in education', defines educational leadership and management and distinguishes between these twin concepts. It examines the international trend towards decentralisation in education and notes that this has considerable implications for the leadership and management of people. The chapter assesses the impact of globalisation and the paradoxical parallel emphasis on culture and context. It explores the currently fashionable transformational leadership model and concludes by discussing leadership development in education.

In Chapter 2, 'Leading and managing people for performance', the focus is on defining the purpose of education. Increasingly, external pressures lead to assessing staff performance in terms of public examination results but this both narrows the purpose of education and creates negative stress for teachers and support staff. This chapter examines the nature of performance in education and considers an alternative 'people-centred' approach, involving motivation, professional development, mentoring and empowerment. It concludes that enhanced, and sustainable, performance can be achieved only by harnessing human potential, a key dimension of transformational leadership, rather than simply by using narrowly defined performance indicators.

Chapter 3 considers 'The importance of support staff in schools and colleges'. There has been a marked increase in research and literature on this topic since the first edition of this book, an acknowledgement that the nature of staffing in schools is undergoing radical change. The chapter examines some of this new work and concludes that, whilst restructuring of school staffing is likely to continue, the way support staff are led and managed as people is critical to their job satisfaction and to educational success.

Part II, 'Key Concepts Underpinning Educational Leadership', examines some of the main factors influencing the leadership and management of people. Chapter 4, 'Organisational cultures', explains the contemporary interest in culture and its significance for educational leaders and managers. It distinguishes between national, or societal, culture, which provides a context for school leaders, and organisational culture, which may be susceptible to change. A case study of South African schools illustrates the difficulty of re-establishing a culture of teaching and learning following systemic trauma and the chapter concludes by stressing the importance of attitudinal change to educational success.

In Chapter 5, 'Organisational structures and roles', the focus is on the framework for educational leadership and management. The chapter examines the nature and purpose of structure, links it to the concept of hierarchy and assesses the various ways in which organisational theory portrays structure. The chapter also addresses role theory and its applicability to school and college leadership. A central issue is the extent to which people simply take on roles prescribed by managers or use their specific talents and experience to design and develop their own approach. The chapter concludes by examining the links between structure and roles, and by stressing the need for flexibility in interpreting both concepts.

In Chapter 6, 'Staff motivation and job satisfaction' are seen as key to staff commitment and organisational effectiveness. Job satisfaction is presented as a focus on present conditions whereas motivation enables the person to take a positive attitude to future work. The importance of context, including different cultures, is stressed and leaders need to recognise that factors such as gender, and 'ownership' of innovation, influence these attitudes in individual organisations. The chapter concludes by noting that leaders should also be strongly motivated if they are to influence others.

Chapter 7 focuses on 'Leading and managing for equal opportunities'. It stresses the importance of ensuring equal opportunities in schools and colleges. Several ways of managing this effectively are proposed and the issues within particular contexts and cultures are discussed. The chapter then examines the implications for leaders, looking at ways in which various processes need to be managed so that all employees feel equally valued and, therefore, committed to the organisation.

Chapter 8, 'Leading and managing through teams', explains the rationale for team work and considers the composition of leadership and management teams in several countries. It notes how teamwork can be developed and examines the notion of team learning within a learning organisation. It gives case examples of teamwork in New Zealand and England and notes that, despite the pervasive nature of teams, they do have limitations when applied to education, not least because teaching tends to be a solitary activity.

The final part, 'Managing Key Processes', addresses five central aspects of the leadership and management of people in education. Chapter 9 deals with the essential starting point, 'Leading and managing staff recruitment and selection'. This is an under-researched area in education but much practice in business, for example, has been adapted for schools and colleges. The recognition of fallibility and subjectivity in selectors needs to be acknowledged but the attempt to make the process as objective as possible remains important for leaders for both moral and legal reasons. As the nature of staffing in education is undergoing change in many countries, the need for effective recruitment and selection processes becomes even more important.

Chapter 10, 'Induction and retention', focuses on the stage following appointment, that of staff induction, and on an increasingly important issue for school and college leaders, that of retention. An effective start to an individual's employment is shown to increase the chances of that person remaining longer in the organisation. The chapter stresses that induction is a process not a programme and that socialisation is a key element. In a climate of enhanced staff mobility in some countries, the need to retain part-time and temporary colleagues is equally important, and the chapter also examines how best to support such staff.

In Chapter 11, 'Mentoring and coaching', the focus is on these important processes for supporting and developing staff. It begins by defining these terms and distinguishing between them. It examines mentoring practice in Hong Kong, Singapore, England and Wales, and the USA. The chapter notes the benefits of mentoring, for mentors and the educational system as well as mentees, and it concludes by proposing a model for effective mentoring.

'Performance appraisal and review' is the focus of Chapter 12, building on the performance issue raised in Chapter 2 and including a discussion of the ways in which performance can be appraised. Two dimensions of performance management, professional development and accountability, are explored and schemes which reconcile the two are described. The chapter considers different schemes to manage performance in various countries, for example performance related pay, but concludes that the main factor in successful schemes continues to be the relationship between the appraisee and their leaders and managers, and that mutual trust remains the crucial component of this relationship.

In the final chapter, 'Leading and managing staff and organisational learning', attention is paid to the ways in which schools and colleges focus on their core purpose, learning, through becoming learning organisations. In such contexts, staff as well as students are regarded as learners and the chapter considers how organisational learning can be integrated into leaders' plans for the development of learning. The chapter, and the book, conclude by stressing the need for training for all staff and by encouraging positive attitudes to learning for everyone. The leader's task includes being a role model, by prioritising personal learning. We hope that this book contributes to this objective.

The authors wish to thank Felicity Murray for her work in producing the manuscript and index for this book, and for all her support for their research, publications and teaching during the past 13 years.

Tony Bush and David Middlewood
University of Lincoln
July 2004

Notes on Authors

Tony Bush is Professor of Educational Leadership at the University of Lincoln, United Kingdom and previously held similar posts at the universities of Leicester and Reading. He has also been a visiting professor in China, New Zealand and South Africa. He has written or edited 29 books, including the third edition of *Theories of Educational Leadership and Management* (Sage 2003). His current and recent research includes directing the evaluations of the National College for School Leadership's (NCSL's) 'New Visions: Induction to Headship' pilot programme and the 'Working Together for Success programme'. He also directed the CfBT funded evaluation of education management development and governor training in the Gauteng province of South Africa. He is the editor of the leading international journal, *Educational Management, Administration and Leadership* (*EMAL*).

David Middlewood was until recently Deputy Director of the Centre for Educational Leadership and Management at the University of Leicester and was previously a secondary school headteacher in England. He is now a research associate for the University of Lincoln. He taught in schools in England for more than 20 years. He acts as consultant and link higher education (HE) person for a number of individual schools, some local education authorities (LEAs) and, currently, Networked Communities of Schools.

David has published on teacher appraisal and performance in particular and explored its links with staff development, including *Managing Teacher Appraisal and Performance: A Comparative Approach* (with Carol Cardno) published by Routledge-Falmer (2001), and a chapter on 'Managing appraisal and performance' in *The Principles and Practice of Educational Management* (edited by Bush and Bell) published by Paul Chapman (2002). David has also published books on strategic management, curriculum management, human resource management, and Practitioner Research in Education. He has recently completed and published research on teaching assistants and is currently involved with research on NCSL's programme for new heads, and with Leadership Teams, (with Tony Bush). David has been a visiting Professor in New Zealand and in South Africa where he has published on human resource management and the curriculum, and was the editor of the UK journals *Headship Matters* and *Primary Headship* from 1999–2005.

PART I

Leading and Managing People: Setting the Scene

1

The context for leadership and management in education

Introduction: leadership and management

The first version of this volume, published in 1997, was titled *Managing People in Education*. The addition of 'leadership' to the title of this book illustrates the growing significance of this concept, notably in England, where a National College for School *Leadership* (our emphasis) was opened in November 2000. The inclusion of both terms in the title of this second version signals the authors' recognition of this trend but also their view that effective 'management' is just as important as visionary leadership if educational organisations are to be successful. As Lumby (2001, p.11) notes in respect of English further education, polarisation of leadership and management should be replaced by an androgynous approach, synthesising these two dimensions.

Bolam (1999, p.194) defines educational management as 'an executive function for carrying out agreed policy'. He differentiates management from educational leadership which has 'at its core the responsibility for policy formulation and, where appropriate, organisational transformation' (p.194). Writing from an Indian perspective, Sapre (2002, p.102) states that 'management is a set of activities directed towards efficient and effective utilisation of organisational resources in order to achieve organisational goals'.

Bush (2003) argues that educational management should be centrally concerned with the purpose or aims of education. These purposes or goals provide the crucial sense of direction which should underpin the management of educational institutions. Management is directed at the achievement of certain educational objectives. Unless this link between purpose and management is clear and close, there is a danger of 'managerialism', 'a stress on procedures at the expense of educational purpose and values' (Bush 1999, p.240). The emphasis is on managerial efficiency rather than the aims and purposes of education (Newman and Clarke 1994; Gunter 1997). This appears to have been the case in further education in both England (Elliott and Crossley 1997) and Scotland (McTavish 2003). The latter refers to the 'dominance' of business managerialism and points to the prioritisation of managerial rather than educational concerns at one of his case study colleges in Glasgow.

3

Despite its contemporary importance, there is no agreed definition of the concept of leadership and Yukl (2002, pp.4–5) argues that 'the definition of leadership is arbitrary and very subjective. Some definitions are more useful than others, but there is no "correct" definition'. Three dimensions of leadership may be identified as a basis for developing a working definition:

1 Leadership involves a process of influence 'exerted by one person [or group] over other people [or groups] to structure the activities and relationships in a group or organisation' (Yukl 2002, p.3). Yukl's use of 'person' or 'group' serves to emphasise that leadership may be exercised by teams as well as individuals.
2 Leadership should be grounded in firm personal and professional values. Wasserberg (2000, p.158) claims that 'the primary role of any leader [is] the unification of people around key values'. The emphasis on 'people' shows the central importance of staff and other stakeholders if schools and colleges are to be successful learning environments for children and students.
3 Leadership involves developing and articulating a vision for the organisation. The vision needs to be specific to the school or college, and be embedded in the organisation, if leadership is to be successful. The contemporary importance of this concept is illustrated by the use of the title, 'New Visions', for the programme for new headteachers developed by the National College for School Leadership

Cuban (1988) provides one of the clearest distinctions between leadership and management. He links leadership with change while management is seen as a maintenance activity. He also stresses the importance of both dimensions of organisational activity:

> By leadership, I mean influencing others' actions in achieving desirable ends. Leaders are people who shape the goals, motivations, and actions of others. Frequently they initiate change to reach existing and new goals … Leadership … takes … much ingenuity, energy and skill. (p.xx)

> Managing is maintaining efficiently and effectively current organisational arrangements. While managing well often exhibits leadership skills, the overall function is toward maintenance rather than change. I prize both managing and leading and attach no special value to either since different settings and times call for varied responses. (p.xx)

Leadership and management need to be given equal prominence if schools and colleges are to operate effectively and achieve their objectives. While a clear vision is essential to establish the nature and direction of change, it is equally important to ensure that innovations are implemented efficiently and that the school's residual functions are carried out effectively while certain elements are undergoing change:

> Leading and managing are distinct, but both are important. Organisations which are over managed but under led eventually lose any sense of spirit or purpose. Poorly managed organisations with strong charismatic leaders may

soar temporarily only to crash shortly thereafter. The challenge of modern organisations requires the objective perspective of the manager as well as the flashes of vision and commitment wise leadership provides. (Bolman and Deal 1997, pp.xiii–xiv)

The dichotomy in England is that NCSL is promoting leadership while the government is encouraging a managerial approach through their stress on performance and public accountability (Glatter 1999, Levačić et al. 1999). Distinctive visions may also be difficult to achieve where, as in most countries, governments prescribe a national curriculum and require schools to comply with it. In practice, schools and colleges require both visionary leadership, to the extent that this is possible with a centralised curriculum, and effective management. Briggs's (2003, p.434) study of middle managers in English further education colleges suggests that these two dimensions have a symbiotic relationship and need to be kept in balance.

Decentralisation and self-management

Educational institutions operate within a legislative framework set down by national, provincial or state parliaments. One of the key aspects of such a framework is the degree of decentralisation in the educational system. Highly centralised systems tend to be bureaucratic and to allow little discretion to schools and local communities. Decentralised systems devolve significant powers to subordinate levels. Where such powers are devolved to the institutional level, there is 'self-management'.

Lauglo (1997) links centralisation to bureaucracy and defines it as follows:

Bureaucratic centralism implies concentrating in a central ('top') authority decision-making on a wide range of matters, leaving only tightly programmed routine implementation to lower levels in the organisation ... a ministry could make decisions in considerable detail as to aims and objectives, curricula and teaching materials to be used, prescribed methods, appointments of staff and their job descriptions, admission of students, assessment and certification, finance and budgets, and inspection/evaluations to monitor performance. (Lauglo 1997, pp.3–4)

Leaders operating in such controlled systems experience particular problems in developing a distinctive vision for their schools. When heads and principals are reduced to implementing directives from national, regional or local government, they lack the scope to articulate school goals. They also cannot lead and manage staff effectively because all the major decisions about staff appointments, promotions and development are made by government officials. This approach is evident in China (Bush et al. 1998), the largest educational system in the world, and also in the Seychelles, one of the smallest.

Decentralisation involves a process of reducing the role of central government in planning and providing education. It can take many different forms:

> Decentralisation in education means a shift in the authority distribution away from the central 'top' agency in the hierarchy of authority … Different forms of decentralisation are diverse in their justifications and in what they imply for the distribution of authority. (Lauglo 1997, p.3)

Self-management occurs where decentralisation is to the institutional level, as Caldwell and Spinks (1992, p.4) suggest: 'A self-managing school is a school in a system of education where there has been significant and consistent *decentralisation* to the school level of authority to make decisions related to the allocation of resources'.

Self-managing schools and colleges may be regarded as potentially more efficient and effective but much depends on the nature and quality of internal management if these potential benefits are to be realised. Dellar's (1998) research in 30 secondary schools in Australia, for example, shows that 'site-based' management was most successful where there was a positive school climate and the involvement of staff and stakeholders in decision-making. Certainly, the scope for leading and managing staff effectively is much greater when the major educational decisions are located within schools and colleges, and not reserved for action outside the school.

Globalisation

Educational leadership and management are exercised at institutional level but are also influenced by a range of contextual variables. A significant 'macro' variable is that of globalisation, described by (Bottery 2001, p.202) as 'a central buzzword'. Globalisation has two main dimensions:

- a reduction in the power of the nation state
- movement of this power, primarily to supra-national bodies (Bottery 2001).

Rikowski (2002, p.1)) refers to globalisation as 'essentially capitalist' but Bottery (2001) identifies five different forms:

- political, e.g. the European Union or the United Nations
- managerial, looking for best practice wherever it can be found
- economic, notably through multinational companies
- cultural, for example through film and music
- environmental, notably through global warming and pollution across national boundaries.

In education, globalisation is manifested through national and local implementation of what are essentially international trends. The shift to decentralisation of education, sometimes involving greater autonomy for schools, for example, is widespread, as we noted earlier. The nature of decentralisation varies across national boundaries but the overarching concept has global significance. Similarly, the fast-paced developments in technology affect the nature of teaching and learning, and leadership and management, in many developed countries.

Leadership development is also strongly influenced by globalisation. Bush and Jackson (2002, pp.420–1) refer to 'an international curriculum for leadership preparation' and note that links between leadership quality and school effectiveness have been demonstrated in many parts of the world. The English National College for School Leadership aims to be a world-class centre as its first corporate plan suggests. It plans:

> To ensure that our current and future school leaders develop the skills, the capability and the capacity to lead and transform the school education system into the best in the world. (NCSL 2001, p.2)

This objective is ambitious, and laudable, but it begs the question of how 'best' may be judged. As Glatter and Kydd (2003, p.233) point out, defining 'best practice' is fraught with difficulty and dependent on context. We turn now to address the contexts for educational leadership and management.

Culture and context

As we noted above, many of the major themes of educational leadership and management have global significance. Notions of bureaucracy, autonomy and control, accountability and quality, for example, are evident in many different countries. However, it is vital to be aware of the powerful differences between countries and not to overestimate their similarities. Some of the problems may be the same but their solutions often depend more on local circumstances than on importing ready-made answers from very different contexts. 'It is easy to become over-impressed by apparent similarities between "reforms" in various countries and to neglect deep differences at the level of implementation and practice' (Glatter 2002, p.225).

Some of the differences between educational systems can be attributed to economics. Many developing countries do not have the resources to ensure universal education, even at primary level, or to provide buildings, equipment or staffing of the quality which is taken for granted in the developed world. These countries are caught in a vicious circle. They lack the resources to develop all their children to their full potential. This contributes to a continuing economic weakness because they do not have the skills to compete effectively with fully developed economies. As a result, the tax base is too weak to fund a really effective educational system (Bell and Bush 2002).

Although the economic issues should not be underestimated, the main differences between countries may be cultural. Dimmock and Walker (2002) explain and compare organisational and societal culture:

> Societal cultures differ mostly at the level of basic values, while organisational cultures differ mostly at the level of more superficial practices, as reflected in

the recognition of particular symbols, heroes, and rituals. This allows organisational cultures to be deliberately managed and changed, whereas societal or
national cultures are more enduring and change only gradually over longer
time periods. (p.71)

Cultural differences play an important part in explaining the varied approaches to
apparently similar issues in many different countries. One example relates to attitudes to bureaucracy. As we noted earlier, it is the preferred approach to management in many countries, including very large and complex systems, for example in
China, and smaller states such as the Seychelles. It is also the dominant model in
South America (Newland 1995). In some Western countries, however, it is associated with inefficiency and excessive centralisation. The differences may be
explained by alternative perspectives on the nature of authority with those favour-
ing bureaucracy more willing to defer to those holding positional power than people who feel constrained by it (Bell and Bush 2002).

Differences within countries

It is also unwise to assume that educational problems are the same within countries
let alone between them. In developing countries, there are often considerable differences between urban and rural schools (Bush et al. 1998; Thurlow et al. 2003). In
both developed and developing nations, socio-economic variables inevitably influence the educational context. South Africa, for example, is still coming to terms
with the institutionalised differences in its schools arising from the apartheid era.
Comparing the best schools in the major cities with those in remote rural areas provides as sharp a contrast as the differences between developed and developing
countries (Thurlow et al. 2003).

There are also significant differences amongst schools within developed nations.
Harris (2002) reports on the particular issues faced by the leaders of schools in challenging circumstances in England. She paints a picture of schools with multiple
indicators of difficulty:

- low levels of achievement in public examinations
- high proportions of children eligible for free school meals
- categorised as requiring 'special measures' or being in 'serious weaknesses' by the
  Office for Standards in Education (Ofsted)
- located in urban areas with low socio-economic status.

She conducted research with ten such schools that were showing evidence of school
improvement. Her findings provide valuable evidence about the nature of successful leadership in such schools. The main features of such leadership were:

Vision and values
'An alignment to a shared set of values' (Harris 2002, p.18) and a vision, built

around these core values, that was communicated to staff and students. 'The heads in the study did display *people-centred* leadership in their day-to-day dealings with individuals' (p.18) (present authors' emphasis).

Distributing leadership

Harris points to a shift from autocratic styles of leadership to a greater focus on teams and distributed leadership as the schools improved. 'I think leadership styles have to match the needs of that school at that particular point in time' (head, p.20).

Investing in staff development

These heads invested in staff development as a means of maintaining staff morale and motivation as well as improving their capability. Development included support staff as well as teachers.

Relationships

These heads were perceived to be good at developing and maintaining relationships with staff, students and parents. 'They placed an emphasis on *people not systems* and invited others to lead' (p.22) (present authors' emphasis).

Community-building

These heads emphasised the need to establish the interconnectedness of home, school and community, aware that forces within the community impeded learning. Their leadership involved managing both internal and external environments.

Harris (2002, p.24) concludes that these successful leaders displayed people-centred qualities and skills: 'The context in which people work and learn together is where they construct and refine meaning leading to a shared purpose or set of goals.'

These dimensions of successful leadership could arguably be applied to schools in any situation. The distinguishing feature is the recognition that leaders' approaches have to be tailored to the specific needs of the school and the context in which it operates. A 'one size fits all' approach is unlikely to be effective, as a teacher researched by Harris (2002) suggests: 'The head displays a range of leadership styles really, much depends on the situation or circumstance' (p.20).

Leading and managing people

There is ample evidence that high-quality leadership is vital in achieving successful schools and colleges. The Commonwealth Secretariat (1996), for example, states that ' the head ... plays the most crucial role in ensuring school effectiveness'. Similarly, the National College for School Leadership (2001, p.5) refers to 'the pivotal role of effective leadership in securing high quality provision and high standards'.

Given this widely held assumption that high-quality leadership and management are required to develop and sustain good educational institutions, two further questions arise:

- Which types of leadership are most likely to produce positive outcomes?
- What is the best way to develop successful leaders?

The nature of successful educational leadership

There is convincing evidence that successful leaders focus most strongly on motivating and developing people rather than establishing and maintaining systems
and structures. The latter is important but should always be a second-order priority.
In education, as in many other settings, people are most likely to show commitment if they are valued by those who have responsibility for them. This applies to
teachers just as much as to the children and students. It also applies to the many
support staff who work in schools and colleges. An inclusive approach, involving
all categories of staff, is most likely to produce the teamwork which is also a feature
of successful organisations.

It is an oft-stated axiom that leaders should develop a specific vision for the
school and communicate it to all staff and stakeholders. Less attention is generally
given to the process of vision development. It can be argued that people are more
likely to understand, and to seek to implement, the vision if they have been
involved in its development. If the school is to be democratic, it is inadequate for
the head or principal to enunciate the vision without the participation of others
with a legitimate interest in the outcome.

Begley's (1994) four-level analysis of 'the principal as visionary' shows that the
most sophisticated leaders involve the whole community in developing school
vision. The 'vision derived goals' aspect (one of five used by Begley) illustrates the
approach (see Table 1.1).

Table 1.1 The principal as visionary

Level	Vision derived goals
Basic	Possesses a set of goals derived from Ministry and Board expectations.
Intermediate	Develops school goals consistent with the principal's articulated vision.
Advanced	Works with the teaching staff to develop school goals which reflect their collaborative vision.
Expert	Collaborates with representative members of the school community to develop goals which reflect a collaboratively developed vision statement.

Source: Begley 1994

Table 1.1 shows that 'vision' may operate at different levels. The shift from 'basic'
to 'expert' provides a useful way of categorising the extent to which leaders are able
to develop a distinctive vision, and of the level of involvement of staff and other
stakeholders in the process of developing vision.

Even if leaders involve the school or college community in vision-building, this
does not inevitably lead to effective leadership and management. It is just as important to ensure successful implementation of that vision. A clear sense of purpose is

vital but it requires careful management for it to be achieved. There needs to be a close relationship between vision, goals, activities and school outcomes. Mintzberg (1994) suggests that poor strategic implementation may inhibit the attainment of vision, leading to frustration rather than satisfaction. Even the most inspiring vision, attracting widespread support throughout the school community, will fail to generate improvement if it is not supported by effective management practices.

Transformational leadership

The model most often linked to vision is 'transformational leadership'. Gunter (2001, p.69) says that this is about building a unified common interest between leaders and followers.

Transformational approaches are often contrasted with transactional leadership:

> Transactional leadership is leadership in which relationships with teachers are based upon an exchange for some valued resource. To the teacher, interaction between administrators and teachers is usually episodic, short-lived and limited to the exchange transaction. Transformational leadership is more potent and complex and occurs when one or more teachers engage with others in such a way that administrators and teachers raise one another to higher levels of commitment and dedication, motivation and morality. Through the transforming process, the motives of the leader and follower merge. (Miller and Miller 2001, p.182)

Leithwood (1994) notes that 'building school vision' is a key dimension of leadership but also refers to the need for goals and structures. He reports on seven quantitative studies and concludes that:

> Transformational leadership practices, considered as a composite construct, had significant direct and indirect effects on progress with school-restructuring initiatives and teacher-perceived student outcomes. (p.506)

The transformational model is comprehensive in that it provides a normative approach to school leadership which focuses primarily on the process by which leaders seek to influence school outcomes rather than on the nature or direction of those outcomes. It may also be criticised as being a vehicle for control over teachers and more likely to be accepted by the leader than the led (Chirichello 1999). Allix (2000) goes further and alleges that transformational leadership has the potential to become 'despotic' because of its strong heroic and charismatic features.

The contemporary policy climate within which schools have to operate also raises questions about the validity of the transformational model, and about the possibility of developing a vision specific to the needs and aspirations of the school community. The English system increasingly requires school leaders to adhere to government prescriptions which affect aims, curriculum content and pedagogy, as well as values. There is 'a more centralised, more directed, and more controlled educational system [that] has dramatically reduced the possibility of realising a genuinely transformational education and leadership' (Bottery 2001, p.215).

Webb and Vulliamy (1996, p.313) take a similar view, arguing that 'the current climate ... encourages headteachers to be powerful and, if necessary, manipulative leaders in order to ensure that the policies and practices agreed upon are ones that they can wholeheartedly support and defend'.

Such approaches are questionable and likely to produce negative long-term outcomes. Sustainable success needs a focus on the needs and wishes of students, staff and the community rather than on a vision based on external demands or the head's personal wishes.

Conclusion: developing school leaders

There is considerable international interest in leadership development, evidenced strongly in England by the opening of the National College for School Leadership and by the subsequent proposals for equivalent bodies for further education and for universities. Bush and Jackson's (2002) review of provision in seven developed countries shows that there are diverse approaches to leadership development but policy-makers in all these systems recognise its vital importance. Such major initiatives suggest that this is a national policy issue in many countries, but the purpose of this section is to argue that principals and headteachers also have a role in leadership development.

The increasing range and complexity of leadership and management responsibilities in schools and colleges means that it is no longer possible, if it ever was, for the principal to be the sole leader. Deputy and assistant heads, and middle-level leaders such as heads of department or subject leaders, are increasingly important for effective management in schools (Woods et al. 2004) and colleges (Briggs 2003). This emphasis requires specific and sustained attention to leadership and management development as a central part of the wider staff development agenda.

Developing middle and senior managers has two main advantages. First, it increases the likelihood that they will perform effectively in their present role. Secondly, it provides a cadre of trained people for advancement to more senior posts as they become available. It is a mode of succession planning, a 'grow your own' model of securing a successful future for the school or college.

The development of future leaders may take several forms but it is underpinned by an approach which is 'people' orientated. It begins with the needs of the individual and might involve a formal staff development or appraisal process. It should provide a means of meeting the aspirations of the person while also anticipating the needs of the institution. When it works well, the requirements of the individual and the organisation are harmonised to promote learning for all who work or study in the school or college.

References

Allix, N.M. (2000), 'Transformational leadership: Democratic or despotic?', *Educational Management and Administration*, 28 (1), 7–20.

Begley, P.T. (1994), *School Leadership: A Profile Document*, www.oise.utoronto.ca/~vsvede.

Bell, L. and Bush, T. (2002), 'The policy context', in Bush, T. and Bell, L. (eds), *The Principles and Practice of Educational Management*, London, Paul Chapman Publishing.

Bolam, R. (1999), 'Educational administration, leadership and management: towards a research agenda', in Bush, T., Bell, L., Bolam, R., Glatter, R. and Ribbins, P. (eds), *Educational Management: Redefining Theory, Policy and Practice*, London, Paul Chapman Publishing.

Bolman, L.G. and Deal, T.E. (1997), *Reframing Organizations: Artistry, Choice and Leadership*. San Francisco, CA, Jossey-Bass.

Bottery, M. (2001), 'Globalisation and the UK competition state: no room for transformational leadership in education?', *School Leadership and Management*, 21 (2), 199–218.

Briggs, A. (2003), 'Finding the balance: exploring the organic and mechanical dimensions of middle manager roles in English further education colleges', *Educational Management and Administration*, 31 (4), 421–436.

Bush, T. (1999), 'Crisis or crossroads? The discipline of educational management in the late 1990s', *Educational Management and Administration*, 27 (3), 239–252.

Bush, T. (2003), *Theories of Educational Leadership and Management: Third Edition*, London, Sage.

Bush, T. and Jackson, D. (2002), 'Preparation for school leadership: international perspectives', *Educational Management and Administration*, 30 (4), 417–29.

Bush, T., Coleman, M. and Si, X. (1998), 'Managing secondary schools in China', *Compare*, 33 (2), 127–138.

Caldwell, B. and Spinks, J. (1992), *Leading the Self-Managing School*, London, Falmer Press.

Chirichello, M. (1999), 'Building capacity for change: transformational leadership for school principals', paper presented at ICSEI Conference, 3–6 January, San Antonio, TX.

Commonwealth Secretariat (1996), *Better Schools: Resource Materials for Heads: Introductory Module*, London, Commonwealth Secretariat.

Cuban, L. (1988), *The Managerial Imperative and the Practice of Leadership in Schools*, Albany, NY, State University of New York Press.

Dellar, G. (1998), 'School climate, school improvement and site-based management', *Learning Environments Research*, 1 (3), 353–367.

Dimmock, C. and Walker, A. (2002), 'School leadership in context – societal and organisational cultures', in Bush, T. and Bell, L. (eds), *The Principles and Practice of Educational Management*, London, Paul Chapman Publishing.

Elliott, G. and Crossley, M. (1997), 'Contested values in further education: findings from a case study of the management of change', *Educational Management and Administration*, 27 (3), 253–266.

Glatter, R. (1999), 'From struggling to juggling: towards a redefinition of the field of educational leadership and management', *Educational Management and Administration*, 27 (3), 253–266.

Glatter, R. (2002), 'Governance, autonomy and accountability in education', in Bush, T. and Bell, L. (eds), *The Principles and Practice of Educational Management*, London, Paul Chapman Publishing.

Glatter, R. and Kydd, L. (2003), 'Best practice in educational leadership and management: can we identify it and learn from it?', *Educational Management and Administration*, 31 (3), 231–243.

Gunter, H. (1997), *Rethinking Education: The Consequences of Jurassic Management*, London, Cassell.

Gunter, H. (2001), *Leaders and Leadership in Education*, London, Paul Chapman Publishing.

Harris, A. (2002), 'Effective leadership in schools facing challenging circumstances', *School Leadership and Management*, 22 (1), 15–26.

Lauglo, J. (1997), 'Assessing the present importance of different forms of decentralisation in education', in Watson, K., Modgil, C. and Modgil, S. (eds), *Power and Responsibility in Education*, London, Cassell.

Leithwood, K. (1994), 'Leadership for school restructuring', *Educational Administration Quarterly*, 30(4), 498–518.

Levačić, R., Glover, D., Bennett, N. and Crawford, M. (1999), 'Modern headship for the rationally managed school: cerebral and insightful approaches', in Bush, T., Bell, L., Bolam, R., Glatter, R. and Ribbins, P. (eds) *Educational Management: Refining Theory, Policy and Practice*, London, Paul Chapman Publishing.

Lumby, J. (2001), *Managing Further Education: Learning Enterprise*, London, Paul Chapman Publishing.

McTavish, D. (2003), 'Aspects of public sector management: a case study of further education ten years from the passage of the Further and Higher Education Act', *Educational Management and Administration*, 31 (2), 175–187.

Miller, T.W. and Miller, J.M. (2001), 'Educational leadership in the new millennium: a vision for 2020', *International Journal of Leadership in Education*, 4 (2), 181–189.

Mintzberg, H. (1994), *The Rise and Fall of Strategic Planning*, Englewood Cliffs, NJ, Prentice-Hall.

National College for School Leadership (NCSL) (2001), *Leadership Development Framework*, Nottingham, NCSL.

Newland, C. (1995), 'Spanish American elementary education 1950–1992: bureaucracy, growth and decentralisation', *International Journal of Educational Development*, 15 (2), 103–114.

Newman, J. and Clarke, J. (1994), 'Going about our business? The managerialism of public services', in Clarke, J., Cochrane, A. and McLaughlin, E. (eds), *Managing*

School Policy, London, Sage.

Rikowski, G. (2002), 'Globalisation and education', paper prepared for the House of Lords Select Committee on Economic Affairs, January.

Sapre, P. (2002), Realising the potential of educational management in India', *Educational Management and Administration*, 30 (1), pp.101–108.

Thurlow, M., Bush, T. and Coleman, M. (2003), *Leadership and Strategic Management in South African Schools*, London, Commonwealth Secretariat.

Wasserberg, M. (2000), 'Creating the vision and making it happen', in Tomlinson, H., Gunter, H. and Smith, P. (eds), *Living Headship: Voices, Values and Vision*, London, Paul Chapman Publishing.

Webb, R. and Vulliamy, G. (1996), 'The changing role of the primary headteacher', *Educational Management and Administration*, 24 (3), 301–315.

Woods, P., Bennett, N., Harvey, J. and Wise, C. (2004), 'Variabilities and dualities in distributed leadership: findings from a systematic literative review', *Educational Management, Administration and Leadership*, 32 (4), 439–457.

Yukl, G.A. (2002) *Leadership in Organizations, Fifth Edition*, Upper Saddle River, NJ, Prentice-Hall.

2

Leading and managing people for performance

Introduction: defining purpose in education

All organisations are established for a purpose. For schools and colleges, the main purpose is to promote learning for their pupils and students. The specific aims vary, and are subject to external pressure, notably from government, but all are expected to facilitate learning for children, young people and adults. The school's targets may be determined and encapsulated through a formal process, such as development planning, or arise from a more informal arrangement, but they provide the basis for subsequent evaluation of performance.

Once the specific purposes of an organisation have been determined and agreed, it becomes possible to assess the extent to which they have been achieved. This is likely to involve analysis of both organisational and individual variables. The main focus of this chapter is on the performance of staff, whose skill and motivation are critical to the achievement of organisational objectives. Schools and colleges have to find an appropriate balance between meeting the needs of individual pupils and staff, and having a clear sense of the wider purpose of the institution, perhaps enunciated in a mission statement. This leads to the possibility that there may be conflict between organisational aims and individual aspirations. It is simplistic to assume that all staff will actively endorse the purposes set out by organisational leaders:

> A potential problem is that individual and organisational objectives may be incompatible, or that organisational aims satisfy some, but not all, individual aspirations. It is reasonable to assume that most teachers want their school or college to pursue policies which are in harmony with their own interests and preferences. (Bush 2003, p.3)

Lumby (2001) refers to the English further education context where managers were being 'persuaded' to endorse organisational aims, even where they conflicted with their own individual aspirations, through a process of coercion. Such an approach is seen by Elliott and Hall (1994) as the 'hard variant' of human resource management and Betts (1994) says that it is likely to lead to resentment rather than improved performance.

Managing for performance

The concept of performance relates to the extent to which an individual carries out the responsibilities assigned to them; 'the accomplishment of a task or activity' (Riches 1997, p.17). This appears to be a straightforward requirement; either the task has been completed or it has not. In practice, however, particularly but not exclusively in professional occupations such as teaching, there may be room for interpretation about the quality of the performance. 'The problem may arise as to how one is to know *if* what has been done is *the* accomplishment of something (performance) and what is the required *standard* ... there is a good deal of subjectivity surrounding the evaluation of performance' (Riches 1997, p.17, original author's emphasis).

In England and Wales, performance in schools is subject to evaluation by the Office for Standards in Education (Ofsted). Staff performance is evaluated in terms of the quality of teaching provided and its impact on the quality of learning and on pupil achievement. Since 1997, this process has included grading teachers for their classroom performance. As Middlewood and Lumby (1998) stress, 'the perspective is clearly one of external accountability in which priority is given to educational attainments, or outcomes, rather than to the process of teaching and learning in its own right' (p.19).

One example of the Ofsted approach relates to its assessment of school leadership and management which are also graded, using a seven-point scale. The following extracts relate to perceived 'very good', 'satisfactory' and 'poor' leadership:

Very good
Leadership is dedicated to ensuring the highest possible standards and achievements in all areas of the school's work. It is reflective, self-critical and innovative and articulates a clear vision of the school in the future, so that all staff know what they are working towards. It results in clear strategic thinking and planning for improvement.

Satisfactory
Leadership is firm, competent and committed, and there are clear lines of responsibility. Staff reflect the school's aims and policies in their work; they understand the school's goals and their role in achieving them. The school monitors its performance and tackles weaknesses.

Poor
Poor leadership is muddled, besieged or incompetent. The school lacks a sense of direction. Senior staff are preoccupied with daily tasks and incidents and find it difficult to prioritise the most important issues and focus their efforts accordingly. Teamwork is weak or little in evidence.
(Adapted from Ofsted 2003, p.141)

Riches (1997) outlines four problems in assessing performance:

1 Reliability of performance over time. Very good performance may be observed during the evaluation period but this may not be typical.
2 Reliability of performance observations. Different criteria, or different observers, may produce different performance ratings.
3 The criteria used to assess performance may be too limited to enable valid judgements to be made.
4 Performance is likely to be affected by the context or 'situational variables' (Adapted from Riches 1997, p.17).

These problems, and the Ofsted criteria outlined above, suggest that performance evaluation is subjective. Confidence in the accuracy of performance measurement is essential if it is to be accepted by teachers and leaders, but this is likely to be undermined if it is seen to be subjective. Fitz-Gibbon (1996), for example, criticises both the reliability and the validity of the Ofsted inspection model.

Eraut et al. (1997) illustrate performance management through four case examples in financial organisations and point to the contradiction between 'performance' and 'human resource development':

> These examples ... demonstrate the tension between performance management systems, which focus on short term results and key activities which directly affect the 'bottom line', and a human resource development approach focused on the development of staff capability over a longer time scale. (p.3)

The 'bottom line' in education may be the next inspection, or complaints by students or parents. It is a truism that each child only has one chance of a good education and is entitled to be taught by a competent teacher. Longer-term approaches may work but some learners may be disadvantaged if the process of development is elongated.

Gleeson and Husbands (2003) address the same issue in their critique of performance management in schools: 'A consequence of performance measures is to redefine the concerns of schools and teachers with the measurable and the short-term at the expense of the less quantifiable and the longer-term' (p.502). They add that performance management frameworks are dependent upon policy prescription about the intended outcomes of teaching. They express concern about 'mandated' schools and claim that 'performance management brings its own tensions, complications and cynicism' (p.509).

Gleeson and Husbands (2003) attribute the performance management culture to government prescription but research in five European countries (Bolam et al. 2000) shows that school managers are also drivers for improved performance. Their survey of 700 new primary and secondary headteachers showed that 40 per cent regarded 'ineffective teachers' as a 'serious or very serious problem' while 33 per cent were concerned about 'getting teachers to accept new ideas'. These are significant findings, suggesting that support for performance management goes well beyond government intentions to develop 'a more skilled, effective and globally competitive workforce' (Gleeson and Husbands 2003, p.503).

Yariv's (2004) research in 40 Israeli primary schools suggests that 7.2 per cent of teachers have 'profound shortcomings' (p.158). He explains why this is a significant problem:

> Problematic teachers present one of the toughest challenges school principals may ever face. Poor performing teachers not only do not bring the expected results, but also their bad behaviour may distract others from doing their work. They consume much of the principal's time and take the place of other workers who might be of more help to the organisation. Their bad behaviour damages the school's reputation. (p.149)

Headteacher support for enhanced performance may be dismissed as the internal manifestation of 'managerialism' but teacher attitudes to performance management are sometimes positive also, as we shall see later in this chapter and in Chapter 12.

Leading People

The alternative to a performance-led approach is one that is people oriented. Here, people are valued in their own right and not simply because they can 'deliver' an appropriate level of performance. This stance also assumes a more dynamic relationship in which people can be developed and motivated to produce higher levels of performance. This is akin to transformational leadership in which people are inspired to achieve an agreed vision of a better future for the organisation and its clients. It is about building a unified common interest between leaders and followers (Gunter 2001, p.69).

Leithwood et al.'s (1999) definition of transformational leadership links to 'people-led' notions of human resource management:

> This form of leadership assumes that the central focus of leadership ought to be the commitments and capacities of organisational members. Higher levels of personal commitment to organisational goals and greater capacities for accomplishing those goals are assumed to result in extra effort and greater productivity. (p.9)

Performance management may be likened to transactional leadership (Miller and Miller 2001) with its focus on short-term, exchange relationships. Achieving the required level of performance, in terms of specific outcomes, is likely to lead to a reward in terms of managerial approval and, perhaps, improved salary or conditions of employment. In contrast, transformational leadership may well produce beneficial changes in the process of teaching and learning, leading to a qualitative and sustained improvement in performance arising from enhanced motivation and commitment.

Briggs (2003) shows that transformational and transactional approaches may both be adopted by leaders who need to find a balance appropriate to their specific context. In relation to middle managers in English further education colleges, she notes that:

> There was an instinctive 'pull' towards a transformational style, followed by a realisation that the efficient working of the systems indicated by the transactional style was an essential factor for enabling their role ... effective enactment of their role depends upon their perceiving the balance between transactional and transformational styles. (p.435)

Foskett and Lumby (2003) express the people/performance debate in terms of control or support. They argue that external pressures on teachers in many countries are damaging:

> The last decade of the twentieth century saw ... an unremitting demand for changes, for improved teaching and for improved outcomes. Teachers have been subject to requirements which for many have become overwhelming. The incidence of stress has become epidemic and stress-related illness an ever present hazard. (p.74)

Foskett and Lumby claim that such negative outcomes arise from government pressure to raise educational standards, leading to greater regulation and strong accountability regimes evidenced, for example, through 'punitive' inspection systems. As a result, 'management of teachers' performance has negative connotations' (p.75).

The alternative to control and regulation is to develop a framework to optimise staff contributions through a 'softer', more supportive, approach. This involves valuing people as individuals and providing opportunities for all staff to develop and work towards fulfilling their aspirations. Two key aspects of this approach are staff motivation and professional development.

Motivation

Handy (1993), Foskett and Lumby (2003) and Hall and Rowland (1999) all refer to the ambiguity of the concept of motivation. It has attracted a 'plethora of definitions' (Foskett and Lumby 2003, p.76) and there is 'no overarching or single theoretical model which explains [it]' (Riches 1994, p.224).

Turner (1992, p.2) states that 'motivation ... involves arousal, direction and persistence'. Handy (1993) refers to the importance of motivation for managers:

> If we could understand, and could then predict, the ways in which individu-
> als were motivated, we could influence them by changing the components of
> that motivation process ... Early work on motivation was indeed concerned to
> find ways by which the individual could be 'motivated' to apply more effort
> and talent to the service of his or her employer. (pp.29–30)

Handy (1993) divides motivation theories into three categories:

1 *Satisfaction theories.* The assumption here is that satisfied workers are more productive but Handy says that there is little evidence to support this, although they
are more likely to remain with the organisation. Much careers advertising refers
to 'satisfaction', including the English Teacher Training Agency's recruitment
campaign in the early twenty-first century.
2 *Incentive theories.* The assumption of these theories is based on the principle of
reinforcement, the 'carrot' approach. Individuals work harder given specific
rewards or encouragement for good performance. Handy (1993, p.32) says that
incentive approaches might work if:

   (a) the individual perceives the extra reward to be worth the extra effort
   (b) the performance can be measured and attributed to the individual
   (c) the individual wants that particular kind of reward
   (d) the increased performance will not become the new minimum standard.

The incentive theory underpins the notion of performance related pay, as we
shall see later.
3 *Intrinsic theories.* The assumption here is that people work best if given a worthwhile job and allowed to get on with it. The reward will come from the satisfaction in the work itself. Foskett and Lumby (2003, p.78) claim that 'teaching is
rich in intrinsic motivation' but add that 'large numbers of teachers are not satisfied with their job' (p.78). Certainly, the problem of teacher retention in many
countries suggests that intrinsic motivation is insufficient to counter the perceived excessive bureaucracy, heavy workloads, low pay and inadequate professional development. In England 30 per cent of newly qualified teachers leave the
profession within five years while in the USA 20 per cent leave within the first
three years (Bush 2002).

All these theories are based on the assumption that motivation is essential if
employees are to perform well. People are motivated in different ways and knowing
what works for each person provides the potential for enhanced long-term performance. Chapter 6 provides a fuller discussion of this issue.

Professional development

Foskett and Lumby (2003) claim that 'providing staff with opportunities to develop is the final step which closes the circle of managing performance' (p.82). Bolam (2002, p.103) adds that 'professional development is widely accepted as fundamental to the improvement of organisational performance' and defines it as:

- an ongoing process of education, training, learning and support activities
- taking place in either external or work-based settings
- proactively engaged in by professional teachers, headteachers and other school leaders
- aimed primarily at promoting learning and development of their professional knowledge, skills and values
- to help them to decide on and implement valued changes in their teaching and leadership behaviour
- so that they can educate their students more effectively
- thus achieving an agreed balance between individual, school and national needs (Bolam 2002, pp.103–4).

The international significance of professional development is evident from a study of 700 new headteachers in five European countries. Twenty-five per cent of respondents referred to the importance of professional development for their teachers (Bolam 2002).

Bush (2002) makes the case for professional development:

> The notion of teaching as a career, rather than just a job, depends on the provision of structured professional development opportunities. Schools and LEAs need to help teachers to access development opportunities at every stage of their careers. This gives teachers the sense of direction which is an essential component of a long term approach. Professional development should include subject knowledge and pedagogy ... [Leaders] should ensure that there is ample opportunity for teachers to access professional development opportunities at every career stage. (p.6)

Professional development can be regarded as a vital dimension in improving teachers' professional skills and capabilities. It is an essential part of lifelong learning and is likely to be beneficial for schools for two reasons. First, effective professional development is likely to improve motivation which, in turn, provides the basis for teacher retention (Cockburn 2000; Odland 2002) and at least the potential for enhanced performance. Secondly, it also makes a direct contribution to performance development in two ways:

- In developing and extending teachers' knowledge and skills, it provides the essential underpinning for improved classroom performance.
- In developing teachers' confidence and motivation, it provides the opportunity to innovate and to 'transform' their professional work.

Managing performance in South African schools

Thurlow (2003) notes that the major educational policy concerns in South Africa include 'poor performance and inadequate outcomes of schooling' (p.33). These issues relate to what has been described as the absence of a 'culture of teaching and learning' in many South African schools (Bush and Anderson 2003).

The predominant culture in South African schools reflects the wider social structure of the post-apartheid era. Decades of institutionalised racism and injustice have been replaced by an overt commitment to democracy in all aspects of life, including education (Bush and Anderson 2003).

The years of struggle against apartheid inevitably affected schools, particularly those in the townships. One of the 'weapons' of the black majority was for youngsters to 'strike' and demonstrate against the policies of the white government. Similarly, teacher unions were an important aspect of the liberation movement and teachers would frequently be absent from school to engage in protest activity. In the immediate post-apartheid period, it was difficult to shift from struggle and protest to a culture of learning. Badat (1995, p.143) claims that 'the crisis in black education, including what has come to be referred to as the "breakdown" in the "culture of learning" ... continued unabated'.

Thurlow (2003, p.33) summarises the main performance issues arising from this 'breakdown':

1 The organisational performance of schools, in respect of their prime functions (teaching and learning), generally needs substantial improvement.
2 The key resources for the improvement of school performance are the people who work in them.
3 Improvements in the performance of schools, and people's contributions to these, have to be managed.

Enhanced performance is a major goal for the South African schools' system, endorsed at the highest political level:

> The transformation of the education and training system has only begun. Our task is to bring redress, establish quality, open the doors of opportunity, enable a true culture of learning and teaching to take root, [and] strive for ever higher levels of performance. (Minister of Education, cited in Smith 1997, p.165)

This ambitious set of objectives was reflected in the establishment of a National Directorate for Quality Assurance, intended, in part, to develop a 'coherent model for quality management' (Department of Education 1998, p.45). As Thurlow (2003, p.37) points out, 'notions of performance must always be referred to notions of quality'.

We referred earlier to the importance of context in assessing performance. This is a vital ingredient for South African schools:

South African school managers are confronted by very serious concerns about the performance of their schools, generally in extremely difficult conditions. In particular, they are concerned with encouraging the highest levels of performance possible from their colleagues despite severely limited resources and a widespread, and documented, demoralisation of the teaching profession. (Thurlow 2003, p.42)

Performance management in England and Wales

The enhanced interest in 'performance' at policy level, notably in England and Wales, has led to the introduction of several formal schemes of performance management. Jennings and Lomas (2003) refer to this as 'the process of monitoring employee performance in an objective manner', adding that it is perceived as a control mechanism. Their survey of all 53 headteachers of secondary schools in one part of England (East Kent) showed a generally positive response to performance management for heads, an unexpected outcome:

Performance management has been introduced without pain and has not been seen as a threat. (p.376)

There is no debate about the purpose of performance management, they are all agreed. (p.376)

This research applies only to heads, and not to teachers, but the authors conclude that 'the first phase has been generally successful and there is evidence from this study that a cultural change is occurring ... there was very little empirical evidence to support the general criticisms of performance management' (Jennings and Lomas 2003, p.380).

James and Colebourne (2004) examined the nature of performance management for staff in 20 local education authorities (LEAs) in Wales. They note that target-setting is a key element in 13 of the 15 LEAs which had performance management schemes in operation. Their evidence suggests that linking individual targets to institutional plans is problematic, not least because 'linking outcomes to individual performance is very shaky' (p.54). The officers interviewed by the authors raised issues about staff ownership of the schemes. 'The challenge is to overcome reluctance from staff, who may see [performance management] as more paper work' (p.57).

These authors develop a four-part model of performance management:

- non-performance management: 'laissez faire'
- accountable: goals are clear but capability is not developed
- development: focuses on developing performance but goals may not be set

- performance management: purposeful in setting goals for individuals and in developing their capability to achieve them.

The research reported here provides mixed evidence on the efficacy of official performance management schemes in education. Heads in Kent generally welcomed it while LEA staff in Wales were concerned about it becoming overly bureaucratic. These findings confirm Foskett and Lumby's (2003) view that performance management does not provide a panacea for teacher development or for addressing under-performance. 'Motivation and development are intensely personal and individual, and no formal process will succeed in improving performance if the individuality of each member of staff is not recognised' (p.85).

Performance related pay

We noted earlier (page 21) that Handy (1993) includes 'incentive' theories as one of his three major types of motivation. These theories assume that people are motivated by such extrinsic rewards as pay, working conditions and holiday arrangements. Performance related pay is an important example of the application of incentive theories.

Foreman (1997) reports on the official moves towards performance related pay in Britain during the 1990s. From 1995, school governing bodies in England have been able to reward excellent performance for both teachers and headteachers. He is sceptical about its value but anticipates that support for performance related pay will continue:

> PRP does not appear to motivate and it can certainly damage organisational culture. Teachers react adversely to incentive measures which they see as inequitable, and dedicated funding is less likely to be set aside for this purpose as school and college budgets remain under pressure. But there seems little doubt that the impetus to measure individual performance and reward it accordingly will continue. (Foreman 1997, p.217)

Burgess et al. (2001) review the performance threshold scheme introduced in England and Wales in 2000. Teachers have historically been paid on a single scale with nine basic increments. Under the new scheme, teachers who have reached the ninth increment are eligible to pass a performance threshold. Their personal performance is assessed against specific factors, including professional development and pupil attainment. If successful, they receive an annual bonus of £2,000 and move on to a new, upper pay scale. Ingvarson (2001, p.170) notes that this is virtually identical to the Australian experience.

Burgess et al. (2001) summarise the findings of the large-scale research undertaken by Wragg et al. (2001). They note that 88 per cent of eligible teachers applied and of those 97 per cent were awarded the additional payment. Significantly, 75 per cent of heads report that the assessment made little or no difference to what teachers did. Burgess et al. (2001) conclude that the scheme

> operated more as a general pay increase for (almost) all teachers at the eligible point of the scale ... If the scheme continues to operate to give almost all eligible staff a pay rise, then we would not expect much impact on effort, as teachers would expect to get the bonus irrespective of whether they increase their effort. (p.27)

Morris and Farrell (2004) report on their research with teachers in 49 primary and secondary schools in Wales. They surveyed 1,125 teachers with a 'disappointing' response rate of 29.3 per cent. Of the respondents, 79.6 per cent agree that pay should take more account of the different jobs carried out by teachers but 65.4 per cent disagree with the principle of performance related pay (PRP). Specific responses to related questions confirm teachers' hostility to this notion (see Table 2.1).

Table 2.1 Teachers' views about the principle of linking pay to performance

PRP proposition	Level of disagreement
The introduction of PRP will lead to greater motivation of teachers	80.6%
The introduction of PRP will have a positive impact on recruitment	83.0%
The introduction of PRP will have a positive impact on teacher retention	83.9%
PRP will result in better and more effective teaching	77.2%
PRP will result in an improvement in pupil learning	73.1%

Source: adapted from Morris and Farrell 2004, p.90

Despite these negative views, most of Morris and Farrell's (2004) respondents did apply to cross the threshold. Most did so for monetary reasons or for the related reason that 'they did a good job but were not paid enough' (p.96). The authors conclude that 'resigned compliance' characterises teachers' responses. 'Why say no to £2,000 per year, just on principle. My not applying would clearly not change what is happening anyway' (p.97).

Conclusion: improving performance

It is evident from the research reviewed in this chapter that 'incentive' schemes, such as performance related pay, are unlikely to have much impact on teacher performance or on pupil outcomes. This confirms the widely held view that extrinsic factors do not contribute in a significant way to staff motivation in education.

Rather, teachers are motivated by intrinsic factors such as altruism, affiliation to the school and their colleagues, and personal growth (Thompson 2000).

Despite this evidence, the quality of staff performance remains an important issue, in education and elsewhere. Drucker (1988, p.361) says that 'the focus of the organisation must be on performance. The first requirement of the spirit of performance is high performance standards, for the group, as well as the individual'. The challenge for educational leaders is to generate optimum performance from all staff.

Transformational leadership (see page 19) provides the potential to increase commitment to the aims of the organisation and to motivate staff to perform at their best for the sake of their pupils and colleagues. The alternative model, transactional leadership, provides only extrinsic rewards which are unlikely to generate long-term improvement. If 'performance management brings its own tensions, complications and cynicism' (Gleeson and Husbands 2003, p.509), leaders must find other ways to inspire their colleagues to achieve at their best. This requires an approach based on the individual needs and aspirations of all staff.

Mentoring and coaching

We noted earlier (page 22) the importance of professional development for teachers. It is self-evident that pre-service training, however effective, is insufficient for a career that might last for 40 years. Professional updating is essential for teachers and associate staff. This is likely to involve enhanced knowledge of both content and pedagogy. It should also include leadership development in recognition of the increasing awareness of distributed leadership in schools and colleges.

Professional development provides a 'win–win' situation for school leaders as it meets the individual's needs for career development while contributing to school improvement and encouraging staff retention. There are several types of professional development and all may be helpful at different times and for certain circumstances. An approach focused on individuals, however, suggests that personal support, such as that provided by effective induction, mentoring and coaching, is most likely to be successful. These processes will be given detailed consideration in subsequent chapters but their collective impact is likely to be of considerable significance in encouraging good performance at all career stages. All these modes of professional development depend on the strength of interpersonal relationships, the availability of suitable mentors or coaches and the priority given to these approaches by leaders and managers. Coleman (1997, p.167) notes that 'good practice with regard to induction and mentoring is likely to be found in schools with a strong commitment to staff development'. For Spindler and Biott (2000), good practice lies in developing a 'sense of belonging', not in adherence to a 'universal set of standards or competences' (p.283).

Empowerment

Performance management is underpinned by 'top-down' assumptions as schools and colleges comply with externally imposed schemes for appraisal and target-setting. It also assumes a control mechanism with judgements being made on an essentially hierarchical basis. An alternative approach is to empower staff by allowing them significant autonomy. Crowther et al. (2002) see this as central to the 'learning organisation':

> Because empowerment has been seen for several decades as critical to the creation of a learning organisation, it follows that principals who want to see their schools develop as learning organisations must empower their teachers in meaningful ways. In effect, they must know how and when to step back from their own leader roles and, in so doing, to encourage teacher colleagues to step forward. (p.59)

Muijs and Harris (2003) also advocate empowering teachers and add that 'the quality of leadership matters in determining the motivation of teachers' (p.437). Empowerment helps staff to develop confidence and to feel ownership of change. Where there are many leaders in an organisation, there are multiple sources of innovation and greater potential for enhanced individual and team performance leading to school improvement. Inspiring optimum performance is vital, but this is most likely to be achieved through sensitive management of people. There is no dichotomy between people and performance. Caring for, and developing, people are the best ways of securing significant and sustainable improvements in performance.

References

Badat, S. (1995), 'Educational politics in the transition period', *Comparative Education*, 31 (2), 141–159.

Betts, A. (1994), *A Focus for Human Resource Management*, Mendip Paper 069, Blagdon, Staff College.

Bolam, R. (2002), 'Professional development and professionalism', in Bush, T. and Bell, L. (eds), *The Principles and Practice of Educational Management*, London, Paul Chapman Publishing.

Bolam, R., Dunning, G. and Karstanje, P. (2000), *New Heads in the New Europe*, Munster/New York, Waxmann.

Briggs, A. (2003), 'Finding the balance: exploring the organic and mechanical dimensions of middle manager roles in English further education colleges', *Educational Management and Administration*, 31 (4), 421–436.

Burgess, S., Croxson, B., Gregg, P. and Propper, C. (2001), *The Intricacies of the Relationship between Pay and Performance for Teachers: Do Teachers Respond to Performance Related Pay Schemes?* Bristol, CMPO.

Bush, T. (2002), *Teacher retention: research evidence*, paper prepared for the Education and Lifelong Learning Scrutiny Panel, London Borough of Greenwich, November.

Bush, T. (2003), *Theories of Educational Leadership and Management, Third Edition*, London, Sage.

Bush, T. and Anderson, L. (2003), 'Organisational culture', in Thurlow, M., Bush, T. and Coleman, M. (eds), *Leadership and Management in South African Schools*, London, Commonwealth Secretariat.

Cockburn, A. (2000), 'Elementary teachers' needs: issue of retention and recruitment', *Teaching and Teacher Education*, 16 (2), 223–238.

Coleman, M. (1997), 'Managing induction and mentoring', in Bush, T. and Middlewood, D. (eds), *Managing People in Education*, London, Paul Chapman Publishing.

Crowther, F., Kaagan, S., Ferguson, M. and Hann, L. (2002), *Developing Teacher Leaders*, Thousand Oaks, CA, Corwin Press.

Department of Education (1998), *Annual Report of the Department of Education: 1998*, Pretoria, Department of Education.

Drucker, P. (1988), *Management*, Oxford, Heinemann.

Elliott, G. and Hall, V. (1994), 'FE Inc – business orientation in further education and the introduction of human resource management', *School Organisation*, 14 (1), 3–10.

Eraut, M., Alderton, J., Cole, G. and Senker, P. (1997), 'The impact of the manager on learning in the workplace', paper given to the BERA Conference, York, September.

Fitz-Gibbon, C. (1996), 'Judgements must be credible and fair', *Times Educational Supplement*, 29 March, 21.

Foreman, K. (1997), 'Managing individual performance', in Bush, T. and Middlewood, D. (eds), *Managing People in Education*, London, Paul Chapman Publishing.

Foskett, N. and Lumby, J. (2003), *Leading and Managing Education: International Dimensions*, London, Paul Chapman Publishing.

Gleeson, D. and Husbands, C. (2003), 'Modernising schooling through performance management: a critical appraisal', *Journal of Education Policy*, 18 (5), 499–511.

Gunter, H. (2001), *Leaders and Leadership in Education*, London, Paul Chapman Publishing.

Hall, R. and Rowland, C. (1999), 'Teaching managers how to learn: the changing role of management educators', paper presented at the 28th Annual SCUTREA Conference, University of Exeter, July.

Handy, C. (1993), *Understanding Organisations*, London, Penguin.

Ingvarson, L. (2001), 'Developing standards and assessments for accomplished teaching: a responsibility of the profession', in Middlewood, D. and Cardno, C. (eds), *Managing Teacher Appraisal and Performance: A Comparative Approach*, London, RoutledgeFalmer.

James, C. and Colebourne, D. (2004), 'Managing the performance of staff in LEAs in Wales: practice, problems and possibilities', *Educational Management, Administration and Leadership*, 32 (1), 45–66.

Jennings, K. and Lomas, L. (2003), 'Implementing performance management for headteachers in English secondary schools: a case study', *Educational Management and Administration*, 31 (4), 369–384.

Leithwood, K., Jantzi, D. and Steinbach, R. (1999), *Changing Leadership for Changing Times*, Buckingham, Open University Press.

Lumby, J. (2001), *Managing Further Education: Learning Enterprise*, London, Paul Chapman Publishing.

Middlewood, D. and Lumby, J. (1998), *Human Resource Management in Schools and Colleges*, London, Paul Chapman Publishing.

Miller, T.W. and Miller, J.M. (2001), 'Educational leadership in the new millennium: a vision for 2020', *International Journal of Leadership in Education*, 4 (2), 181–189.

Morris, J. and Farrell, C. (2004), 'Resigned compliance: teacher attitudes towards PRP in schools', *Educational Management, Administration and Leadership*, 32 (1), 81–104.

Muijs, D. and Harris, A. (2003), 'Teacher leadership – improvement through empowerment? An overview of the literature', *Educational Management and Administration*, 31 (4), 437–448.

Odland, J. (2002), 'Professional development schools: partnerships that work', *Childhood Education*, 78 (3), 160–162.

Office for Standards in Education (Ofsted) (2003), *Framework 2003 – Inspecting Schools*, London, Ofsted.

Riches, C. (1994), 'Motivation', in Bush, T. and West-Burnham, J. (eds), *The Principles of Educational Management*, Harlow, Longman.

Riches, C. (1997), 'Managing for people and performance', in Bush, T. and Middlewood, D. (eds), *Managing People in Education*, London, Paul Chapman Publishing.

Smith, W. (1997), 'School performance, change and education management', in Smith, W., Thurlow, M. and Foster, W. (eds), *Supporting Education in South Africa: International Perspectives, Vol. 1*, Montreal and Pretoria, Canada-South African Education Management Programme.

Spindler, J. and Biott, C. (2000), 'Target setting in the induction of newly qualified teachers: emerging colleagueship in a context of performance management', *Educational Research*, 42 (3), 275–285.

Thompson, M. (2000), 'Performance management: new wine in old bottles?', *Professional Development Today*, 3, 9–19.

Thurlow, M. (2003), 'Managing people and performance', in Lumby, J., Middlewood, D. and Kaabwe, E. (eds), *Managing Human Resources in South African Schools*, London, Commonwealth Secretariat.

Turner, C. (1992), *Motivating Staff*, Mendip Paper 033, Blagdon, Staff College.

Wragg, E., Haynes, G., Wragg, C. and Chamberlin, R. (2001), *Performance Related Pay: The Views and Experiences of 1000 Primary and Secondary Head Teachers*, Exeter, University of Exeter.

Yariv, E. (2004), 'Challenging teachers: what difficulties do they pose for their principals?', *Educational Management, Administration and Leadership*, 32 (2), 149–170.

3

The importance of support staff in schools and colleges

Introduction

Although the focus in effective leadership and management of staff in schools and colleges has always been – and remains – on teachers, since they are at the heart of the organisations' central purpose of promoting learning, there has been a significant increase in research and literature on other staff employed there. Although the importance of, for example, school bursars and secretaries, librarians and caretakers/janitors has always been acknowledged, little literature exists before 1990 and in some countries there has been since the 1990s a particular interest in those who work in direct support of teachers. This interest and scrutiny is by no means universal and appears to relate very much to each country's prevailing culture. The USA tends to use the word 'paraprofessionals' for employees other than teachers, and Kerry and Kerry (2003, p.71) point to a Kansas State list of duties for such staff that dates back to 1977. In many developing counties, the issue of unqualified teachers is far more pressing than the roles of other staff (see, for example, Middlewood 2003, on South Africa, and Dalin and Rust 1994, on Columbia, Ethiopia and Bangladesh). Literature concerning those in a support role for teachers in many countries is very limited, and in some countries such staff simply do not exist.

In the UK, the importance of support staff in schools in particular has become a significant issue, for two main reasons. The first is the increasing appreciation of the need to recognise and utilise the skills of all employees to support the increased focus on learning. The second is that since the movement towards self-governance, and particularly delegated budget responsibility, schools have become much more conscious of cost-effectiveness. In the first major research in this area, Mortimore et al. (1994) found much innovative use of what they termed 'associate staff', most of it originating in a desire for value for money.

This chapter examines who support staff are and the leadership and management issues relating to their effectiveness, looking at both the operational and the strategic aspects. In focusing on these staff specifically, it is important to remember that most of the issues concerning leadership and management of people in other chapters of this book relate equally to support staff.

The culture in British schools, whereby schools are expected to deal with the 'whole child', has inevitably meant that the role of the teacher has developed into one of being responsible, at least collectively, for all aspects of their pupils' development, not just learning in the classroom. The increase in teachers' workloads, at the same time as a demand for the increased focus on pupils' learning achievement, accentuated the need for developing the roles of people who could:

- support the teacher directly in helping the pupils' learning
- take over some of the tasks done by teachers which did not require their professional skills, thus releasing the teachers to focus even more on teaching.

The confusion over these two key purposes is reflected in the plethora of terms that developed during the 1990s to describe various support staff roles. Clayton (1993) identified seven different terms for assistants working in classrooms with teachers! By 1999, Adamson suggested that 'teaching assistant' had become the most widely accepted term in schools in England, whilst the research of Wilson et al. (2003) confirms that 'classroom assistant' had been adopted in Scotland. More significant in the development of this role, however, is that common National Occupational Standards were drawn up by 2001 'for all staff in England, Scotland, Wales and Northern Ireland who work with teachers in classrooms supporting the learning process in primary, special and secondary schools' (LGNTO 2001). The final official recognition was the UK government's proposal (DfES 2002) that from September 2003 teachers would not be required to do a number of administrative tasks (e.g. photocopying, examination entries, displays, cataloguing resources, etc). This would require an increase in support staff from 216,000 to 266,000. It is thus clear that the importance of these staff is increasing and will continue to do so. The confusion is added to by the further proposal that assistants, with training, should take over supervision of classes on occasions, which, perhaps inevitably, brought divided reactions from teachers' unions.

Because of the complex situation described above, most current literature focuses on the operational aspects of the management of support staff and not upon a strategic view of what is in the best interests of pupil learning and therefore the best way to lead and manage these staff. Most research has focused on what assistants actually do (e.g. Moyles and Suschitzky (1997); Wilson et al. 2003). It is appropriate now to try to describe the various kinds of support staff in schools, identify some of the issues in leading and managing them, and propose principles for effective practice in their leadership and management.

Who are support staff?

Classification is most helpfully done by task and purpose, especially because several of these tasks officially coming under different roles are actually done by the same people. It is quite common for someone to have two separate employment contracts in one school, for example, one as a cleaner and one as a midday supervisor. Confining the list to those regularly employed, the following is suggested:

1 Those who carry out clerical, administrative, and reception tasks – normally in offices.
2 Those who prepare, develop and maintain resources of various kinds – e.g. technicians, librarians, reprographic assistants.
3 Those who maintain the premises – caretakers, cleaners, etc.
4 Those who are responsible for the pupils during periods between formal lessons – normally lunchtime or midday supervisors.
5 Those who assist the teachers by relieving them of various administrative, physical and routine tasks.
6 Those who work directly with pupils in conjunction with the teachers, in developing their learning. This will include those who support pupils with learning difficulties and also pupils with behavioural problems, since this is essentially a learning issue also.
7 Those with a management responsibility for the finance and business administration, such as bursars or business managers.

The last named category are seen, for the purposes of this chapter, to be in a different category from the others since such posts are often filled in secondary schools and colleges by people with professional qualifications and it is common now for bursars or business managers to be members of a school or college leadership team. They are therefore referred to elsewhere in this volume, including in the chapter on teams.

Any classification of support staff, not only highlights the wide range of personnel deployed in a school or college but also helps to emphasise the need to apply key leadership and management principles to all the people working in the organisation. Although most literature focuses on schools, the roles of employees other than lecturers in further education colleges have also developed since greater funding flexibility was introduced. Kedney and Brownlow (1994 p.12) noted that such roles were becoming:

• more flexible
• more involved directly in support of students
• more like to offer guidance and support
• more likely to be directly concerned with instruction, supervision and design.

Later Simkins and Lumby (2002 p.19) also referring to English further education colleges, noted that 'Role distinctions between academic and other staff may also be becoming more blurred.'

For key principles to be applied, some of the most important issues need to be identified first.

Issues in the leadership and management of support staff

1 Who should lead and manage support staff?

It could be argued that, given the diversity of roles in the above classification, there is a risk of having too many managers, but it is important that the responsibility is clear in any organisation. Middlewood (1997 p.188), writing about staff development, asked whether the needs of a science technician, for example, could be best met by considering that person as a member of the science departmental team or as a member of the school's support staff. A reasonable answer is that both are essential but there is a potential tension in the situation for the technicians and their managers.

Each of the above categories of support staff may be viewed as a team but designated leaders and managers vary. In most organisations, there is an office manager who leads the clerical/administration team and premises staff have a Head of Premises or equivalent to lead that team. However, this is not usually the case with midday supervisors, and technicians are usually managed by a teacher in charge of the relevant curriculum area. Most learning support assistants (LSAs) who support pupils with special educational needs (SEN) are led by the school or college's head of learning support (a senior teacher or lecturer) or, in the case of smaller schools, by the teacher who is SEN co-ordinator (SENCO).

Many schools or colleges have a member of the leadership team who has overall responsibility for support staff and, with the development of teaching assistants (TA) and (in 2003) higher level teaching assistants (HLTA), this responsibility may belong to the leader with teaching and learning as a brief. However, Curtis (2002, p.5) describes how, in one school, a specific department was created for support staff:

> With the business manager as its head, the support staff department at Churchdown School was born. Technicians, site management staff, lunchtime supervisors, secretarial staff, the librarian, the receptionist, catering staff and cleaners all stood on an equal footing with teachers. They now have department meetings and have a head of department to whom they can turn.

This department is different from other teaching departments because its size (80 people) is about the same size as the entire teaching staff; therefore, a number of its processes are necessarily different, e.g. in identifying training needs, performance management interviews. One of the key advantages of this department appears to be the status and value that its existence gives to support staff and the vehicle it offers to allowing support staff views to be represented and acted upon.

2 Training and development

All staff in a school or college may be perceived as having an entitlement to training, but whereas the training and development of teachers has generated a whole literature in its own right, including relevant journals, the training of certain groups of support staff is much less widespread. Naylor (1999) noted that the LEA training he described for lunchtime supervisors was rare among such bodies, probably no more than one school in 20 being estimated as providing them with training of any kind, regardless of its quality.

Not only does a lack of training hinder a member of support staff's opportunity to develop skills in areas where they can contribute to the organisation, it also signals the undervaluing of them and what they do. Offering no training may indicate that this is a job that anyone can do! In fact, the lunchtime supervisors' role encapsulate the two aspects of the support work referred to earlier. First, they relieve the teachers of the onerous task of supervising pupils or students between formal sessions and, secondly, they support pupil learning in that more structured behaviour or relaxation between lessons has an effect on behaviour, and therefore learning, in the classroom lessons following a break (Fenner 1998).

The concern therefore for leaders and managers is to ensure that effective and relevant training is available to support staff of all kinds in a way that is 'enriching' as Stoll et al. (2003 p.126) describes it: 'Involve them, training them to perform roles that will enhance the school, build their personal efficacy, use their skills ... '.

As other chapters in this book show, the importance of training and development is also that it contributes to the 'collective learning' (Stoll et al. 2003, p.140) of the organisation. Those in support roles may have access to aspects of the organisation's culture which need to be explored and developed. Using this access can have practical value for leaders who wish to move the organisation forward as a whole. Middlewood (1999) described how John, a learning support assistant in a special school, joined an in-house course for staff and undertook a piece of in-house research on pupil behaviour between lessons, as a result of which the school re-examined its whole practice in this area. John had an access to the pupils which teachers could not have and was able therefore to gain additional insights. More structured, relevant and consistent training for support staff clearly brings additional benefits to the organisation. Ryall and Goddard's (2003) case studies of the training of midday assistants and specialist teaching assistants led in both cases to the conclusion that 'investment in the training of support staff is worthwhile both for the individuals and the organisation ... The school has to reflect on the implications emerging from the training and modify their structures and procedures to maximise benefits. It is an investment that is well worth the cost' (p.78).

3 Career structure and development

Various studies (Mortimore et al. 1994; Farrell et al. 1999; Wilson et al. 2003) have shown that, for classroom support staff, levels of pay are low, many contracts are temporary and there is no career structure. This, ironically, means that those receiving training can become among the most frustrated if no development opportunities are given for them to use the received benefits.

However, as attention is paid to the issue of reducing teachers' workloads in Eng-land and Wales (DfES 2003), significantly increased opportunities emerge for vari-ous support staff to have access to training which is structured to enable them to gain precise and coherent qualifications and to plan career progression. New foun-dation degrees were begun in a few higher education institutions in 2001 offering teaching assistants the chance to study, in a work-based link between schools and HE, for a qualification as a higher level assistant, an associate teacher and, for those that wished, to proceed to gain full qualified teacher status. The high demand for places on these courses has underlined the need for them but also the frustration at the lack of opportunity offered up till then. Official evaluations of these degrees (e.g. Foreman-Peck and Middlewood 2002) indicate that they are likely to expand as well as be refined.

4 Valuing their contributions

The studies referred to above found that many support staff feel undervalued in the schools or colleges where they work. They feel that because they are seen as of lower status than teachers or lecturers, they are perceived as being less important and their contributions are not recognised. They feel they are not often consulted when deci-sions are made which affect them or their work. Indeed, at the wider level, Todd (2003) pointed out, that while extensive consultations were taking place with teacher unions and leaders of schools about how assistants might be used to decrease teachers' workloads, no one was consulting the assistants themselves.

In further education Simkins and Lumby (2002) show that little attention is paid to support staff and Lumby (2001) found an intensely felt 'them and us' culture between lecturers and support staff.

This undervaluing of support staff has often included lack of formal processes, such as induction (Middlewood 1999, p.129) and appraisal (DES 1992) where HMI reported that their effectiveness was limited by 'a lack of formal or informal appraisal of performance'. However, it can reveal itself in other less overt ways that are reflected in the culture of the organisation.

For example, the leaders and managers may well reflect upon the actual practice of what is commonly stated in organisations about 'equally valuing all staff' by reflecting upon the following questions:

- Do all staff have equal access to staffroom and facilities?
- Do 'staff lists' reflect hierarchical values?
- Do 'staff' photographs include all members of staff?
- Are staff events, including social occasions, open to all staff?
- Are achievements of support staff recognised in the same way as those of others?

One important consideration sometimes overlooked is that many support staff tend to live within the school or college's immediate community, compared with teachers and lecturers who are able to travel a considerable distance to work. This means that support staff are potentially powerful voices within the local community and should be valued as such – not least because of their importance in informal 'word of mouth', marketing!

Where members of support staff feel undervalued, the effect on their self-esteem can be significant, and there are ways in which the contribution made by them can be acknowledged. Williams et al. (2001, p.56) describe a case study in which a headteacher deliberately adopted strategies to enhance the self-esteem of midday supervisors:

> Midday supervisors are difficult to recruit, but having got together a team I set out to build up the self-esteem of the group and raise the profile of the job. I appointed an intelligent and caring MDSA and sent her for training in first aid and managing challenging behaviour. We had daily briefings before lunch to update her on children causing concern. I gave her a budget to choose new uniforms in agreement with the others. The other members of the team were offered options on a rota basis and began to ask, 'When is it my turn for training?' *I allow them odd days off (without pay) to take up cheaper holidays within school time*. Staff meetings are held after lunch once per term and problems are raised with me. I now have a committed team and a list of people wanting to join! The importance of backing up the team and then working with staff and not against them cannot be stressed enough. The benefits can be seen in a vast improvement in playground behaviour.

This example contain strategies both of formal processes (giving access to training) and informal recognition (giving days off for cheaper holidays), both crucially important in enabling staff to feel valued.

Whilst there is comparatively little research into support staff outside Britain, some that has been done has important implications for their perceived value. Whilst Kerry's (2001) study of paraprofessionals in Portugal found them to be well integrated, the focus in the Czech Republic in using assistants to support an ethnic minority (Romany children) had significant effects. On the one hand, the assistants enhanced the Romany children's education significantly; on the other, the fact that they had assistants rather than teachers raised the same ethical issue as was raised about support staff being used to meet the needs of students of racial, ethnic and language minority groups in the USA, i.e. 'Is one of the constructs of the support staff role that they are to be seen as second class instructors for second class students?' (Kerry and Kerry 2003 p.70).

5 Working relationships

The phrase 'support staff' itself implies a working relationship with another professional and in most cases this will be a teacher or lecturer. The research of Lee (2002) into the developing role of teaching assistants found that time for assistants and teachers to collaborate was crucial to the assistants' effective working. Although this effectiveness would lead to the reduction in some of the teachers' work, it was also pointed out that teachers themselves have to oversee and manage the work of assistants, and this takes additional time. Proposals related to the reduction in teachers' working load in England and Wales (DfES 2003) imply a range of relationships between teachers and support staff, ranging from personal assistants (who may do photocopying, stock-taking, etc.) to higher level teaching assistants (who will have considerable autonomy and will take responsibility for classes under the teacher's general direction). As with all working relationships, the effectiveness of the partnership between support staff and teachers or lecturers will depend upon:

- clarity of roles – who does what
- recognition of the different but complementary skills each brings to the partnership
- mutual respect
- agreement about what are the common goals
- opportunity for good communication, resources, training, etc.

New technology may provide better opportunities for improved co-operation in this area. Rai (2003) describes how, since a resources manager was appointed to the school where she works and lesson plans are on the networked laptop computers, she has had more time to work effectively with the teacher since they both come better prepared to their meetings. Palmer (2003) argues that in this relationship teachers too need training and development in how to manage support staff. She points out that, as teaching has traditionally been an autonomous and thereby solitary occupation, there are still many teachers who are not naturally comfortable with another adult within 'their' classroom and to these 'a classroom assistant can sometimes seem more like a hindrance than a help' (p.6). Foreman-Peck and Middlewood (2002) also found that, while the vast majority of teachers welcomed and encouraged assistants studying the foundation degree, the assistants felt there were a small number who resented and even felt threatened by the new learning and skills they were acquiring. Lorenz (1999) concluded from a number of studies that the training together of assistants and teachers was often the most beneficial way to develop new learning for the benefit of the pupils and also was most likely to develop the working relationship.

Effectiveness in leadership and management of support staff

Working on the premise that all employees are entitled to be led and managed in a sensitive, professional and efficient way, it is clear that support staff in educational organisations require many of the same principles applied to them as any other members of staff. In this way, optimum staff performance is more likely to be achieved and, most importantly, the performance of the pupils or students is more likely to be improved.

As discussed elsewhere in this book, the context within which schools and colleges operate is continually changing and, in particular, the factors affecting the organisations' key purpose, i.e. learning, are being transformed. It is inevitable, therefore, that the roles of those facilitating learning – especially teachers and lecturers – will continue to change also. Accordingly, the roles in schools and colleges developed dramatically following schools' and colleges' increased self-governance. As Busher and Saran (1995, p.177) noted, 'the job of the caretaker had been transformed into that of a site manager and the secretary had become a principal administrative officer in both name and duties'. Interestingly, such transformed roles belong to the 'business' side of school and college management, concerning finance and premises. As organisations took control of their own resources, it was inevitable that they needed first to manage these matters efficiently. As the focus moves now much more to what these resources exist for, i.e. learning, so the roles related more closely to that must change. As the use of all resources ultimately needs to be shown to be related to learning, so the human resource – as the most important and expensive of all – comes under scrutiny. In this context, support staff need to be led and managed to the greatest possible effectiveness. The following aspects may be significant.

Awareness and implementation of general entitlement

Support staff have the same entitlement as other staff to the best possible practices in human resource management such as:

- job description
- induction
- mentoring
- performance review or appraisal
- training and development
- opportunities for promotion and career development.

It has already been noted how some of these are limited at a national level but there is much that can be done in individual organisations. In some areas, practice will need to be 'customised' to ensure it is appropriate for these staff. For example, where applicants are likely to come from within the nearby community, more limited advertising for certain posts is allowable. To ensure that all staff are seen to be equally valued, leaders and managers need to ensure that all such procedures apply to everyone. It should be stressed that this applies to needing to be hard on under-performance just as much as valuing positively. As Fidler and Atton (1999) show, the poor performance of a receptionist at a school and college cannot be tolerated any more than that of a teacher or lecturer. If it is, it gives out the signal that that particular job or task does not matter and, by implication, the people affected do not matter either.

Recognition of issues special to support staff

What is required of support staff demands particular skills specific to the job as well as a number of attributes common to all or most effective employees. If these are to be acknowledged and used effectively, it is important that they are not seen as a weaker or 'watered down' version of skills of teachers or lecturers. In healthcare, for example, surgeons have high-level skills but paramedics such as ambulance staff have particular skills which surgeons do not possess because each is specific to the job they do. Yet, ultimately, the patient is likely to need both. Similarly, in the case of teaching or classroom assistant and the teacher, they will work best as a team when their complementary roles and skills are recognised and used accordingly. Indeed, any idea that assistants are all inherently frustrated teachers can be dispelled by research undertaken with assistants (e.g. Moyles 1997; Farrel et al. 1999; Foreman-Peck and Middlewood 2002). Some assistants, such as Todd (2003) and Rai (2003), are clear that they want to be in this role because it is important and fulfilling. They believe it is just as important as the teachers', but brings a different dimension to the learning process. As Todd (2003, p.9) explains:

> Pupils are more likely to ask me about a problem (either scholastic or personal) because I am not such an authoritative figure ... When we (the teachers and assistant) work well, we work as a team – but our functions are different and should be respected as such.

Similarly, effective midday supervisors employ a whole range of specific skills relevant to the situations that they manage. A case study by Ryall and Goddard (2003, p.74) identified 'use of effective communications with pupils and teaching staff and strategies for behaviour management including the non-confrontational handling of misbehaviour' as key elements in the improvement of this category of support staff. From this case study emerged also the significant issue that to enable these skills to be effectively deployed, there were several things that school leaders needed to address. For example, supervisors had in many contexts authority to punish but none to reward, and received no feedback from teachers to whom they referred disciplinary problems (p.75). It was hardly surprising that these staff were perceived by children as negative, and by teachers as ineffective. The involvement of the supervisors in revision of procedures, sanctions and rewards proved invaluable.

Need for a holistic view

As this chapter indicates, many recent studies focus on the role of various support staff, especially those working directly with teachers and learners. However, virtually all of them focus on the operational aspects of support staff roles and recommendations on the way to improve the situation for them, other staff, the organisation and, of course, the students or pupils. However, the effective leader should take a strategic view, related to the organisation's key purpose, develop a staffing model and profile which best suits that purpose, and aim to work towards that. Much current thinking appears to start from the current posts and not from what should be achieved and what kind of roles best serve that.

Middlewood and Parker (2001) offer one model in terms of support for learning against which specific roles can be developed. Acknowledging the teacher as the key manager of learning, they suggested that there may be three levels of support provided for learning:

1 The compensatory level – where support is needed to relieve pressure on teachers, to enable teachers to concentrate on their key tasks. This will inevitably involve some 'technical' work and operate directly under teacher direction.
2 The interpretative level – where support is focused on the learners being helped to understand the task required of them. This may involve, for example, re-emphasising, rephrasing the original task for the learner.
3 The extension level – where the students' learning is extended from the original task to understanding what comes next. This will involve interpreting the *learning* taking place to enable the students to make their own decisions (Middlewood and Parker 2001, p.198).

Such a model, as they explain, allows leaders and managers to decide which skills and qualities are needed at each specific level, and the deployment and training of support staff can therefore develop appropriately. It also, of course, offers clear opportunities for individual professional progression for those filling the roles, thereby supporting motivation and job satisfaction.

Kerry and Kerry (2003, p.80) see the changing nature of 'the support staff phenomenon' as part of a whole new reconstruction of schools and schooling in the postmodernist era. The leaders with a vision of what the organisation is likely to be will be aware of what kind of human resources will be needed to fulfil that vision. The kind of people, and the kinds of roles and tasks needed to achieve the vision, are a crucial part of this. Of course, except where a brand new school or college is being started, leaders and managers always have to start from where they are now. They can, however, try to ensure that they take as few, if any, steps which take them in a different direction from that of achieving the vision. In the early years of the twenty-first century, it can be argued that leaders are fortunate in doing this at a time when many roles are evolving anyway. The roles of support staff in schools and colleges seem destined for significant change in the next few years, giving leaders an opportunity to build that vision and make these staff a key part of its achievement. If the opportunity is missed, it may be harder when roles are more entrenched.

Conclusion

The nature of the support workforce, especially in schools in the UK, will continue to evolve and probably at a considerable speed. Rather than dealing with this on a piecemeal basis, just by replacing one person with another, the effective leader may wish to develop a staffing model for the future of the particular school or college, based upon the most effective way of enhancing pupil/student learning and continuing to improve achievement. This model will inevitably include a range of employees, with a variety of skills, some of which cannot necessarily be foreseen at present because of the evolving nature of learning in the twenty-first century and consequent evolving ways of supporting this. Just as the role of the teacher will develop, so will that of all those in supporting roles.

One staffing model, outlined by Hargreaves (1996), is that of having fewer, highly trained and specialised, teachers supported by a workforce of 'professionals'. This latter group will have a variety of skills available to support learning, directly or indirectly, just a 'paramedics' have between them a whole range of skills to help the patients in the hospital or health service, whilst the actual medical practitioners concentrate on using their specialist skills. This will inevitably be accompanied by an appropriate career structure and reasonable pay and conditions. Leading and managing support staff in such a context will be not only coherent but also more rewarding, for the staff and their leaders and managers.

References

Adamson, S. (1999), Review of published literature on teaching assistants, unpublished report for DfEE Teaching Assistants Project.

Busher, H. and Saran, R. (1995), 'Working with support staff', in Busher, H. and Saran, R. (eds), *Managing Teachers as Professionals in Schools*, London, Kogan Page.

Clayton, T. (1993), 'From domestic helper to assistant teacher: the changing role of the British classroom assistant', *European Journal of Special Needs Education*, 8 (1), 32–44.

Curtis, R. (2002,) 'The management of support staff', *Headship Matters*, (20), pp. 5–6, London, Optimus Publishing.

Dalin, P. and Rust, V. (1994), *How Schools Improve*, London, Cassell.

Department of Education and Skills (DES) (1992), *Use of Support Staff in Special Educational Needs Education*, London, DES.

Department of Education and Skills (DfES) (2002), *Raising standards and tackling workload: a national agreement*, London, DfES.

Farrel, D., Balshaw, M. and Polat, R. (1997) 'The management, role and training of learning support assistants', *Research Report No. 161*, London, DfEE.

Fenner, J. (1998), Effects of healthcare and diet on students learning, unpublished MBA dissertation, University of Leicester.

Fidler, B. and Atton, T. (1999), *Poorly Performing Staff in Schools and How to Manage Them*, London, Routledge.

Foreman-Peck, L. and Middlewood, D. (2002), *A Formative Evaluation of the Foundation Degree Arts – Learning and Teaching (Schools)*, Northampton, University College Northampton.

Hargreaves, D. (1996), 'Teaching as a research-based profession: possibilities and prospects', in *Teacher Training Agency Annual Lecture*, London, TTA.

Kedney, B. and Brownlow, S. (1994), *Funding Flexibility*, Mendip Paper 62, Blagdon, Staff College.

Kerry, C. and Kerry, T. (2003), 'Government policy and the effective employment and deployment of support staff in UK schools', *International Studies in Educational Administration*, 31 (1), 65–81.

Kerry, T. (2001), *Working with Support Staff*, London, Pearson Education.

Lee, B. (2002), 'The developing role of teaching assistants', *Headship Matters*, no. 20, London, Optimus Publishing, pp.11–12.

Local Government National Training Organisation (LGNTO) (2001), *National Occupational Standards for Teaching/Classroom Assistants*, London, Local Government National Training Organisation.

Lorenz, S. (1999), *Effective In-Class Support: The Management of Support Staff in Mainstream and Special Schools*, London, David Fulton.

Lumby, J. (2001), *Managing Further Education: A Learning Enterprise*, London, Paul Chapman Publishing.

Middlewood, D. (1997), 'Managing staff development', in Bush, T. and Middlewood, D. (eds), *Managing People in Education*, London, Paul Chapman Publishing.

Middlewood, D. (1999), 'Engendering change', in Middlewood, D., Coleman, M. and Lumby, J., *Practitioner Research in Education*, London, Paul Chapman Publishing, pp.119–136.

Middlewood, D. (2003), 'Teacher professionalism and development', in Lumby, J., Middlewood, D. and Kaabwe, S. (eds), *Managing Human Resources in South African Schools*, London, Commonwealth Secretariat.

Middlewood, D. and Parker, R. (2001), 'Managing curriculum support staff for effective learning', in Middlewood, D. and Burton, N. (eds), *Managing the Curriculum*, London, Paul Chapman Publishing, pp.190–203.

Mortimore, P., Mortimore, J. and Thomas, H. (1994), *Managing Associate Staff*, London, Paul Chapman Publishing.

Moyles, J. and Suschitzky, W. (1997), *Jill of All Trades*, London, ATL Publications.

Naylor, D. (1999), 'The professional development needs of mid-day assistants', *Professional Development Today*, 3 (1), 51–60.

Palmer, S. (2003), 'Learning to manage teaching assistants: a new role for teachers', in *CPD Update*, London, Optimus Publishing.

Rai, A. (2003), 'Finding more hours in the day', *Education Guardian*, 13 May.

Ryall, A. and Goddard, G. (2003), 'Support staff in primary schools: reflections upon the benefits of training and implications for schools', *Education 3–13*, 31 (1),

72–78.

Simkins, T. and Lumby, J. (2002), 'Cultural transformation in further education? Mapping the debate', *Research in Post-Compulsory Education*, 7 (1), 9–25.

Stoll, L., Fink, D. and Earl, L. (2003), *It's About Learning (and It's About Time!)*, London, RoutledgeFalmer.

Todd, D. (2003), 'Not in front of the children', *Education Guardian*, April, p.9.

Williams, S., Macalpine, A. and McCall, C. (2001), *Leading and Managing Staff through Challenging Times*, London, Stationery Office.

Wilson, V., Schlapp, U. and Davidson, J. (2003), 'An extra pair of hands? Managing classroom assistants in Scottish primary schools', *Educational Management and Administration*, 31 (2), 189–205.

PART II

Key Concepts Underpinning Educational Leadership

4

Organisational cultures

Introduction: defining culture

The concept of culture has become increasingly significant in education during the 1990s and into the twenty-first century. This enhanced interest may be understood as an example of dissatisfaction with the limitations of those leadership and management models which stress the structural and technical aspects of schools and colleges. The focus on the intangible world of values and attitudes is a useful counter to these bureaucratic assumptions and helps to produce a more balanced portrait of educational institutions.

Culture relates to the informal aspects of organisations rather then their official elements. They focus on the values, beliefs and norms of individuals in the organisation and how these individual perceptions coalesce into shared meanings. Culture is manifested by symbols and rituals rather than through the formal structure of the organisation:

> Beliefs, values and ideology are at the heart of organisations. Individuals hold certain ideas and value-preferences which influence how they behave and how they view the behaviour of other members. These norms become shared traditions which are communicated within the group and are reinforced by symbols and ritual. (Bush 2003, p.156)

The developing importance of culture arises partly from a wish to understand, and operate more effectively within, this informal domain of the values and beliefs of teachers, support staff and other stakeholders. Morgan (1997) and O'Neill (1994) both stress the increasing significance of cultural factors in leadership and management. The latter charts the appearance of cultural 'labels' and suggests why they have become more prevalent:

> The increased use of such cultural descriptors in the literature of educational management is significant because it reflects a need for educational organizations to be able to articulate deeply held and shared values in more tangible ways and therefore respond more effectively to new, uncertain and potentially

threatening demands on their capabilities. Organizations, therefore, articulate values in order to provide form and meaning for the activities of organizational members in the absence of visible and certain organizational structures and relationships. In this sense the analysis and influence of organizational culture become essential management tools in the pursuit of increased organizational growth and effectiveness. (O'Neill, 1994, p.116)

The shift towards self-management in many countries reinforces the notion of schools and colleges as unique entities with their own distinctive features or 'culture'. It is inevitable that self-management will lead to greater diversity and, in England, this is one of the Government's explicit aims. Caldwell and Spinks (1992) argue that there is 'a culture of self- management'. The essential components of this culture are the *empowerment* of leaders and their acceptance of *responsibility*.

Societal culture

Most of the literature on culture in education relates to organisational culture and that is also the main focus of this chapter. However, there is also an emerging literature on the broader theme of national or societal culture. Dimmock and Walker (2002a, p.3) claim that 'the field of educational administration ... has largely ignored the influence of societal culture' but their work has contributed to an increasing awareness of this concept.

Given the globalisation of education, issues of societal culture are increasingly significant. Walker and Dimmock (2002) refer to issues of context and stress the need to avoid 'decontextualized paradigms' (p.1) in researching and analysing educational systems and institutions:

> The field of educational leadership and management has developed along ethnocentric lines, being heavily dominated by Anglo-American paradigms and theories ... Frequently, either a narrow ethnicity pervades research and policy, or an implicit assumption is made that findings in one part of the world will necessarily apply in others. It is clear that a key factor missing from many debates on educational administration and leadership is context ... context is represented by societal culture and its mediating influence on theory, policy and practice. (Walker and Dimmock 2002, p.2)

Walker and Dimmock are by no means alone in advocating attention to issues of context. Crossley and Broadfoot (1992, p.100) say that 'policies and practice cannot be translated intact from one culture to another since the mediation of different cultural contexts can quite transform the latter's salience' while Bush et al. (1998, p.137) stress that 'all theories and interpretations of practice must be "grounded" in the specific context ... before they can be regarded as useful'.

Dimmock and Walker (2002b, p.71) have given sustained attention to these issues and provide a helpful distinction between societal and organisational culture:

> Societal cultures differ mostly at the level of basic values, while organizational cultures differ mostly at the level of more superficial practices, as reflected in the recognition of particular symbols, heroes and rituals. *This allows organizational cultures to be deliberately managed and changed*, whereas societal or national cultures are more enduring and change only gradually over longer time periods. School leaders influence, and in turn are influenced by, the organizational culture. Societal culture, on the other hand, is a given, being outside the sphere of influence of an individual school leader. (Our emphasis)

Dimmock and Walker (2002b) identify seven 'dimensions' of societal culture, each of which is expressed as a continuum:

1 *Power-distributed/power concentrated*: power is either distributed more equally among the various levels of a culture or is more concentrated.
2 *Group-oriented/self-oriented*: people in self-oriented cultures perceive themselves to be more independent and self-reliant. In group-oriented cultures, ties between people are tight, relationships are firmly structured and individual needs are subservient to the collective needs.
3 *Consideration/aggression*: in aggression cultures, achievement is stressed, competition dominates and conflicts are resolved through the exercise of power and assertiveness. In contrast, consideration societies emphasise relationships, solidarity and resolution of conflicts by compromise and negotiation.
4 *Proactivism/fatalism*: this dimension reflects the proactive or 'we can change things around here' attitude in some cultures, and the willingness to accept things as they are in others – a fatalistic perspective.
5 *Generative/replicative*: some cultures appear more predisposed towards innovation, or the generation of new ideas and methods, whereas other cultures appear more inclined to replicate or to adopt ideas and approaches from elsewhere.
6 *Limited relationship/holistic relationship*: in limited relationship cultures, interactions and relationships tend to be determined by explicit rules which are applied to everyone. In holistic cultures, greater attention is given to relationship obligations, for example kinship, patronage and friendship, than to impartially applied rules.
7 *Male influence/female influence*: in some societies, the male domination of decision-making in political, economic and professional life is perpetuated. In others, women have come to play a significant role (adapted from Dimmock and Walker 2002b, pp.74–6).

This model can be applied to educational systems in different countries. Bush and Qiang (2000) show that most of these dimensions are relevant to Chinese education:

- *Power is concentrated* in the hands of a limited number of leaders. 'The principal has positional authority within an essentially bureaucratic system ... China might be regarded as the archetypal high power-distance (power-concentrated) society' (p.60).
- Chinese culture is *group oriented*. 'Collective benefits [are] seen as more important than individual needs' (p.61).
- Chinese culture stresses *consideration* rather than aggression. 'The Confucian scholars advocate modesty and encourage friendly co-operation, giving priority to people's relationships. The purpose of education is to mould every individual into a harmonious member of society' (p.62).
- *Patriarchal leadership* dominates in education, business, government and the Communist Party itself. There are no women principals in the 89 secondary schools in three counties of the Shaanxi province. Coleman et al. (1998, p.144) attribute such inequalities to the continuing dominance of patriarchy.

Societal culture is one important aspect of the context within which school leaders must operate. Leaders and managers must also be aware of organisational culture which provides a more immediate framework for leadership action. Principals and others can help to shape culture but they are also influenced by it. Chapter 7, for example, refers to the need for educational leaders to be aware of the societal culture underpinning schools and colleges so that appropriate equal opportunities policies and practices can be developed.

Central features of organisational culture

Organisational culture has the following major features (Bush 2003):

1 It focuses on the *values and beliefs* of members of organisations. These values underpin the behaviour and attitudes of individuals within schools and colleges but they may not always be explicit. These individual beliefs coalesce into shared values: 'Shared values, shared beliefs, shared meaning, shared understanding, and shared sensemaking are all different ways of describing culture ... These patterns of understanding also provide a basis for making one's own behaviour sensible and meaningful' (Morgan, 1997, p.138).

   This does not necessarily mean that individual values are always in harmony with one another. Morgan (1997, p.137) suggests that 'there may be different and competing value systems that create a mosaic of organizational realities rather than a uniform corporate culture'. Dissonance is more likely in large, multipurpose organisations such as colleges and universities but Nias et al. (1989) note that they may also exist in primary education. Fullan and Hargreaves (1992, pp. 71–2) argue that some schools develop a 'balkanized' culture made up of separate and sometimes competing groups:

Teachers in balkanized cultures attach their loyalties and identities to particular groups of their colleagues. They are usually colleagues with whom they work most closely, spend most time, socialize most often in the staffroom. The existence of such groups in a school often reflects and reinforces very different group outlooks on learning, teaching styles, discipline and curriculum.

Staff working in sub-units, such as departments, may develop their own distinctive 'subculture' and middle managers, or 'middle level leaders' as the NCSL prefers to call them, may wish to cultivate this as a way of developing and enhancing team effectiveness. However, as Fullan and Hargreaves (1992) imply, such subcultures may not be consistent with the whole-school or college culture.

2 Organisational culture emphasises the development of *shared norms and meanings*. The assumption is that interaction between members of the organisation, or its subgroups, eventually leads to behavioural norms that gradually become cultural features of the school or college. Nias et al.'s (1989, pp.39–40) research shows how group norms were established in their case-study schools:

> As staff talked, worked and relaxed together, they began to negotiate shared meanings which enabled them to predict each other's behaviour. Consequently each staff developed its own taken-for-granted norms. Because shared meanings and ways of behaving became so taken for granted, existing staff were largely unaware of them. But they were visible to newcomers ... Researchers moving between schools were constantly reminded of the uniqueness of each school's norms.

These group norms sometimes allow the development of a monoculture in a school with meanings shared throughout the staff – 'the way we do things around here'. We have already noted, however, that there may be several subcultures based on the professional and personal interests of different groups. These typically have internal coherence but experience difficulty in relationships with other groups whose behavioural norms are different. Wallace and Hall (1994, pp.28 and 127) identify senior management teams (SMTs) as one example of group culture with clear internal norms but often weak connections to other groups and individuals:

> SMTs in our research developed a 'culture of teamwork' ... A norm common to the SMTs was that decisions must be reached by achieving a working consensus, entailing the acknowledgement of any dissenting views ... there was a clear distinction between interaction inside the team and contact with those outside ... [who] were excluded from the inner world of the team.

3 Culture is typically expressed through *rituals and ceremonies* which are used to support and celebrate beliefs and norms. Schools, in particular, are rich in such symbols as assemblies, prize-givings and corporate worship. Hoyle (1986, pp.150

and 152) argues that ritual is at the heart of cultural models: 'Symbols are a key component of the culture of all schools ... [they] have expressive tasks and symbols which are the only means whereby abstract values can be conveyed ... Symbols are central to the process of constructing meaning'. (Hoyle 1986, pp.150–2).

School culture may be symbolized through three modes:

(a) *Conceptually or verbally*, for example through use of language and the expression of organisational aims.
(b) *Behaviourally*, through rituals, ceremonies, rules, support mechanisms, and patterns of social interaction.
(c) *Visually or materially*, through facilities, equipment, memorabilia, mottoes, crests and uniforms (Beare et al. 1989, p.176).

Schein (1997, p.248) argues that 'rites and rituals [are] central to the deciphering as well as to the communicating of cultural assumptions'.

4 Organisational culture assumes the existence of *heroes and heroines* who embody the values and beliefs of the organisation. These honoured members typify the behaviours associated with the culture of the institution. Campbell-Evans (1993, p. 106) stresses that heroes or heroines are those whose achievements match the culture: 'Choice and recognition of heroes ... occurs within the cultural boundaries identified through the value filter ... The accomplishments of those individuals who come to be regarded as heroes are compatible with the cultural emphases.'

This feature is evident in South Africa, for example, where the huge interest in school sport means that sporting heroes are identified and celebrated. This was noted in a Durban school visited by one of the authors, where former student Shaun Pollock, the South African fast bowler, had numerous photographs on display and a room named after him. In celebrating the achievements of this cricketing 'hero', school managers are seeking to emphasise the centrality of sporting achievement to the ethos and culture of the school.

Developing a culture of learning in South Africa

As we noted earlier (p.48), societal or national culture underpins the organisational culture of individual schools and colleges. Nowhere is this more apparent than in South African schools where the predominant culture reflects the wider social structure of the post-apartheid era. Decades of institutionalised racism and injustice have been replaced by an overt commitment to democracy in all aspects of life, including education.

Ngcobo (2003) addresses issues of cultural diversity and, drawing on Irvine (1990), identifies nine dimensions of African culture:

• Spirituality: life is viewed as vitalistic rather than mechanistic.
• Harmony: humans and nature live interdependently and in harmony.

- Movement: rhythm, music and dance.
- Verve: high levels of stimulation.
- Affect: emotions and feelings.
- Communalism: social connectedness and an awareness of responsibilities to the group transcending individual privileges.
- Expressive individualism: genuine personal expression.
- Oral tradition: oral/aural metaphors and colourful forms.
- Social time perspective: time as social rather than material space (adapted from Ngcobo 2003, p.224).

Ngcobo (2003) notes that these cultural features are very different from European cultures. Such cultural differences became particularly significant as schools began to change their racial composition in response to the South African Schools Act (1996), which made it illegal to deny admission to students on the basis of race. Formerly white schools, with a predominantly 'European' culture, began to assimilate learners, and to a lesser extent educators, from different cultural backgrounds. Ngcobo (2003) gives two contrasting examples of how school leaders responded to these cultural changes. Vryburg high school avoided cultural diversity by dividing the premises into two sections (white and black). This had several deleterious consequences, including conflict leading to charges of assault being laid against 14 black learners and seven parents of white students. Greenland secondary school in Durban adopted a different approach, aiming at cultural diversity and encouraging learners and staff to express and celebrate their own cultures. This school has been very successful academically which the principal attributes to 'the strong integrative culture it promotes' (Ngcobo 2003, p.230).

During the Apartheid era, many of the 'black' schools became centres of resistance to the unpopular regime. Both learners and educators were frequently absent to take part in protest activity or simply because they were demoralised by government policies. They were also deeply concerned about the inequitable funding regimes for different racial groups. As a result, it became difficult for school principals to establish and sustain a 'culture of learning' in township and many deep rural schools. Both educators and learners became more involved with the struggle than they were in their own learning and teaching. They did not want to co-operate with a racist system even if they were disadvantaged by such a stance.

This issue surfaced in Bush and Anderson's (2003) survey of school principals in the KwaZulu-Natal province. In response to a question about the aims of their school, principals stated that:

- the school is striving to instill in the minds of learners that 'education is their future'
- to show the importance of education within and outside the school
- to provide a conducive educational environment
- to develop a culture of learning.

The absence of a culture of learning in many South African schools illustrates the long-term and uncertain nature of cultural change. The long years of resistance to apartheid education have to be replaced by a commitment to teaching and learning if South Africa is to thrive in an increasingly competitive world economy. However, educational values have to compete with the still prevalent discourse of struggle and also have to reconcile the diverse value systems of the different sub-cultures in South Africa's integrated schools. It seems likely that the development of a genuine culture of learning will be slow and dependent on the quality of leadership in individual schools.

Leadership and culture

We noted earlier (p.49) that societal culture is beyond the control of educational leaders but heads and principals are able to influence organisational culture. Arguably, they have the main responsibility for generating and sustaining culture and communicating core values and beliefs both within the organisation and to external stakeholders (Bush 1998, p.43). Heads and principals have their own values and beliefs arising from many years of successful professional practice. They are also expected to embody the culture of the school or college. Hoyle (1986, pp.155–6) stresses the symbolic dimension of leadership and the central role of heads in defining school culture:

> Few heads will avoid constructing an image of the school. They will differ in the degree to which this is a deliberate and charismatic task. Some heads ... will self-consciously seek to construct a great mission for the school. Others will convey their idea of the school less dramatically and construct a meaning from the basic materials of symbol-making: words, actions, artefacts and settings.

Schein (1997, p.211) argues that cultures spring primarily from the beliefs, values and assumptions of founders of organisations. Nias et al. (1989, p. 103) suggest that heads are 'founders' of their school's culture. They refer to two of their English case study schools where new heads dismantled the existing culture in order to create a new one based on their own values. The culture was rebuilt through example: 'All the heads of the project schools were aware of the power of example. Each head expected to influence staff through his/her example. Yet their actions may also have been symbolic of the values they tried to represent.' Nias et al. (1989) also mention the significance of co-leaders, such as deputy heads and curriculum co-ordinators, in disseminating school culture.

Deal (1985, pp.615–18) suggests several strategies for leaders who wish to generate culture:

- Document the school's history to be codified and passed on.
- Anoint and celebrate heroes and heroines.

- Review the school's rituals to convey cultural values and beliefs.
- Exploit and develop ceremony.
- Identify priests, priestesses and gossips, and incorporate them into mainstream activity. This provides access to the informal communications network.

One of the ways in which leaders can shape or change culture is through the appointment of other staff who have the same values and beliefs, leading to cultural consonance. In this view, the staff selection process provides an opportunity to set out the values of the school, or its leaders, in the hope that those who hold similar values will be attracted to the post while others will be deterred from making or pursuing an application. Over time, the culture of the school will shift in the direction sought by the principal. The literature on collegiality (e.g. Bush 2003) shows that leaders are more likely to cede power to others when they are confident that their own educational values will not be compromised by doing so.

Foskett and Lumby (2003) point out that staff selection processes are themselves subject to cultural variables. They draw on Akinnusi (1991) to distinguish between 'universalistic' and 'particularistic' approaches to selection. The universalistic approach, as discussed in Chapter 9 of this volume, for example, attempts to match applicants to objective criteria and is thought to be 'more successful in identifying the best match to the vacant post' (Foskett and Lumby 2003, p.71). These authors contrast this model with the particularistic approach adopted, for example, in Africa and in China. Here, 'selection is shaped by the personal affiliation of the players, for example kinship, religion, ethnic or political similarities' (p.70). This approach is likely to be successful in ensuring that the appointees have similar values to the leaders.

Using cultural criteria to appoint new staff may help to modify culture but the established staff, and inertia, may still ensure that change is highly problematic. Reynolds (1996) refers to one school where the prevailing culture was 'posing severe difficulties for any purported change attempts' (p.153). He points to 'multiple barriers to change' including:

- staff wanted 'top down' change and not 'ownership'
- 'we've always done it this way'
- individual reluctance to challenge the prevailing culture
- staff blaming children's home background for examination failure
- numerous personality clashes, personal agendas and fractured interpersonal relationships (Reynolds 1996, pp.153–4).

This example illustrates the difficulty of attempting to impose cultural change. As one former college principal stresses, '[it is] dangerous … for managers to move too fast on cultural change' (Bridge 1994, p.197). Turner (1990, p.11) acknowledges the pressures on leaders to 'mould' culture but rejects the belief that 'something as powerful as culture can be much affected by the puny efforts of top managers'.

Hargreaves (1999, p.59) makes a similar point, claiming that 'most people's beliefs, attitudes and values are far more resistant to change than leaders typically allow'. He identifies three circumstances when culture may be subject to rapid change:

- The school faces an obvious crisis, for example a highly critical inspection report or falling pupil numbers, leading to the prospect of staff redundancies or school closure.
- The leader is very charismatic, commanding instant trust, loyalty and fellowship. This may enable cultural change to be more radical and be achieved more quickly.
- The leader succeeds a very poor principal. Staff will be looking for change to instil a new sense of direction
(adapted from Hargreaves 1999, pp.59–60).

These points may also apply to sub-units and subcultures. Hargreaves (1999, p.60) concludes that, 'if none of these special conditions applies, assume that cultural change will be rather slow'.

Leaders also have responsibility for sustaining culture, and cultural maintenance is often regarded as a central feature of effective leadership. Sergiovanni (1984, p.9) claims that the cultural aspect is the most important dimension of leadership. Within his 'leadership forces hierarchy', the cultural element is more significant than the technical, human and educational aspects of leadership:

> The net effect of the cultural force of leadership is to bond together students, teachers, and others as believers in the work of the school ... As persons become members of this strong and binding culture, they are provided with opportunities for enjoying a special sense of personal importance and significance.

Limitations of organisational culture

The concept of organisational culture contributes several useful elements to the leadership and management of people in schools and colleges. The focus on the informal dimension is a valuable counter to the rigid and official components of the formal models. By stressing the values and beliefs of participants, culture reinforces the human aspects of management rather than their structural elements. However, this approach has three significant weaknesses (Bush 2003):

1 The notion of 'organisational culture' may simply be the imposition of the leaders' values on other members of the organisation. The search for a monoculture may mean subordinating the values and beliefs of some participants to those of leaders or the dominant group. 'Shared' cultures may be simply the values of leaders imposed on less powerful people. Morgan (1997) refers to 'a process of ideological

control' and warns of the risk of 'manipulation':

> Ideological manipulation and control is being advocated as an essential managerial strategy ... such manipulation may well be accompanied by resistance, resentment and mistrust ... where the culture controls rather than expresses human character, the metaphor may thus prove quite manipulative and totalitarian in its influence. (pp.150–1)

Prosser (1999, p.4) refers to the 'dark underworld' of school culture and links it to the concept of micropolitics: 'The micro-political perspective recognized that formal powers, rules, regulations, traditions and rituals were capable of being subverted by individuals, groups or affiliations in schools'. Hargreaves (1999, p.60) uses the term 'resistance group' to refer to sub-units seeking to subvert leaders and their intended cultural change. However, this may simply be a legitimate attempt to enunciate the specific values of, for example, departmental culture.

2 The portrayal of culture may be unduly mechanistic, assuming that leaders can determine the culture of the organisation (Morgan 1997). While they have influence over the evolution of culture by espousing desired values, they cannot ensure the emergence of a monoculture. As we have seen, secondary schools and colleges may have several subcultures operating in departments and other sections. This is not necessarily dysfunctional because successful sub-units are vital components of thriving institutions, and successful middle-level leadership and management are increasingly regarded as essential to school and college effectiveness (Harris 2002; Briggs 2003).

In an era of self-managing schools and colleges in many countries, lay influences on policy are increasingly significant. Governing bodies often have the formal responsibility for major decisions and they share in the creation of institutional culture. This does not mean simple acquiescence to the values of the head or principal. Rather, there may be negotiation leading to the possibility of conflict and the adoption of policies inconsistent with the leader's own values.

3 Hoyle (1986) argues that symbols may misrepresent the reality of the school or college. He suggests that schools may go through the appearance of change but the reality continues as before:

> A symbol can represent something which is 'real' in the sense that it ... acts as a surrogate for reality ... there will be a mutual recognition by the parties concerned that the substance has not been evoked but they are nevertheless content to sustain the fiction that it has if there has been some symbolization of the substance ... in reality the system carries on as formerly. (p.166)

Schein (1997, p.249) also warns against placing too much reliance on ritual.

> When the only salient data we have are the rites and rituals that have survived over a period of time, we must, of course, use them as best we

can … however … it is difficult to decipher just what assumptions leaders have held that have led to the creation of particular rites and rituals.

Conclusion: people and culture

The belief that schools and colleges are unique entities is gaining ground as people increasingly recognise the importance of the specific contexts, internal and external, which provide the frameworks within which leaders and managers must operate. Despite the pressures of globalisation, understanding and managing the school context is a vital dimension of leadership in the twenty-first century. Values and beliefs are not universal and a 'one size fits all' model does not work for nations any more than it does for schools.

The recognition that school and college development needs to be preceded by attitudinal change is also salutary, and is consistent with the view that teachers must feel 'ownership' of change if it is to be implemented effectively. Externally imposed innovation often fails because it is out of tune with the values of the teachers who have to implement it. 'Since organization ultimately resides in the heads of the people involved, effective organizational change always implies cultural change' (Morgan 1997, p.150).

The emphasis on values and symbols may also help to balance the focus on structure and process in many of the other models. The informal world of norms and ritual behaviour may be just as significant as the formal elements of schools and colleges. 'Even the most concrete and rational aspects of organization – whether structures, hierarchies, rules, or organizational routines – embody social constructions and meanings that are crucial for understanding how organization functions day to day' (Morgan 1997, p.146).

Culture also provides a focus for organisational action. Effective leaders often seek to influence values so that they become closer to, if not identical with, their own beliefs. In this way, they hope to achieve widespread support for, or 'ownership' of, new policies. By working through this informal domain, rather than imposing change through positional authority or political processes, heads, principals and other leaders, including middle managers, are more likely to gain support for innovation.

An understanding of both societal and organisational culture also provides a sound basis for leading and managing people in education. In many countries, schools and colleges are becoming multicultural, and recognition of the rich diversity of the cultural backgrounds of students, parents and staff is an essential element in school management. Similarly, all educational organisations have certain distinctive features and understanding and managing this cultural apparatus is vital if leadership is to be 'in tune' with the prevailing norms and values. An appreciation of the relevance of both societal and organisational culture, and of the values, beliefs and rituals that underpin them, is an important element in the leadership and management of schools and colleges.

References

Akinnusi, D. (1991), 'Personnel management in Africa', in Brewster, C. and Tyson, S. (eds), *International Comparisons in Human Resource Management*, London, Pitman.

Badat, S. (1995), 'Educational politics in the transition period', *Comparative Education*, 31 (2), 141–159.

Beare, H., Caldwell, B. and Millikan, R. (1989), *Creating an Excellent School: Some New Management Techniques*, London, Routledge.

Bridge, W. (1994), 'Change where contrasting cultures meet', in Gorringe, R. (ed.), *Changing the Culture of a College*, Blagdon, Coombe Lodge Reports.

Briggs, A. (2003), 'Finding the balance: exploring the organic and mechanical dimensions of middle managers' roles in English further education colleges', *Educational Management and Administration*, 31 (4), 421–436.

Bush, T. (1998), 'Organisational culture and strategic management', in Middlewood, D. and Lumby, J. (eds), *Strategic Management in Schools and Colleges*, London, Paul Chapman Publishing.

Bush, T. (2003), *Theories of Educational Leadership and Management: Third Edition*, London, Sage.

Bush, T. and Anderson, L. (2003), 'Organisational culture', in Thurlow, M., Bush, T. and Coleman, M. (eds), *Leadership and Strategic Management in South African Schools*, London, Commonwealth Secretariat.

Bush, T. and Qiang, H. (2000), 'Leadership and culture in Chinese education', *Asia Pacific Journal of Education*, 20 (2), 58–67.

Bush, T., Qiang, H. and Fang, J. (1998), 'Educational management in China: an overview', *Compare*, 28 (2), 133–140.

Caldwell, B. and Spinks, J. (1992), *Leading the Self-Managing School*, London, Falmer Press.

Campbell-Evans, G. (1993), 'A values perspective on school-based management', in Dimmock, C. (ed.), *School-Based Management and School Effectiveness*, London, Routledge.

Coleman, M., Qiang, H. and Li, Y.(1998), 'Women in educational management in China: experience in Shaanxi province', *Compare*, 28 (2), 141–154.

Crossley, M. and Broadfoot, P. (1992), 'Comparative and international research in education: scope, problems and potential', *British Educational Research Journal*, 18, 99–112.

Deal, T. (1985) 'The symbolism of effective schools', *Elementary School Journal*, 85 (5), 605–20.

Dimmock, C. and Walker, A. (2002a), An international view of the principalship and its development: allowing for cultural context – no one 'best practice' model, paper presented at the National College for School Leadership International Conference, Nottingham, October.

Dimmock, C. and Walker, A. (2002b), 'School leadership in context – societal and organizational cultures', in Bush, T. and Bell, L. (eds), *The Principles and Practice of Educational Management*, London, Paul Chapman Publishing.

Foskett, N. and Lumby, J. (2003), *Leading and Managing Education: International Dimensions*, London, Paul Chapman Publishing.

Fullan, M. and Hargreaves, A. (1992) *What's Worth Fighting for in Your School?*, Buckingham, Open University Press.

Hargreaves, D. (1999), 'Helping practitioners explore their school's culture', in J.Prosser (ed.), *School Culture*, London, Paul Chapman Publishing.

Harris, A. (2002), 'Effective leadership in schools facing challenging circumstances', *School Leadership and Management*, 22 (1), 15–26.

Hoyle, E. (1986), *The Politics of School Management*, Sevenoaks, Hodder and Stoughton.

Irvine, J. (1990), *Black Students and School Failure*, New York, Greenwood Press.

Morgan, G. (1997), *Images of Organization*, Newbury Park, CA, Sage.

Nias, J., Southworth, G. and Yeomans, R. (1989), *Staff Relationships in the Primary School*, London, Cassell.

Ngcobo, T. (2003), 'Managing multicultural contexts', in Lumby, J., Middlewood, D. and Kaabwe, E. (eds), *Managing Human Resources in South African Schools*, London, Commonwealth Secretariat.

O'Neill, J. (1994), 'Organizational structure and culture', in Bush, T. and West-Burnham, J. (eds), *The Principles of Educational Management*, Harlow, Longman.

Prosser, J. (1999), *School Culture*, London, Paul Chapman Publishing.

Reynolds, D. (1996), 'Turning round ineffective schools: some evidence and some speculations', in Gray, J., Reynolds, D., Fitz-Gibbon, C. and Jesson, D. (eds), *Merging Traditions: The Future of Research on School Effectiveness and School Improvement*, London, Cassell.

Schein, E. (1997), *Organizational Culture and Leadership*, San Francisco, CA, Jossey-Bass.

Sergiovanni, T. (1984) 'Cultural and competing perspectives in administrative theory and practice', in Sergiovanni, T. and Corbally, J. (eds), *Leadership and Organizational Culture*, Chicago, IL, University of Illinois Press.

Turner, C. (1990), *Organisational Culture*, Blagdon, Mendip Papers.

Walker, A. and Dimmock, C. (2002), 'Introduction', in Walker, A. and Dimmock, C. (eds), *School Leadership and Administration: Adopting a Cultural Perspective*, London, RoutledgeFalmer.

Wallace, M. and Hall, V. (1994) *Inside the SMT: Teamwork in Secondary School Management*, London, Paul Chapman Publishing.

5

Organisational structures and roles

Introduction: the nature and purpose of organisational structure

Structure refers to the formal pattern of relationships between people in organisations. It expresses the ways in which people relate to each other in order to achieve organisational objectives. O'Neill's (1994, p.109) definition captures the main features of structure and shows its relationship with the concept of 'role': 'Structure embodies … a formal description of roles, authority, relationships and positions within the organisation.' Everard and Morris (1996, p.x) also demonstrate the links between structure and roles: 'An organisation's structure embraces the organisation chart, the committees, the departments, the roles, [and] the hierarchical levels and authority.'

Structure is often represented by diagrams or charts which show the authorised pattern of relationships between members of the organisation. However, there is a tension between the focus on structure and the individual characteristics which people bring to their workplaces. If structure is regarded as a framework for individual role holders, it must also reflect the perspectives of these individuals. As Lumby (2001, p.82) suggests, 'the very concept of an organisational structure is problematic, as the organisation is a theoretical concept which exists in reality only as a set of buildings and people … Whatever the "structure" on paper, the reality will be a maelstrom of loosely connected beliefs and activities'. Despite this recognition of the importance, and variability, of individuals, all organisations have some form of structure which is recognisable and provides the framework for organisational activity. Lumby (2001, p.83) extends the notion of structure to embrace the external environment which interacts with the organisation and may enable or constrain its activities.

Mullins (1989, p.113) stresses that structure provides a means of improving organisational performance. He identifies six objectives of structure:

1 The economic and efficient *performance* of the organisation.
2 *Monitoring* the activities of the organisation.
3 *Accountability* for areas of work undertaken by groups and individuals.
4 *Co-ordination* of different parts of the organisation.

5 *Flexibility* in responding to future demands and developments, and in adapting to changing environmental influences.
6 The social *satisfaction* of people working in the organisation.

Fidler (1997) argues that structures have two overarching purposes, control and co-ordination, and both these dimensions are evident in Mullins's (1989) list. Structures are often tightened in an attempt to achieve greater control. Changing school management structures is one of the ways in which new heads can exert their influence over the school or college. However, creativity is more likely to be encouraged with a looser framework designed to co-ordinate rather then to control. Fullan (1999, p.5) notes that too little structure creates chaos while too much leads to 'grid-lock'. Lumby (2001, p.85) concludes that 'any structure will be a compromise which cannot achieve all that is required. It may be necessary to identify the primary objectives the structure is to achieve from the myriad that are possible'.

Structures and hierarchy

An abiding feature of structure is its emphasis on hierarchy. Organisations are almost always portrayed in terms of a vertical, or pyramidal, structure. Briggs's (2002, p.66) 'generalised hierarchy of management in further education colleges' includes middle managers as being at the third or fourth tier of the college hierarchy. They are subordinate to the principal and the senior management team but superordinate to staff working in their teams. Harper (2000) also emphasises the dominance of hierarchy in English further education. Her study of 107 such colleges leads her to conclude that 'one broad type of structure has become dominant which ... has become labelled as "the new college hierarchy"' (p.434):

> In the new college hierarchy no two colleges are identical. However, the common features are that the senior management team most typically consists of a chief executive and two, three or four senior managers, each accountable for one or more broad areas of operational management. Academic and support functions are centralised and middle managers coordinate varying aspects of support for teaching and learning within flatter organisational structures. (p.434)

Lumby's (2001) work in this sector suggests that the hierarchy is being modified as college principals respond to funding constraints. 'Management posts have been deleted, leading to flatter organisations' (p.86). She adds that the need for responsiveness has influenced restructuring in many colleges. More flexible structures are required to provide creativity and innovation:

> Organisational structures tend to get in the way of this process. The more hierarchic, bureaucratic and sectionalised they are, the more obstructive they tend

to be ... Self-organising units with their high level of autonomy are likely to be able to respond to the external and internal environment more swiftly and also motivate staff more effectively. (pp.87–8)

Despite this need, Lumby (2001, p.92) notes that 'some degree of bureaucratic hierarchy will always assert itself' and that structural change is often presented as a way of 'softening the rather negative connotations of hierarchy' (p.91).

The pervasiveness of hierarchy is demonstrated by its prevalence in other sectors of education. Smith (2002) joins with Deem (1998) to note that higher education structures are highly managerial and bureaucratic, notably in the new, or statutory, universities. Wallace and Hall's (1994) study of secondary school management teams also shows the significance of hierarchy. Within such teams, 'distinctions between levels of individual management responsibility variably reflected the formal status hierarchy within each team' (p.50). They identify four such status levels:

- head
- deputy heads
- other professional staff
- bursars or administrators
  (Wallace and Hall 1994, p.51).

Heads are superordinate because of their overall responsibility for the school, leading to a 'major hierarchical distinction' (p.52) at one school, while the most 'senior' deputy acted in the head's absence, contributing to 'a perception of hierarchy' (p.52). Hierarchy may also be manifested in a 'two tier' approach, as at 'Longrise', where only the most senior staff attended certain meetings, leading to less senior staff feeling excluded from the 'inner cabinet'. Bursars are perceived to be at the base of the hierarchy:

The most clear cut hierarchical distinction operated between the senior administrative officer at Drake, the bursar at Underhill and senior teaching staff in these two SMTs. They were not members of the teaching profession, they were paid less, and their contribution to the SMT was ... limited ... They did not attend all SMT meetings and their involvement in major policy decisions was largely restricted to considering the financial or administrative implications of proposals for action. (p.54)

This research demonstrates that, even in ostensibly collaborative frameworks, such as teams, hierarchy remains a powerful determinant of structure and process (see Chapter 8).

Hierarchy is also a dominant feature of structure in many other countries. In South Africa, for example, there are six levels external to the school and powerful bureaucratic constraints on the nature of internal structures (Bush 2003a). Similarly, Bush et al. (1998) note that in China there is 'a complex and elaborate structure

with five separate levels external to the school' (p.133) and bureaucratic requirements for the nature of internal structures.

The determinants of structure

A significant determinant of structure, as noted above, is the extent to which organisations are able to design or modify it to meet institutional needs. The central control in China means that there is little scope for local initiative, and structures are
very similar in all schools. The administrative structure has four main divisions:

- the principal's office, including one vice-principal in schools with 12–24 classes
  and two vice-principals in larger schools
- the Teaching Affairs section, responsible for the management of teaching and
  political (or moral) education
- the General Affairs section, responsible for infrastructure, including finance,
  buildings and equipment
- the school factory or farm, whose profits contribute to school income
  (Lewin et al. 1994 ; Bush et al. 1998).

There are also teaching and research groups, or *jiaoyanzu*, which comprise teachers
working together to develop curriculum and pedagogy. There is also a parallel Communist Party structure headed by a branch secretary in each school. Bush et al.
(1998) note that the structure is unwieldy with limited scope for principals to influence its design or to modify it as circumstances change.

The external control of school structures is also evident in South Africa where this
is largely determined by the provincial department of education. In KwaZulu-Natal,
for example, the distribution of promoted posts such as deputy principals and heads
of department is made by the Department of Education and Culture. While these
prescriptions are inevitably influential, many principals circumvent such restric-
tions by creating unofficial, and unpaid, subject leader posts to augment the formal
structure (Bush 2003a).

In England, structure is usually one of the discretionary elements of organisations. Leaders inherit structure but are free to adapt it to meet local needs:

> Local management for further education colleges, as for schools and universi-
> ties, leaves each college free to determine how its human and financial
> resources are best deployed to carry out the functions of the institution. The
> internal management structures of colleges, and the contexts in which they
> operate, are therefore largely developed in response to local management
> need, and shaped by the philosophies of those who manage them. (Briggs
> 2002, p.64)

The institutional context is a major variable in determining structure. Scale is one key dimension and larger organisations tend to have more complex structures. This is illustrated by one college, studied by Briggs (2002), whose staff refer to 'imperfections and frustrations' (p.71) which can be attributed to the college being both large and located on several sites.

Lumby (2001) shows how English colleges use the management structure as a tool for cultural change. Of the 164 colleges responding to her survey, only four had not restructured within the previous six years. Most had done so more than once in a 'belief in the efficacy of achieving the right structure to support effective management' (p.82). As Lumby's (2001) research demonstrates, restructuring is often undertaken in an attempt to promote change. However, Clark (1983, p.114) points out that 'the heavy hand of history' is an important aspect of educational organisations and simply changing structures does not mean that the previous framework simply fades away. Rather, the values implied by the former structure remain in place and continue to influence events and behaviour.

Wildy and Louden (2000), referring to restructuring in the USA, point to three dilemmas for school principals:

1 The *autonomy* dilemma, where principals are expected to share power with professional colleagues.
2 The *efficiency* dilemma, where principals are expected to minimise the wastage of resources such as time, energy and commitment. This requirement conflicts with the pressures for participation.
3 The *accountability* dilemma, where the principal has to be answerable to the district. This requirement also limits the scope for autonomy and participation.

School structures are likely to be a compromise, taking account of each of these dilemmas. In England, there may be a strong rhetorical commitment to participation but a residual reliance on formal structure. Wallace and Hall (1994) show that their six case study secondary schools 'all exhibited a strong commitment among members to a team approach to management' while retaining a significant measure of hierarchy both within, and external to, their senior management teams. The nature and significance of structure may also be influenced by gender. Coleman's (2002) study of English secondary school headteachers suggests that women are more likely than men to favour collaboration and teamwork.

Structures and organisational theory

Structure is an important aspect of the theory of educational leadership and management. The treatment of structure varies according to the conceptual assumptions underpinning each theory (Bush 2003b).

Bureaucracy

As we have noted, most organisational structures in education, particularly those in secondary schools and colleges, tend to be consistent with bureaucratic assumptions and some could be regarded as pictorial representations of democracy. Evetts (1992) stresses the bureaucratic nature of school structures and shows how it reinforces the headteacher's power. 'A high degree of authority is vested in the headteacher and transmitted through heads of departments/years ... [it implies] agreement about the headteacher's ability to direct the management of the school without disagreement or opposition' (p.84).

The hierarchical pyramid, referred to earlier, is based on bureaucratic theories (Turner 1991). This is reflected in the structure of English further education colleges (Lumby 2001). It is also evident in South Africa where there is an 'ethos of top down management' (Johnson 1995, p.224). 'It [is] important to bear in mind the nature of power relations within schools. In most cases, power resides with the principal who has legal authority and is legally accountable' (p.225).

Collegiality

An alternative to hierarchy is a collegial structure. In this model, structures are flattened and communication tends to be lateral rather than vertical, reflecting the view that all teachers should be involved in decision-making and 'own' the outcome of discussions. Authority in collegial structures is based on professional expertise rather than formal position. Ad hoc working parties, rather than committees whose membership is determined by position, may be more effective in promoting collegiality, as Brown et al. (1999) suggest in relation to English secondary schools. 'We have working parties who report back to faculties after consultation with the senior management team and collaborative policies are produced and implemented' (p.323).

There is some evidence of collegiality even within the largely bureaucratic structures prevalent in China and South Africa. As we noted earlier, Chinese schools have teaching and research groups (*jiaoyanzu*) which operate on the 'assumption that teachers would work together in almost every aspect of their work' (Paine and Ma 1993, p.676). In many South African schools, there is at least a rhetorical commitment to shared decision-making. Principals at all five KwaZulu-Natal schools studied by Bush (2003a) claimed to be working towards participatory decision-making. The main forum for this approach was the weekly staff meeting.

Referring to English further education, Harper (2000, p.442) suggests that 'team-based, non-hierarchical structures are far more appropriate for today's changing environment' but warns that 'flat organisations, by their very nature, present few opportunities for promotion, whereas in a Weberian bureaucracy there is a clearly defined career structure'.

English primary schools usually have flat and unstratified structures. Teachers are accountable directly to the head, rather than via an intermediate authority, limiting the extent and importance of the hierarchy (Bush 1997).

Micropolitics

The departmental structure of many secondary schools and colleges may allow micropolitics to thrive with subunits competing for resources and influence (Bush 2003b). The formal structure becomes the setting for conflict between interest groups and the structure may be subject to change through a process of bargaining and negotiation. 'Organisational structure[s] ... are often best understood as products and reflections of a struggle for political control ... organisational structure is frequently used as a political instrument' (Morgan 1997, pp.175–6).

Hoyle (1986) argues that schools are particularly prone to micropolitics because of their 'loosely coupled' structure based around the sectional interests of the different sub-units. This is evident, for example, in the Netherlands where there are two parallel structures representing subject departments and student guidance units. Imants et al. (2001, p.290) argue that these are 'conflicting sub-structures', leading to tension, fragmentation and barriers between teachers of different subjects. Micropolitics are also evident in Wildy and Louden's (2000) study of high schools in the USA, where the case study principals worked with a 'balkanised senior staff group'.

There is also significant evidence of micropolitics influencing structure in England. This is often related to scale, as Bolton (2000) suggests in relation to higher education. 'Larger units – those with more than, say, 30 staff – tend in any case to form themselves into interest groups or cliques' (p.57).

In further education, micropolitical 'territories' (Briggs 2005) exist while Lumby (2001) points out that restructuring can be seen as 'an internal political process of reshaping power' (p.89). Harper (2000, p.443) claims that 'there are serious conflicts between managers and lecturers in the sector'.

Wallace and Hall's (1994) study of secondary school teams also provides evidence of micropolitical activity:

> One head of science felt his first loyalty was to his faculty: 'when do you defend the faculty and when do you defend the general policy?'. His desire to serve partisan faculty interests, according to his beliefs and values about his role as a faculty leader, clashed on occasions with the expectation of other SMT members that he should adopt a 'school-wide' perspective within the SMT culture of teamwork.

This example illustrates the ease with which apparently collegial frameworks can become the settings for micropolitical activity. In this model, the structure may be unstable and be subject to change as different interest groups seek to shape it to their advantage.

Subjective models

Subjective models regard organisational structure as an outcome of the interaction of participants rather than a fixed entity. Structure is a product of the behaviour of individuals and serves to explain the relationships between members of organisations. Subjective theories stress the different meanings placed on structure by individuals. Structural change may be ineffective if it does not address the underlying concerns of individuals:

> Shifting the external trappings of individuals, which we may call organisation if we wish, turns out to be easier than altering the deeper meanings and purposes people express through organisation ... we are forced to see problems of organisational structure as inherent not in 'structure' itself but in the human meanings and purposes which support that structure. Thus it appears that we cannot solve organisational problems by either abolishing or improving structure alone; we must also look at their human foundations. (Greenfield 1973, p.565)

Lumby's (2001) study of English further education colleges addresses this issue. 'As the goals and experience of each individual are unique, from the subjective standpoint, an organisation cannot exist as a coherent whole, but merely as the sum of the range of different perspectives and experiences' (pp.82–3).

Ambiguity

Ambiguity models regard organisational structure as problematic. Institutions are portrayed as aggregations of loosely coupled sub-units with structures that may be both ambiguous and subject to change. Enderud (1980) argues that organisational structure may be subject to a variety of interpretations because of the ambiguity and sub-unit autonomy that exists in many large and complex organisations. 'What really matters to the way in which the formal structure influences the process is not what the structure formally "looks like" but how it is actually used' (p.248). One aspect of this process is the extent of participation in committees and working parties. People who are members of such committees may not participate regularly, may arrive late or leave early. 'One consequence of such structural ambiguities is that decisions may be possible only where there are enough participants. Attempts to make decisions without sufficient participation may founder at subsequent stages of the process' (Bush 2003b, p.146).

Large organisations are particularly prone to structural ambiguity. Briggs (2002, p.70) refers to a 'mismatch of role expectations' in English further education and subsequently adds that 'ambiguity and role overload are common features of the managers' situation' (Briggs 2005, p.46). Lumby (2001, p.100) states that 'whether the official place within the structure of any role had changed or not, the way the role was seen by the role holder and by others continued to change, and was likely to be subject to ambiguity, conflict and overload'.

Culture

Structure may be regarded as the physical manifestation of the culture of the organisation. 'There is a close link between culture and structure: indeed they are interdependent' (Stoll 1999, p.40). The values and beliefs of the institution are expressed in the pattern of roles and role relationships established by the school or college.

The larger and more complex the organisation, the greater the prospect of divergent meanings leading to the development of subcultures and the possibility of conflict between them. 'The relationship between organisational structure and culture is of crucial importance. A large and complex organisational structure increases the possibility of several cultures developing simultaneously within one organisation' (O'Neill 1994, p.108). This phenomenon is evident in English further education where managers are perceived to have a different value system from that of academic staff (Randle and Brady 1997; Harper 2000). Elliott (1996) contrasts the student-centred pedagogic culture of lecturers with the managerialist culture of managers.

Leadership and management roles

Structure is usually expressed in two distinctive features of the organisation. First, there is a pattern of committees and working parties which have regular or ad hoc meetings. Secondly, individual roles are established and there is a prescribed or recommended pattern of relationships between role holders. The relationship between structure and management roles is deceptively simple. As Hall (1997, p.61) explains, 'functionalist views of role theory suggested that, as long as a school's or college's purposes and structures could be identified, roles could be ascribed and subsequent behaviour predicted'. Subjective theorists, however, see roles as 'merely clusters of related meanings perceived to be appropriate to certain social settings' (Silverman 1971, p.134). Hall (1997) contrasts these two perspectives:

> Schools and colleges [are] in a transitional state between bureaucratic certainties (including tightly defined structures, roles and responsibilities) and the postmodern uncertainties (in which boundaries are permeable, roles blurred and tasks constantly changing) ... Researchers have, in the main, moved away from [a] formal description of tasks and responsibilities. (p.62)

Lumby (2001, p.95) endorses this latter view: 'Each individual will have a job description which delineates duties and responsibilities, but this is at best only a sketchy approximation of their role. The concept of role is more dynamic and exists at the interface of formal duties and responsibilities, the expectations of the role set and the status accorded to the role by the players.'

A distinction can be made between 'role-taking', accepting the role as it is presented, and 'role-making', actively reconstructing it (Turner 1969; Hall 1997). In the former model, roles are used to match people with tasks and responsibilities through job descriptions and other formal processes. In the latter approach, individuals behave differently from their job descriptions by responding to both the expectations of their role set and their own interpretation of the requirements of the post. 'Teachers, lecturers and principals, within the framework of their understanding of others' expectations of their roles, attempt to interpret them in ways which are comfortable, rewarding and manageable' (Hall 1997, p.64).

The dynamic nature of roles is illustrated by the changing patterns of teaching and management in English further education. Lumby (2001) refers to one such change, where lecturers have become de facto managers by taking on programme manager roles. Similarly, many support staff had enhanced status as a result of taking on management functions as colleges became autonomous in the early 1990s. Also, managers were increasingly appointed from outside education and 'imported' role expectations from their previous experience.

Briggs (2002, p.69) notes that role expectations varied according to management level in her study of middle managers in colleges:

- Senior managers expected middle managers to translate strategy into action.
- Middle managers saw themselves as 'bridging the gap', by interpreting college objectives.
- Team members saw the middle managers as 'bridges and brokers' and 'information managers'.

One team member expressed the dilemma more starkly, referring to middle managers 'mediating between those who actually do the work and those who institute unworkable policies' (p.70). Middle managers are affected by all three sets of perceptions as all contribute to their received role.

Smith's (2002) study of English universities shows that middle managers have to balance academic leadership with line management. While most of his respondents regard these dimensions as of equal significance, a significant minority disagreed, with those from chartered universities stressing academic leadership while those in the newer statutory universities gave primacy to line management.

Hall (1997) points to the changing role expectations in schools. These include:

- greater dependence on teamwork
- increased responsibilities for bursars and other support staff
- enhanced expectations on lay governors in self-managing schools.

These changes all point to the need for a flexible approach in interpreting the role of teachers, leaders and managers in educational organisations. Leaders and managers need to recognise that skills and talent can be found throughout the school or college and are not located only in the upper echelons of the hierarchy. Creativity is most likely to be facilitated by reducing the emphasis on formal structures and through empowering all staff.

Role conflict and ambiguity

The need to respond to differing expectations often leads to role strain, conflict or ambiguity. Role strain occurs when individual expectations are either contradicted or not shared with others. Hall (1997, p.69) regards role strain as 'inevitable' given the nature and scale of change in education. This also links to the problem of role overload where expectations increase to the point where strain, and sometimes stress, is evident. This can be seen in primary schools where headship may be not just a job but a way of life (Southworth 1995). It is also evident in further education where 'role overload was reported as universal and serious, leading to severe stress for staff' (Lumby 2001, p.101).

Role conflict occurs when there are contradictory expectations held for a person occupying a particular position. The conflict can occur between roles, within a role or within a role set (Hall 1997). Briggs (2002) says that strain or conflict can occur when there is a lack of role clarity. Smith (2002) makes a similar point in relation to the problem of managing 'difficult' members of staff in higher education. He refers to Bolton's (2000, p.62) explanation of this issue:

> The main culprit is the vagueness of the academic contract which implicitly acknowledges that research creativity cannot be predicated on a nine to five basis and that excellence in teaching cannot be imparted. If the HoD [head of department] decides, therefore, to question formally the performance of a particular member of staff, he or she will be faced with a major stumbling block – where is the written statement of what, in detail, is expected or required?

Lumby (2001) notes that conflict may also arise from 'boundary spanning' where external organisations may adopt a different view from internal stakeholders.

Role ambiguity occurs when an individual is uncertain about the precise nature of the role at any given time. This can be a particular problem for teachers undertaking management roles for the first time, usually without any specific preparation for their new responsibilities (Hall 1997). Briggs (2005, p.46) claims that role overload and ambiguity are 'common features of the [middle] managers' situation' in further education, a view endorsed by Lumby (2001).

The ubiquitous presence of role strain, conflict, ambiguity and overload suggests that leading and managing educational organisations is a thankless task, and it is little surprise that there are many early retirements and that there is a shortage of applications for headships in many English regions. However, the situation is less bleak than might be imagined. The many uncertainties create the space and 'structural looseness' to enable managers to shape their roles according to their own sense of what is important, taking account of, but not slavishly following, the expectations of others. Given the changing educational landscape, individual interpretation of roles is essential if they are to be creative and innovative. Hall (1997) and Lumby (2001) both point to the value of utilising 'space' flexibly to enhance the role:

> There is a positive side to role ambiguity. It is located in the space it allows for an individual to shape his or her own role. (Hall 1997, p.72)

> The gains from the creativity and energy of people liberated to build their own part of the organisation outweighed the disadvantages of the disagreements that arise as a consequence. (Lumby 2001, p.97)

Conclusion: linking structure and role

Structures are familiar elements of educational organisations. Because they are usually on 'display' as figures or charts, they provide an apparently clear description of school or college management. Structure also expresses the formal set of roles and role relationships for an organisation, setting out management responsibilities and accountabilities for all to see. These pictorial representations of structure, based essentially on the bureaucratic model, are also remarkably similar across educational contexts, leading to the misleading assumption that educational management operates in the same way regardless of national or school culture. The reality is much more complex and raises important questions about the validity of both structure and management roles.

1 The formal structure, expressed in a 'solid' form, may be misleading because it takes little account of the differing meanings of participants. When a manager leaves and is replaced, the new person rarely operates in the same way as the predecessor. Rather, they bring their own unique mix of values, qualifications and experience to interpret the role in their own way. This serves to modify the role and also produces subtle but important changes to the structure itself. The structure influences role behaviour but does not determine it.

2 The essentially Weberian structure (Bush 2003b) also raises wider questions about the nature of school and college management. The various points in the hierarchy are inevitably represented by role rather than person, 'principal' not 'Ann Smith' or 'Joseph Wong'. This means that the apparent structure remains unchanged as people move in or out of the organisation but it also implies a lack of respect for individual talents and personalities. The assumption is that people are 'role-takers' rather than 'role-makers' but the evidence is that successful lead-

ers and managers in the twenty-first century require space to create and recreate their roles in response to changing demands from the external environment.

3 The bureaucratic structure also underestimates the significance of alternative portrayals of school and college organisation. By emphasising hierarchy and vertical accountability, it neglects lateral and participative models, such as teamwork. It also downplays the potential for ambiguity and micropolitics to undermine the formal structure and, by adopting a 'one size fits all' model, underestimates the importance of societal and organisational culture.

These reservations demonstrate the limitations of bureaucratic structures and formal roles as the 'building blocks' of schools and colleges. However, they do not mean that structure is redundant. It provides an essential framework for organisational management and a valuable starting point for new teachers, leaders and managers. As long as structure can be *interpreted* flexibly, and is capable of being adapted to accommodate new people and a rapidly changing context, it remains helpful and relevant in understanding organisations and in helping them to operate effectively. Formal structures have their limitations but they are remarkably resilient.

References

Bolton, A. (2000), *Managing the Academic Unit*, Milton Keynes, Open University Press.

Briggs, A, (2002), 'Facilitating the role of middle managers in further education', *Research in Post-Compulsory Education*, 7 (1), 63–78.

Briggs, A, (2005), 'Middle managers in English further education colleges: understanding and modelling the role', *Educational Management, Administration and Leadership*, 33 (1) 27–50.

Brown, M., Boyle, B. and Boyle, T. (1999), 'Commonalities between perception and practice in models of school decision-making in secondary schools', *School Leadership and Management*, 21 (2), 199–218.

Bush, T. (1997), 'Management structures', in Bush, T. and Middlewood, D. (eds), *Managing People in Education*, London, Paul Chapman Publishing.

Bush, T. (2003a), 'Organisational structure', in Thurlow, M., Bush, T. and Coleman, M. (eds), *Leadership and Strategic Management in South African Schools*, London, Commonwealth Secretariat.

Bush, T. (2003b), *Theories of Educational Leadership and Management: Third Edition*, London, Sage.

Bush, T., Qiang, H. and Fang, J. (1998), 'Educational management in China: an overview', *Compare*, 28 (2), 133–141.

Clark, B.R. (1983), 'The contradictions of change in academic systems', *Higher Education*, 12, 101–116.

Coleman, M. (2002), *Women as Headteachers: Striking the Balance*, Stoke-on-Trent, Trentham Books.

Deem, R. (2000), *'New Managerialism' and the Management of UK Universities*, End of Award Report, Economic and Social Research Council.

Elliott, G. (1996), *Crisis and Change in Vocational Education and Training*, London, Jessica Kingsley.

Enderud, H. (1980), 'Administrative leadership in organised anarchies', *International Journal of Institutional Management in Higher Education*, 4 (3), 235–253.

Everard, B. and Morris, G. (1996), *Effective School Management: Third Edition*, London, Paul Chapman Publishing.

Evetts, J. (1992), 'The organisation of staff in secondary schools: headteachers' management structures', *School Organisation*, 12 (1), 83–98.

Fidler, B. (1997),'Organisational structure and organisational effectiveness', in Harris, A., Bennett, N. and Preedy, M. (eds), *Organisational Effectiveness and Improvement in Education*, Buckingham, Open University Press.

Fullan, M. (1999), *Change Forces: The Sequel*, London, Falmer.

Greenfield, T. (1973), 'Organisations as social inventions: rethinking assumptions about change', *Journal of Applied Behavioural Science*, 9 (5), 551–574.

Hall, V. (1997), 'Management roles in education', in Bush, T. and Middlewood, D. (eds), *Managing People in Education*, London, Paul Chapman Publishing.

Harper, H. (2000), 'New college hierarchies? Towards an examination of organisational structures in further education in England and Wales', *Educational Management and Administration*, 28 (4), 433–446.

Hoyle, E. (1986), *The Politics of School Management*, Sevenoaks, Hodder and Stoughton.

Imants, J., Sleegers, P. and Witziers, B. (2001), 'The tension between organisational sub-structures in secondary schools and educational reform', *School Leadership and Management*, 19 (2), 213–222.

Johnson, D. (1995), 'Developing an approach to educational management development in South Africa', *Comparative Education*, 31 (2), 223–241.

Lewin, K., Xu, H., Little, A. and Zheng, J. (1994), *Educational Innovation in China: Tracing the Impact of the 1985 Reforms*, Harlow, Longman.

Lumby, J. (2001), *Managing Further Education: Learning Enterprise*, London, Paul Chapman Publishing.

Morgan, G. (1997), *Images of Organisation*, Newbury Park, CA, Sage.

Mullins, L. (1989), *Management and Organisational Behaviour*, London, Pitman.

O'Neill, J. (1994), 'Organisational structure and culture', in Bush, T. and West-Burnham, J. (eds), *The Principles of Educational Management*, Harlow, Longman.

Paine, L. and Ma, L. (1993), 'Teachers working together: a dialogue on organisational and cultural perspectives of Chinese teachers', *International Journal of Educational Research*, 19, 675–697.

Randle, K. and Brady, N. (1997), 'Further education and the new managerialism', *Journal of Further and Higher Education*, 21 (2), 229–239.

Silverman, D. (1971), *The Theory of Organisations: A Sociological Framework*, London, Heinemann.

Smith, R. (2002), 'The role of the university head of department: a survey of two British universities', *Educational Management and Administration*, 30 (3), 293–312.

Southworth, G. (1995), *Looking into Primary Headship: A Research Based Interpretation*, Lewes, Falmer Press.

Stoll, L. (1999), 'School culture: black hole or fertile garden for school improvement?', in Prosser, J. (ed.), *School Culture*, London, Paul Chapman Publishing.

Turner, R. (1969), 'Role-taking: process versus conformity', in Lindesmith, A. and Strauss, A. (eds), *Readings in Social Psychology*, New York, Rinehart and Winston.

Turner, C. (1991), *Structures – fact and fiction*, Mendip Paper 007, Blagdon, Staff College.

Wallace, M. and Hall, V. (1994), *Inside the SMT: Teamwork in Secondary School Management*, London, Paul Chapman Publishing.

Wildy, H. and Louden, W. (2000), 'School restructuring and the dilemmas of principals' work', *Educational Management and Administration*, 28 (2) 173–184.

6

Staff motivation and job satisfaction

Introduction

Most employees recognise that the way they feel about their work and their job is affected by a number of factors. If they move from one job to another they may feel better or worse about it or, even in the same job, their feelings about the work they do may vary from period to period. It is almost certain that the better they feel about the work, the better they will carry it out. This chapter deals with the leader's role in trying to maintain and develop those positive feelings in employees in educational organisations. The ability and strategies to motivate staff, to develop staff morale and to try to ensure job satisfaction are central to the leader's role in raising performance. It is, however, a complex issue. Some of the theories related to motivation and job satisfaction are explored and the barriers to achieving them within organisations are described. Acknowledging the limitations to leaders' influence, the chapter suggests principles for leaders and managers to follow, recognising that perhaps the most significant task is to establish the particular context within which these can flourish. This context is essentially an individualised one, since external factors, often outside the leader's control, may actually work against individual notions of what motivates employees. Nevertheless, effective leaders and managers of staff recognise the crucial importance of motivation and job satisfaction, not least because they acknowledge its significance for their own performance!

Clarifying the terms

Motivation

As Riches (1994, p.224) pointed out, the 'increasing sophistication of technology in industry, and to a lesser extent in education, has heightened awareness that machines may be necessary for increasing efficiency and effectiveness but people and their motivation are seen more than ever to be irreplaceable'. He goes on to suggest that, since the early 1990s, 'programmes have come to the fore to help to provide a continuous reservoir of well-trained and highly motivated people ... although the education service with its concepts of "professionalism" and "autonomy" has hitherto paid limited attention to motivation and personal development.'

In examining motivational definitions, Riches (1994) suggested that a basic model included:

a. needs or expectations
b. behaviour
c. goals
d. some form of feedback. (p. 225)

There are many theories of motivation, among the best known being Maslow's (1970) hierarchy of needs, McGregor's (1960) 'X' and 'Y' theory and Herzberg's (1966) 'two factor' theory. Middlewood and Lumby (1998) summarised the main theories into three categories.

- *Needs theories*: the Maslow, McGregor and Herzberg theories all fit into this category, each based on the premise that basic needs or impulses within humans are the key to what motivates us. Maslow's hierarchy of needs from 'survival' and 'security' through to 'self-fulfilment' is readily recognisable to many managers. The important aspect of this theory is that satisfaction of needs is sequential and therefore employees cannot be motivated by self-fulfilment unless lower-level needs have been met. There is value for leaders in recognising the range of needs. However, Maslow's insistence on the need to meet these needs in strict hierarchical order is discredited. McGregor's theory that either people must be pressured by managers because they seek to avoid work or they are self-directed and responsible can be useful in analysing underlying assumptions about the way people behave and may be implicit in staff policies.

  Herzberg suggested that managers need to make staff positively satisfied and remove causes of dissatisfaction but that these two things are independent of each other. His extreme satisfiers were recognition, self-fulfilment and sense of achievement, whilst the main dissatisfiers were related to conditions at work (pay, relationships with employer), which Herzberg called the 'hygiene factors'. However, the theory, whilst offering sensible insights into managing employees, can lead to motivation and satisfaction being confused.
- *Goal theories*: Handy (1993) suggested that all employees make a personal calculation of costs and benefits of how they act and perform accordingly.
- *Equity theories*: these suggest that employees are primarily motivated by a sense of fair play and that perceptions that they are being treated less fairly than others will demotivate them.

As Middlewood and Lumby (1998) point out, many of these well-known theories originate in the west and probably do not pay enough attention to issues of race and culture. Hofstede's (1980) research on certain kinds of leadership suggested that western models are not necessarily motivating in other cultures, a view supported recently by Dimmock and Walker (2002).

Morale

Morale is normally used as the term referring to the general state of motivation and well-being amongst a group of people. Morale will therefore be determined by the overall psychological and physiological state of the staff. Evans (1998, p.30) describes it as 'a state of mind encompassing all the feelings determined by … anticipation of the extent of satisfaction of those needs … significantly affecting the work situation'.

Both motivation and morale therefore clearly involve the notion of anticipation and therefore can be related to the individual or group at work looking forward to what is going to happen or to be achieved.

Job satisfaction on the other hand implies an attitude or internal state which is associated with the work an employee *currently* does. Frase (1992) suggests that the greatest satisfaction comes from doing a good job but this satisfaction is not the cause of doing a good job. Improved performance leads to improved learning and improved learning results in greater employee satisfaction. In this sense, responsibilities and recognition are both seen as key motivators. Each appeals to employees' intrinsic needs related directly to their work, for example, teaching. The benefit of adding more responsibility may not be immediately understood, but it is assumed that teachers with a strong desire to increase their effectiveness, and possibly influence, can 'die on the vine of sameness. These teachers do not want to do a mediocre job; they want to do a good job, because this is where they gain their satisfaction' (p.26).

Job satisfaction and motivation are inextricably linked because staff need to feel they are doing a good job and, when that is established, the leader can build on that to try to motivate them to move forward. If there is basic dissatisfaction, there is little scope for motivation. South Africa's staffing problems in many schools in the second half of the 1990s were largely related to job dissatisfaction. 'A lack of job satisfaction leads to frequent absence from work; behaving aggressively, inclination to quit one's job, and psychological withdrawal from work' (Mwanwenda 1995, p.85).

The link between job dissatisfaction and absence or withdrawal from work is clear. Blauner (1964) identified 'Meaninglessness' as one of his elements in job dissatisfaction. Essentially where the job is seen as having no point, the eventual extreme logic will be that there is no point in going to work and can lead to depression and stress. Mwanwenda's (1995) analysis of a specific situation referred to violence in schools and lack of resources but sheer boredom with routine tasks can equally contribute to a job being seen as meaningless. Rowe (2003) argued that the endless testing of children to achieve artificial targets made teachers in England see teaching as more boring and less creative, and was a direct contributory factor in young people leaving the profession after only a few years. Fisher (1993) also referred to ancillary workers in education as one of the groups suffering from boredom at work, interestingly noting the advantages of those who worked with children at lunchtime over those who cleaned the empty buildings after working hours.

Blauner's (1964) other key elements in job dissatisfaction were:

- powerlessness – where the employee feels he/she has no influence in the job done
- isolation – where an employee appears not to fit in with any group and behaves differently from the norms of the workplace
- self-estrangement – where the employees do not see the job as important in their own lives and only the pay earned is relevant.

Factors influencing motivation and job satisfaction

As the abundance of theories suggests, motivation is an extremely individual matter; since needs and desires are internal states, the task for the leader in trying to analyse those factors influencing staff motivation and morale is complex. Each individual member of staff of a school or college needs to 'come to school in the morning with an understanding that each is valued first and foremost as a person' (Mortimore and Mortimore 1995, p.7). If not, the implication is that the quality of the staff member's experiences that day will be diminished and performance will suffer.

These factors can be categorised into four groups:

- Individual factors – these include a person's gender, their abilities, their age and experience, their personal circumstances. These factors are ones over which the leader or manager has no control or influence.
- Social factors – these particularly relate to relationships at work, which teams they are involved with, mentoring/buddying links, and whether personal relationships are involved or excluded at work. The influence of the leader/manager here is limited, since employees choose their own social groups and relationships.
- Organisational factors – these include the conditions of service, including facilities and physical resources. They also include workload and work incentives, fair distribution of these, and structured opportunities for career development. This is the area where the leaders and managers have full responsibility in creating a fair and appropriate working environment.
- Cultural factors – these are what make the employee feel they work for an organisation in which they believe. Equal opportunities in operation will indicate a sense of fairness, consideration for work/life balance will be seen as a valuing of employees as people. This may be seen as an important long term aim for leaders, and was dealt with fully in Chapter 4.

Limits to influence of leaders

An analysis of the factors influencing motivation and job satisfaction makes it clear that some of them are controlled by forces external to the school or college and therefore the scope for action by the organisation's leaders is restricted. The most usual external power in this context is national government policy and practice.

Prescribed curriculum

Many countries operate a national curriculum, the content of which (and in some cases the form also) is prescribed centrally by government departments. This has the effect of removing choice for teachers about what they teach and may well remove creativity and spontaneity from their daily work (Fryer 1996), both of which may be seen for many professionals as essential to motivation and job satisfaction. Along with prescription of content may come an overemphasis on other routine activities such as testing and recording. In discussing the long hours working culture in Britain, Johnson (2003, p.65) claims that in educational organisations:

> The core of the problem, however, is that a high proportion of those hours is spent in work that is imposed and considered by the workers unproductive in terms of pupil performance. Much of it is concerned with the recording of activity, required to provide documentary evidence to a distrusting government and its agencies.

Centralist control

In countries where there is clear and even authoritarian control of the educational system, the roles of those in educational organisations are more inclined towards those of functionaries, following central directives, and the scope for addressing the motivational needs of individuals is inevitably more restricted. In Greece, for example, 'the centralised, bureaucratised and authoritarian system of control over education' (Ifanti 1995, p.277) has meant a status for teachers as government employees, and with little devolution to regional and local level, the leaders themselves lose motivation. One headteacher in Crete (quoted in Middlewood 2001, p.184) describes how, if a teacher is absent and no one is prepared to take over – 'the children have no classes – they go home. This encourages a culture in which virtually all teachers send their own children to private extra classes, and many of them take on extra jobs outside their teaching hours. Many actually run private schools for an extra income'.

In Malta, Bezzina (2001, p.107) describes how meeting the challenge in moving from a highly centralised system to more local decision-making will be dependent upon the principals' ability to stimulate and motivate their professional colleagues.

Status of educational staff in society

The status of teachers in particular may be quite different in some countries compared with others, simply because of religious and cultural traditions which place a greater or lesser value on learning and education. Reynolds and Farrell (1996, p.54–7), in examining a number of studies, list 'the high status of teachers in the Pacific Rim societies' as one of the key factors in the superior educational achievement of students in East Asia, whilst Lewis (1995) notes the prestige of teaching in Japan as high relative to other professions. Status conferred via a title can be important too. Lumby and Briggs (2002) found that some lecturers employed in sixth form colleges (establishments for 16–19-years-old) much preferred the word 'lecturer' because of its academic associations, although they saw themselves as teaching, not lecturing.

Status is essentially something based on the perceptions of others, and where those that work in schools and colleges perceive themselves as being undervalued in society or by governments, this has clear implications for lower self-esteem and thereby job satisfaction and morale in the workforce. Farrel et al. (1997) point to the perceived low status of school support staff in England and Wales, whilst Johnson (2003, p.66) points out that, although government ministers' statements about teachers since 2001 have nearly all been positive, 'teachers believe the contrary' and he suggests that 'the continuation of policies that show a lack of trust in the profession produces the misapprehension'.

In developed countries, since the marketisation of education in the 1980s and 1990s, Ozga (1995) argues that it is easy for the educational workforce to be marginalised and in some cases scapegoated for the failure to raise standards despite massive restructuring. Her argument is that the workforce can become deskilled and that contributes to 'loss of control over the meaning and purpose of their work' (p.35). This last phrase epitomises a potential dilemma for school or college leaders in trying to eliminate Blauner's 'meaninglessness' from their staff's attitude to work. In a country such as Saudi Arabia, the status of jobs such as teaching may be seen as an inferior one for men (Bjerke and Al-Meer 1993), hence women are in the majority in the teaching profession. This can clearly have implications for motivation for people considering whether to enter the profession, especially men.

External control over incentives

Whether pay is a significant factor or not in motivating employees in schools or colleges, there is little doubt that lack of pay is a cause of job dissatisfaction. The issue of performance related pay is more directly related to the chapter on performance and review (Chapter 12) but here we may note that the scope for offering incentives, financial or otherwise, may be limited by pay, career progression and promotion structures which are uniform and legislated by government. In countries such as New Zealand, Israel and Singapore, teachers' career structures are formalised so that progression to the next stage depends upon some form of assessment, outside of leaders' control. At one extreme, if the assessment is rigorous and only a minority succeed in progressing, the risk is that those that do not succeed feel demotivated. At the other extreme, if the 'assessment' is ritualistic, with the assumption that all will 'pass', the incentive to work hard for success will be little. The introduction of the threshold assessment in the UK was described by the Secretary of State for Education as an important step in providing a 'well motivated' teaching force (DfEE 1998)), and Ingvarson (2001) compared it with a similar move in Australia. He predicted that around 90 per cent would pass and his prediction was correct with 92.5 per cent passing in the first year. 'The assessment gains no respect, there is no recognition and the salary progression quickly becomes automatic, which was what the teacher unions aimed for anyway' (p.170).

In countries where progression and pay is automatic, the risk of a 'job for life' culture developing is considerable. In Slovenia, for example, promotion is based on, primarily, length of service, days of in-service training (unassessed) and additional work (Erculj 2001). Whilst security in a post is important as a basis for satisfaction, it cannot in itself be a motivator for performance.

Importance of leadership at institutional level

Despite the limitations described above, the potential for leaders and managers to make an impact on motivation at institutional level is significant. There are two main reasons for this. The first is simply that motivation *is* an individual issue. National initiatives can never legislate for what employees individually feel or think in their own schools or colleges in the way that the managers in those places can. Figure 6.1 shows a representation of the relative impact of influencers on motivation.

The significance for leaders of schools and colleges is in realising that the people closest to the individual employee will have the most impact upon motivation. In management terms, the actions of the person with direct responsibility for the employee's work (line manager) have a more direct impact than those of organisational leaders.

The second reason is that the evidence is overwhelming that the more immediate the benefit of an action is perceived to be, the greater is likely to be its impact. Not only do people appreciate shorter-term goals (Kakabadse et al. 1988), but adult learners generally need to see practical and relevant outcomes for their learning to be motivated (Knowles 1984; Brookfield 1986).

Furthermore, the actual quality of management at institutional level has been shown to have a direct impact upon staff motivation. Hutchings et al. (2000) found that 40 per cent of demotivated teachers in London schools cited 'poor management' as being central to their demotivation and dissatisfaction. In a survey on *The Quality of Teachers' Working Lives* (2001), the National Foundation for Educational

Research (NFER) found that good quality management was very high on the list of factors that were significant for those teachers in the UK who were 'satisfied' or 'very satisfied' with their working lives. Similarly, in Kremer-Hayon and Goldstein's (1990) study of Israeli secondary school teachers, school managers were found to be central to the attitude to work that the teachers had.

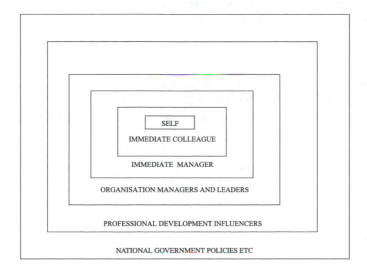

Fig. 6.1 Relative impact of influencers on motivation

Motivational strategies at institutional level

The following may be seen to be relevant to those with responsibility for motivating staff in individual schools or colleges.

Recognising the importance of individuality in motivation

As Whitaker (1997, p.20) notes, 'In managing, treating all people the same is a recipe for difficulty and disappointment'.

All employees need to be treated appropriately, taking into account as far as possible their needs and aspirations. Some of the variations in these needs and aspirations can be appreciated and catered for if attention is paid to the fact that staff can be differently motivated according to the stage of career they are at, their gender, or the culture within which they operate. This is essentially an issue of equal opportunities, which is dealt with fully in Chapter 7.

In terms of stages of career
Leithwood (1990) identified the following career cycle (although it was based on teachers, it is equally relevant to all employees in education):

1 Launching the career.
2 Stabilising: developing mature commitment, feeling at ease, seeking more responsibility.
3 New challenges and concerns, diversifying, seeking added responsibilities.
4 Reaching a professional plateau: reappraisal, sense of mortality, ceasing striving for promotion or stagnating and becoming cynical.
5 Preparing for retirement: focusing, disenchantment, serenity.

Most schools or colleges, even small ones, are very likely to have people on their staff who are at different stages of a cycle such as this. Someone who is at stage 2, for example, may be motivated by being offered the opportunity to get involved in a new initiative or take on a responsibility. Someone at stage 4, possibly a middle manager, may need the challenge of a whole new sense of direction, a fresh challenge, so that their abilities can be acknowledged and they have something new to look forward to. Someone at stage 5 may need to be motivated by the leader offering them a chance to finish their career 'with a flourish' by achieving something not tackled before but relevant to their experience.

Career stages of course cannot be separated from the stages of human development that individuals move through during their lives. Erikson's (1977) model defined the issue for ages 30–60 stage of development for humans as being 'Generativity versus stagnation'. Since this period covers at present the bulk of a working career in education, it suggests that the ability to enable others to be motivated and renewed is one which is not only valuable to the organisation in fulfilling its goals but one which is also contributing to people leading richer, more fulfilled lives.

In terms of gender

Thompson (1992, p.260) states that: 'Comparative studies of 65 occupations found that most men work for money and career advancement. Men are always looking up the ladder to the main chance whereas women seek job satisfaction, a good working atmosphere and flexibility to fit family life into their careers.'

Of course, in many education systems women do not have the same opportunities as men anyway, but the manager still needs to be alert to potential differences in factors affecting motivation for men and for women. Coleman's (2002) research into women as headteachers in England and Wales powerfully brings out the importance of avoiding stereotyping. This has crucial implications for managers of motivation since they need to avoid making assumptions about what motivates someone simply because she is, for example, a single woman who may, according to the stereotype, be a 'career woman (who) are cold, hard and single-minded' (Coleman 2002, p.86). The most common gender stereotypes relevant to motivation relate to women being seen as wanting to carry the caring role from home into the work situation, and to men as seen wanting to take on more disciplinary and competitive roles.

In terms of different cultures

Harrison's (1995) study, building on the work of Hofstede (1980), suggested that as a country's economy developed so the emphasis on individualism increased with its consequent implications for motivation. However, as Foskett and Lumby (2003, p.77) point out, this may be undermined by the many conclusions in published studies. They point to Fisher and Yuan's (1998) study which found that satisfaction factors differed considerably, from 'good wages' (China) to 'promotion and growth of skills' (Russia). All these points underline the principle that a universality of imperatives for motivation and satisfaction cannot be assumed.

Provide opportunities for relevant professional development

Professional development and staff learning is fully dealt with in Chapter 13, but it is worth noting here that, since personal growth and development is closely allied to motivational attitudes, leaders and managers will wish to use this as a powerful means of motivating staff. The opportunity to develop skills, gain new ones and demonstrate to oneself the ability to learn new ideas and apply them, is for adults an important way of gaining the confidence to meet new challenges and adapt to changed situations.

Professional development can be a powerful motivating force even in circumstances where all the usual factors likely to motivate staff appear to be absent. Taylor (2003, p.9) contrasts the motivational attitudes of the staff of two schools she worked in, both of which were designated to close, and attributes the success of one of them to the leadership shown.

> [An] ... important thing that the leadership did was to establish a very full programme of accredited professional development with a local higher education provider. The accreditation was very important because it offered the opportunity for everyone to gain some form of qualification that would benefit them greatly in their applications now and in their future careers.

She describes how she gained a higher degree 'something I believe I never would have been motivated to do if I had stayed in a normal school. Five others at least that I know of from that group have also obtained their Masters degree qualification since and two or three others have diplomas'. She concludes that 'it is a tribute to the programme and above all the staff that the tutor describes the staff group as being one of the most enthusiastic that he had encountered. Thus we must have been well motivated in our circumstances!'

Similarly, Middlewood (1999) describes how school-based research-centred professional development programmes were found to produce significant impact on staff morale. In one school due for closure, the maintaining of motivation was an actual stated aim of the programme. In the second school, the course was established in what was seen as a failing school, and then the news came of its intended closure. One of the school managers felt that the unifying aspect of the course was important in motivating them. Middlewood (1999, p.94) concludes:

The situations in these two schools offered evidence that, since the direct aim for school improvement could hardly be deemed to be relevant as the schools would no longer exist, the benefits must lie in the process, firstly for maintaining and enhancing the motivation of teachers in potentially very demotivating circumstances and, secondly, enabling the schools' students to receive the best possible service during the schools' remaining time.

Provide individuals and teams with a sense of direction

Since motivation is focused on future action, staff's capacity to be motivated will be greater if their organisation, their team and they themselves are able to see that future courses of action are clear and worthwhile. Organisations that 'wander' or 'meander' (Hopkins et al. 1994) or 'cruise' (Stoll and Fink 1998) have great difficulty in motivating staff either because there is complacency ('We're doing alright as we are') or because this new exhortation to work is just another initiative ('Here we go again').

Leaders who provide strategic direction also tend to provide ways of achieving strategic goals to aid motivation. A secondary head (Parker 1997) was fond of quoting the Koran: 'If you do not know where you are going, anywhere will do.' Even in the cases of the closing schools quoted above, a clear end was in view and some leaders used this to motivate colleagues. Howse and MacPherson (2001) showed how, in the development of New Zealand polytechnics, all motivation was lost by lecturing and support staff because they felt no educational focus and direction was being given by their senior managers. A focus on managerialism and financial planning by leaders meant that staff were not willing or able to see their increased workloads as being relevant to what they had believed to be the polytechnics' key purpose, i.e. student learning.

The lesson for leaders is that staff want to work in a school or college that they feel is 'going somewhere' and this offers an opportunity for what leaders aspire to – the alignment of individual and organisational goals.

Give as much recognition as possible

One of the key phrases in motivation is, according to Evans (1998), 'Nothing succeeds like success' and leaders need to take every opportunity to acknowledge and recognise both achievement and effort. Dwight's (1986) work on patterns of motivation emphasised how important it is to place emphasis on the *effort* people have put into their work and subsequent achievement, much more than an emphasis on their ability. Hopefully, many employees will have both ability and effort but Dwight argued that the risk of overemphasis on ability may mean that when someone does not achieve, they may interpret it as the fact they are not as good as they thought and become demotivated, trying less hard next time.

As far as tangible recognition is concerned, especially in the form of payment, Lumby and Li (1998) showed how it was possible for colleges in China, a country not known for its individual enterprise, to use funds generated by initiatives to provide a range of rewards and incentives. In England and Wales in 2002, the government awarded cash rewards to schools whose examination performance had improved significantly over three years. However, Baxter's (2003) study of how three secondary schools passed the money on within their schools showed the influence individual leaders had on staff motivation.

In School A, the head decided simply to divide the sum of money equally among every employee in the school at the time of the award. Thus everyone (principal, teacher, secretary, caretaker, lunchtime supervisor) all received the same sum. The resultant sum was not great, but it was proportionately (of salary) much higher for some than others, and the staff response was that 94 per cent of the employees found it 'very fair'.

In School B, a complex formula was developed to try to ensure that those who had contributed most directly to the improvement received most money, others less so. Every employee received at least a token amount. Thirty-four per cent saw this distribution as being very fair.

In School C, the leadership allocated the money after a discussion among themselves, awarding most of the money to the school managers and heads of those departments that had improved significantly. Here, only 11 per cent of the staff saw this as very fair, a figure well below the numbers who had actually received awards!

Allow as much employee ownership of work as possible

Fisher and Yuan's (1998) study showed that, in Russia and the USA, being kept informed and involved with decisions so these were not left to be passed down from 'on high' was seen as very important to employees. The literature of educational change (Hopkins et al. 1994; Fullan 1999) demonstrates that ownership of an initiative by those who are to implement it is crucial to success. Day et al. (1990) indicate ways in which staff may become demotivated if:

1 People are simply told that 'they must ... '.
2 People are put into a threatened position.
3 It is felt that the plan is a 'gimmick' promoted by a senior member of staff to further his or her own ends.
4 People feel that the plan is mounted merely to satisfy higher authority.
5 People feel alienated from the organisation or from whoever is responsible for the plan.
6 The leader assumes the role of the 'expert' and there is a lack of opportunity for teachers to develop, or to exercise, responsibility (adapted from Day et al. 1990).

Rea (1997) argues that in a complex organisation, such as a school, 'freedom within structure and fun with limits' is essential to optimise achievement, and uses the expression 'serious fun' to stress the importance of teachers and learners having the opportunity to motivate themselves – for the benefit of the organisation.

This ownership at the actual work level is likely also to contribute to the development of the 'secure human relationships' which are seen as important to motivation. Even in places deprived of basic resources, such as Zambia where one in ten families is headed by a child and one out of three children has a parent who has died of AIDS, these relationships are still seen as on a par with the importance for schools of running water (Riley 2000).

Conclusion

Most writers either explicitly or implicitly indicate that only leaders and managers who are themselves motivated will be successful in motivating others. McClelland (1987) followed his original 1970s work on motivation of high achievers by noting: 'What motivates world-class leaders from mediocre ones are specific behaviours such as self-control, self-confidence, an ability to get a consensus from people, and *strong motivation for achievement* ... '. The lesson for those who wish to motivate others effectively appears to be, as so often in people management, begin with yourself!

References

Baxter, G. (2003), 'A fair distribution of rewards?', *Headship Matters*, (25), 5–6.

Bezzina C. (2001), 'From administering to managing and leading: the case of Malta', in Pashiardis, P. (ed.), *International Perspectives on Educational Leadership*, Hong Kong, Commonwealth Council for Educational Administration and Management.

Bjerke, B. and Al-Meer, A. (1993), 'Culture's consequences: management in Saudi Arabia', *Leadership and Organisation Development Journal*, 14 (1), 30–35.

Blauner, S. (1964), *Alienation and Freedom*, Chicago, IL, University of Chicago Press.

Brookfield, S. (1986), *Understand and Facilitating Adult Learning*, Milton Keynes, Open University Press.

Coleman, M. (2002), *Women Headteachers: Striking the Balance*, Stoke-on-Trent, Trentham Books.

Day, C., Johnston, D. and Whitaker, P. (1990), *Managing Primary Schools in the 1990s: A Professional Development Approach*, London, Paul Chapman Publishing.

Department for Education and Employment (DfEE) (1998), *Teachers: Meeting the Challenge of Change*, Green Paper, London, DfEE.

Dimmock, C. and Walker, A. (2002), 'School leadership in context: societal and organisational cultures', in Bush, T. and Bell, L. (eds), *The Principles and Practice of Educational Management*, London, Paul Chapman Publishing.

Dwight, C. (1986), *Patterns of Motivation*, Oxford, Blackwell.

Erculj, J. (2000), 'Appraisal in Slovenia – the headteacher's burden?', in Middlewood,

D. and Cardno, C. (eds), *Managing Teacher Appraisal and Performance: A Comparative Approach*, London, Paul Chapman Publishing.

Erikson, E. (1977), *Childhood and Society*, London, Triad/Granada.

Evans, L. (1998), *Staff Motivation, Morale and Job Satisfaction*, London, Paul Chapman Publishing.

Farrel, D., Balshaw, M. and Polat, R. (1997), *The Management, Role and Training of Learning Support Assistants*, Research Report No 161, London, DfEE.

Fisher, C. (1993), 'Boredom at work: a neglected concept', *Human Relations*, 46 (3), 395–417.

Fisher, C. and Yuan, A. (1998), 'What motivates employees? A comparison of US and Chinese responses', *International Journal of Human Resource Management*, 9 (3), 516–528.

Foskett, N. and Lumby, J. (2003), *Leading and Management in Education: International Dimensions*, London, Paul Chapman Publishing.

Frase, L. (1992), 'Maximising people power in schools: motivating and managing teachers and staff', *Successful Schools*, 5, California, Corwin Press.

Fryer, M. (1996), *Creative Teaching and Learning*, London, Paul Chapman Publishing.

Fullan, M. (1999), *Change Forces: The Sequel*, London, Falmer Press.

Handy, C. (1993), *Understanding Organisations*, 4th edition, Harmondsworth, Penguin.

Harrison, G. (1995), 'Satisfaction, tension and interpersonal relations: a cross-cultural comparison of managers in Singapore and Australia', *Journal of Managerial Psychology*, 10 (8), 13–19.

Herzberg, F. (1966), 'The motivation–hygiene theory', in Pugh, D. (ed.), *Organisation Theory: Selected Readings*, Harmondsworth, Penguin.

Hofstede, G. (1980), *Culture's consequences: International Differences in Work-Related Values*, Beverly Hills, CA, Sage.

Hopkins, D., Ainscow, M. and West, M. (1994), *School Improvement in an Era of Change*, London, Cassell.

Howse, J. and MacPherson, R. (2001), 'New Zealand's educational administration policies 1984–1994 and the strategic management of its polytechnics', in Pashiardis, P. (ed.), *International Perspectives on Educational Leadership*, Hong Kong, Commonwealth Council for Educational Administration and Management.

Hutchings, M., Mentor, I., Ross, A. and Thomson, D. (2000), *Teacher Supply and Retention in London 1998–1999*, London, University of North London School of Education.

Ifanti, A. (1995), 'Policy making, politics and administration in education in Greece', *Educational Management and Administration*, 23 (4), 217–278.

Ingvarson, L. (2001), 'Developing standards and assessments for accomplished teaching: a responsibility of the profession', in Middlewood, D. and Cardno, C. (eds), *Managing Teacher Appraisal and Performance: A Comparative Approach*, London, Paul Chapman Publishing.

Johnson, M. (2003), 'From victims of change to agents of change', *Professional Devel-*

opment Today, 6 (1), 63–68.

Kakabadse, A., Ludlow, R. and Vinnicombe, S. (1988), *Working in Organisations*, Harmondsworth, Penguin.

Knowles, M. (1984), *Andragogy in Action*, London, McGraw-Hill.

Kremer-Hayon, L. and Goldstein, Z. (1990), 'The inner world of Israeli secondary school teachers: work centrality, job satisfaction and stress', *Comparative Education*, 26, 285–289.

Leithwood, K. (1990), 'The principal's role in teacher development', in Joyce, B. (ed.), *Changing School Culture through Staff Development*, Alexandria, Victoria, ASCD.

Lewis, C. (1995), *Educating Hearts and Minds: Reflections on Japanese Pre-School and Elementary Education*, New York, Cambridge University Press.

Lumby, J. and Briggs, A. (2002), *Sixth Form Colleges: Policy, Purpose and Practice*, Leicester, University of Leicester and Nuffield Foundation.

Lumby, J. and Li, Y. (1998), 'Managing vocational education in China', *Compare*, 28 (2), 197–206.

Maslow, A. (1970), *Motivation and Personality*, New York, Harper and Row.

McClelland, D.A. (1987), *Human Motivation*, Cambridge, Cambridge University Press.

McGregor, D. (1960), *The Human Side of Enterprise*, New York, McGraw-Hill.

Middlewood, D. (1999), 'Some effects of multiple research projects on the host school staff and their relationships', in Middlewood, D., Coleman, M. and Lumby, J., *Practitioner Research in Education: Making a difference*, London, Paul Chapman Publishing.

Middlewood, D. (2001), 'The future of managing teacher performance and its appraisal', in Middlewood, D. and Cardno, C. (eds), *Managing Teacher Appraisal and Performance: A Comparative Approach*, London, Paul Chapman Publishing.

Middlewood, D. and Lumby, J. (1998), *Human Resource Management in Schools and Colleges*, London, Paul Chapman Publishing.

Mortimore, P. and Mortimore, J. (1995), *The Secondary Head*, London, Paul Chapman Publishing.

Mwanwenda, T. (1995), 'Job satisfaction among secondary school teachers in Transkei', *South African Journal of Education*, 19 (2), 84–87.

National Foundation for Educational Research (NFER) (2001), *The Quality of Teachers' Working Lives*, Slough, National Foundation for Educational Research.

Ozga, J. (1995), 'Deskilling a profession: professionalism, deprofessionalisation and the new managerialism', in Busher, H. and Saran, R. (eds), *Managing Teachers as Professionals in Schools*, London, Kogan Page.

Parker, R. (1997), Strategic planning and leadership, unpublished MBA dissertation, University of Leicester.

Rea, D. (1997), Achievement motivation as a dynamical system, paper presented at American Educational Research Association, Chicago.

Reynolds, D. and Farrell, S. (1996), *Worlds Apart: A Review of International Surveys of*

Educational Achievement including England, London, HMSO.

Riches, C. (1994), 'Motivation', in Bush, T. and West-Burnham, J. (eds), *The Principles of Educational Management*, Harlow, Longman.

Riley, K. (2000), Speech to National Union of Teachers, Stoke Rochford, April.

Rowe, J. (2003), 'The myth of target-setting', *Primary Headship*, (11), 2–3, London, Optimus Publishing.

Stoll, L. and Fink, D. (1998), 'The cruising school: the unidentified ineffective school', in Stoll, L. and Myers, K. (eds), *No Quick Fixes: Perspectives on Schools in Difficulty*, Basingstoke, Falmer.

Taylor, D. (2003), 'Managing within closing schools', *Headship Matters*, (23), 4–5, London, Optimus Publishing.

Thompson, M. (1992), 'Appraisal and equal opportunities', in Bennett, N., Crawford, M. and Riches, C. (eds), *Managing Change in Education*, London, Paul Chapman Publishing.

Whitaker, P. (1997), 'Changes in professional development; the personal dimension', in Kydd, L., Crawford, M. and Riches, C. (eds), *Professional Development for Educational Management*, Buckingham, Open University Press, pp.11–25.

7

Leading and managing for equal opportunities

Introduction

This chapter explores the importance of ensuring equal opportunities for people in leading and managing a school or college. Definitions and theoretical perspectives on this are examined, with the related issues described. The particular significance of equal opportunities in educational contexts is then discussed with the implications of this for leadership and management. Some of the ways in which equal opportunities can be integrated into leadership and management processes are then proposed and explored, within the framework of a coherent overall strategy.

Definitions and theoretical perspectives

In developed countries with complex rules for the regulation of society, equal opportunity often occurs in a context with slightly negative connotations, i.e. a rule that must be followed, but in fact the phrase is wholly positive. It simply refers to the notions of fairness and equity embodied in the proposition that everyone is entitled to have an equal chance to achieve the same relevant and appropriate goal. It is therefore an aspiration in a democratic society. While much emphasis in this context can be placed on the word 'equal', for leaders and managers in that society the word 'opportunity' is just as important, since whether individuals take those opportunities is their choice but creating or facilitating them is a key task of leadership and management.

Awareness of equal opportunities in the modern developed world relates very much to the legislation which is bound up with it, which was enacted during the second half of the twentieth century, and is regularly adapted and developed. The Human Rights Act (1998), for example, has brought the legislation of many European countries into force in the UK and affected the rights of individuals there. The key rights likely to affect those working in education, are:

- the right to respect for private and family life
- the right of freedom of expression

- the right of freedom of thought, conscience and religion
- the right not to be subjected to degrading treatment
- the right to a fair and public hearing within a reasonable time by an independent and impartial tribunal established by law (adapted from Gold 2001).

It is easy to understand the implications of these in the daily leadership and management of employees in schools and colleges, although some, such as the right of freedom of expression, have particular resonances for managing adults in education and related occupations because of the special responsibilities they hold in relation to others who are dependent upon them.

Such legislation is equally relevant in most other democracies, although emphases will vary. For example, discrimination against employees on grounds of age is prohibited by law in the USA but is only in the form of a proposal for the future in the UK. In the Republic of South Africa, legislation to counter the extreme inequalities of the apartheid regime was obviously essential and, in that context, leaders and managers have to focus on the actual legislation to a degree which may not be seen as quite so essential when what the laws aim to achieve are more embedded – although problems of a different nature clearly exist then.

A focus on legislation inevitably leads to an emphasis on the indicators of success of implementing equal opportunities policies being largely numerical. Thus schools and colleges, like other organisations in the UK, Europe and North America, are required to monitor staff appointments and keep records for submission to show to what extent their employees reflect equal opportunities application, i.e. the number of those from ethnic minorities, balance of gender, able and disabled and, where applicable, age range. This monitoring can have two distinct disadvantages, according to Middlewood and Lumby (1998, p.35).

- It defines 'success' in terms of the *current* system, which may have some highly unsatisfactory features to it in practice.
- It may encourage leaders and managers to focus on certain forms of discrimination, whilst ignoring others. As Acker (1994) points out, just because an organisation has appointed a certain proportion of black employees into what was previously an all-white staff, does not necessarily mean that racism no longer exists there.

Using the issue of women's equality in Australia as her example, Summers (2003) argues that it is tempting for developed countries, having reached a certain level of equality through debate, rhetoric and legislation, to relax the emphasis. Having raised the issue in public consciousness, and the number of women in senior positions in government, business or public service organisations having increased, public focus can move elsewhere. The problem with this, she argues, is that it is only the situation of *some* women that has improved and that many others remain disempowered. Similarly, after highly publicised reports on racism it may be easy to assume racial equality has been 'dealt with'. At organisational level, such as in schools and colleges, it may be tempting to assume that, having appropriate numbers of women in senior positions, or ethnic minority staff adequately represented, equal opportunities has been fulfilled. In fact, such a position may be just the beginning, i.e. that in fact when such representation exists, the real task of leading and managing *all* people in the organisation can be focused on, without that distraction.

Managing for equal opportunities therefore is complex and leaders and managers, whilst needing to be knowledgeable about relevant legislation and statutory requirements, are faced with questions such as those posed by Middlewood and Lumby (1998) in speculating as to what a school or college would look like when it had achieved equality of opportunity.

- Would the school or college have proportions of men and women, both overall and in senior positions, reflecting the percentages of each in the population, or the proportion employed in that educational phase?
- Would the staff not necessarily display these statistical parallels, but simply be an outstanding group of people, indicating that recruitment ensured that the most talented and skilled were attracted and recruited, irrespective of gender, race or disability?
- Does managing for equality of opportunity mean all staff are treated the same, or according to their individual need?
- Does the latter imply treating some more favourably then others to overcome previous and/or current disadvantage? (p.35)

The last of these questions relates to one particular issue which arises from legislation, and the need to meet sometimes prescribed targets, but is also related to the cultural values which clearly concern leaders striving for equal opportunities, that is, what is known as 'positive discrimination'. This term relates to action taken by employers to redress an imbalance of staff representation (e.g. too few women or disabled employees) by deliberately attempting to recruit from these groups at the expense of those already well represented.

Whilst this positive discrimination is allowed and encouraged by legislation in various circumstances, it can be controversial. Those who argue strongly against the practice believe that it actually works against the interests of those it seeks to support. Thus, McElroy (1992) argues that quota systems for employment of women stigmatise women as inferior by rendering it uncertain as to whether they owe any positions of prestige to personal merit or merely to their gender. She also points out the resentment in a workforce of those who have been passed over in favour of the appointee. Both she and Papps (1992) argue that the key element in employment is the value that is placed on the work itself, irrespective of who does it.

This last argument is meant to encourage employers to examine first what each job is worth and to discount opportunities that society may or may not offer people to take. Thus, in a school or college, those serving the meals and refreshments to staff and students are likely to be among the lowest paid employees, and on part-time contracts because of the nature of the work. In the UK, the majority of these employees are women. If the job had a higher value attached to it, would more men be attracted to the work? These are questions and issues that leaders and managers have to ponder, but always within the context of what is manageable in their own institutions and, of course, within their own budgets. The overlap between what is appropriate and acceptable in the organisation and in society itself is particularly relevant to the management of equal opportunities.

Significance of equal opportunities in educational organisations

Important as the management of equal opportunities may be in any kind of organisation, it can be argued that it has a particular significance in educational institutions, such as schools, colleges or universities.

There are three main arguments for this, each of them linked to what many see as the key moral purpose of education, i.e. to improve the human condition, both by developing people's understanding and knowledge in the institution's immediate society and thereby to contribute to progress on a wider scale.

First, future citizens need to be able to see in the adults who guide their learning *role models* who embody the future and improved state. If all that they see in the world presented by their learning environment is that which reinforces what has been, they will learn or deduce that this is the preferred state.

This may include such extremes as:

- only women teach very young children
- only men can be school caretakers or janitors
- only able bodied people can teach
- only adults of certain races can hold senior positions.

In a school or college therefore, pupils and students need to have the opportunity to see the embodiment of equal opportunities in the way adults on the staff hold and perform in particular roles, according to what they do, not who they are. Without this opportunity, the tendency to stereotype certain roles and tasks according to certain types of people is difficult to avoid. The issue of positive discrimination, described above, may be crucial in addressing this issue for schools and colleges in particular contexts.

Secondly, as an educational institution responsible for children and young people, a school or college can provide the best learning environment for them by having a staff which has the *richness of diversity*, bringing together the various strengths of different types and groups of people. For example a staff which has good representation of both genders should theoretically bring the respective strengths of women and of men to education and its leadership and management.

These 'virtues', based on extensive research into management styles of men and women over the last 30 years (Benn 1974; Gray 1993; Coleman 1994), tend to approximate to the stereotypical ones shown in Table 7.1.

Table 7.1 Strengths of both male and female styles

Male	Female
Problem-solving	Creative
Competitive	Collaborative
Objective	Aware of differences
Decisive	Caring
Disciplined	Tolerant

Much debate has focused on the weakness or inadequacies of one particular style compared with the other but this is often in the context of inequity. That is, although the female style can be seen to be more appropriate to effective leadership of people in the changing twenty-first century, there are comparatively few women in such leadership roles (see Coleman 2002a). However, the argument here is that it is the strengths of both approaches that is most likely to be apparent if there is a good balance of men and women among, for example, the teaching staff of a school or college. This is a different argument from the fact that it is *unjust* that one group is less represented than the other, important though that is. It should also be made clear, of course, that many leaders and managers, both men and women, possess characteristics of each of the lists in Table 7.1, what Benn (1974) called 'psychological androgyny'. It is important again to stress that these characteristics are stereotypical ones, which tend to be found as dominant features of a male or female, rather than solely exclusive to one or the other.

An equally relevant example relates to the range of strengths that could exist in a staff that is ethnically diverse. Whilst much debate centres on the value of one ethnic cultural approach compared to another, particularly western models being transposed to Asian or Eastern cultures (Walker and Dimmock 2002; Foskett and Lumby 2003), a more important argument concerns the possibility of utilising the strengths of both – or more – cultures. There are possibilities, at least ideally, in a staff with elements of, for example,

- Japanese group ethic
- Chinese work ethic
- African collaborative approaches
- Western problem-solving abilities,

all being represented through various personnel, thus exposing pupils and students to all the possibilities inherent in these. Again, the above list is stereotypical, representing what have been seen as the dominant features of particular cultures, not exclusive to them.

Thirdly, educational organisations have by their very nature a *moral* imperative to lead change since their task is helping with the formation of the next generation(s). Therefore, they should reflect an attempt to offer signs of that improved future via the environment and ethos within which their learners and employees operate. The ways in which they are led and managed is the clearest signal to their adult employees about what this future is seen to be. Tillotson (2001, p.6), writing about equal opportunities policies in schools, says that their role should be in 'shifting the focus from the managerial systems to relationships among people in our schools (to be) be part of the process'. In other words, school management should be focusing on relationships in which all people are valued, not on systems.

Some implications for leadership and management

There are perhaps three aspects of a leader's understanding of equal opportunities implications that are worth noting.

The leader's personal understanding

As Middlewood and Lumby (1998, p.37) point out: 'The understanding of the causes of inequality will influence how the individual manager plans to remedy the situation ... The choice of means to achieve progress relates to the theoretical understanding of the cause.'

Whether the leader supports economic theories (i.e. that the position of minorities relates to their role in the economy), oppression theories (i.e. that minorities are oppressed and are likely always to be undervalued) or others, he or she would need to focus on a real commitment to equal opportunity, addressing the issue in an holistic and consistent manner over time. One of the difficulties that leaders need to face is that their own power and preferred or at least familiar norms may be threatened by the changes that a movement to equal opportunities may bring about and, as Freeman (1993) suggests, this could affect their own motivation in this field. Ultimately effective equal opportunities practice will be a matter of cultural values in the institution, epitomised by its leaders (see Bush 1998). In listing keys to success for implementation of equal opportunities in further education colleges, Warwick (1990, p.7) places as the first three:

- commitment by leaders to a value system which sees human resource development as vital
- clear leadership in the implementation of this value system
- firm and public support (by leaders) for equal opportunities within this value system.

Understanding of their societal context

Different societies have different understandings and operation of certain human resource management (HRM) practices. For example, Dimmock (2002) says that Chinese leadership is based on influencing relationships and modelling what are deemed to be desirable behaviours, and Begley (2003) suggests that in Canada consensus is usually something established by a group of professionals working locally.

Whilst gender, for example, may be treated as an equal opportunities issue in Western societies, it is a more complex phenomenon in segregated societies and in patriarchal or collective societies where motherhood and age are equated with status and authority. Thus, Debroux (2003) argues that work practices in Japan are based on a mutual agreement, which can be silent and implicit, between leaders and employees which are reflective of widespread social norms. Accordingly, women have to accept to play for ever a subordinate role in the labour market.

In segregated societies, such as Iran (Afshar 1992), Saudi Arabia (Al-Khalifa 1992), face-to-face meetings between men and women at work may be avoided with a reliance on telephone or writing. In Pakistan, separate institutions exist for females including a women's university with only women in leadership positions (Shah 1998). In such contexts, equal opportunities idealism as discussed earlier is not relevant; it becomes more of an issue of valuing those employees equally, once the initial separations have been made.

Understanding of their own institution's context

The individual school or college, in establishing a culture of equal opportunities, needs to be seen in the context of what the society of which it is part is trying to achieve. In the Republic of South Africa, the realisation of a truly democratic society places a huge responsibility on leaders of educational institutions who need to 'realise the important role of cultivating democratic values and norms in the education sphere and, particularly, in the wider South African community' (Bray 1996, p.150).

A leader will be aware of their school or college's own community context and, if they themselves are of a minority group, the challenge to develop equal opportunities is even greater, being both personal as well as role-driven. The female head of a special school in Birmingham described her struggle as: 'it's three times the battle being a woman, an Asian woman in a male-dominated society and then a head in a racialist community' (Abrol 1999, p.65).

In a local community where the population is wholly white, for example some rural areas in certain Northern European countries, the challenge to present to the students a picture of a society with equal opportunities for all races may be very difficult when there are no staff role models to demonstrate this. One headteacher of a school in rural Somerset, in an all-white small town, describes how she agonised over the appointment of the school's first black member of staff, not because she was not able but because it was a relatively low status job and it might send out the wrong signals to the students.

> She (the applicant) was the best person, but how I wished the post was that of Head of Department! I felt that this was the first black member of staff that the students had ever seen and their risk of forming stereotypes – or reinforcing them – was huge. (Gardiner 2004 p.3)

Building equal opportunities into leadership and management

Whilst legislation may require leaders to pay attention to such issues as ethnicity, religion, disability, gender, age and sexual orientation, an institution committed to equal opportunities will also ensure that its valuing of people extends to all areas of people management. For example:

- part-time employees (see Young and Brooks 2004)
- employees on a fixed-term contract
- voluntary workers
- those in low paid or low status jobs
- those called to stand in for staff in an emergency, such as 'supply' or 'cover' staff.

All these categories have the right to have their work valued as making a contribution to the institution's maintenance or development. Whilst this valuing cannot normally be done in terms of finance or contracts, it is the task of leaders with sensitive people management to try to ensure that these people feel their work is recognised and appreciated. As discussed in the previous chapter, this is very important for employee motivation.

The categories mentioned above are by no means separate from those which legislation requires since, in many countries, part-time workers are often women, many voluntary workers may be retired and elderly, and members of ethnic minorities may often be in low status jobs. The challenge for leaders therefore is to focus in all management processes on the people as individuals in their own right. Several of these key processes are examined in Part III of this book but it will be helpful here to examine the equal opportunities implications of them.

Recruitment and selection

An actual policy may be helpful because it gives a clear and consistent message to everyone involved. Middlewood and Lumby (1998, p.64) offer an actual example of a policy which includes:

To recruit ensuring that no one received less favourable treatment on the grounds of race, colour, nationality, ethnic or national origins, disability, gender or martial status or is disadvantaged by conditions on requirements which cannot be shown to be justifiable.

A policy is only as effective as its implementation and O'Neill et al. (1994, p.67) pose the problem of the situation at the selection stage where one of the candidates is seen to be pregnant. This 'temporary disability' (in work terms) should in theory, and legally, play no part in influencing the selectors' decision, but in a situation where the school or college is desperate for, say, a teacher to take up post the following term, with important classes to be taught, and this candidate will not be available for work until several months after that, there would clearly be a temptation for leaders to take the short-term solution and appoint someone immediately available, particularly if two candidates were nearly equal in merit. Considerable sensitivity, and courage to take the longer-term view may be needed in such situations, simple though the solution may be 'on paper'!

There may also be a temptation, especially perhaps for part-time, temporary or low status jobs, to use informal networks to make a selection. A careful judgement has to be made to avoid discriminating against anyone's access of opportunity. For example, jobs with low pay are invariably filled by people living near the school or college since travelling long distances is likely to be uneconomic; thus advertising for cleaning or catering staff may reasonably be confined to local outlets. However, a part-time teaching post may be different. Parker-Jenkins (1994) describes how the following were among the procedures followed, in recruiting and selecting for a part-time post:

- To ensure as wide a field for recruitment as possible, advertisements were placed in locations outside those which only people in the 'normal' educational circles would reach.
- References were not required since those who have been absent from the labour market – or never in it – might feel reluctant to apply because of the lack of 'appropriate' referees.
- Candidates who did not necessarily follow the conventional format of application were still considered if their suitability matched the job criteria.
- Each interviewee was asked the same questions based on the agreed criteria for the post as advertised.

As Middlewood (1997) pointed out, such part-time posts are the very ones which offer opportunities to recruit from unconventional backgrounds, thus widening students' access to a range of staff, as well as fulfilling equal opportunities principles in practice.

Induction and continuing professional support

Probably beginning in the induction process, the way in which professional support is provided to a member of staff can be a critical issue in the development by leaders and managers of an equal opportunities culture. The significance of mentors and critical friends is discussed in full in Chapter 11 but here we can consider some of the related equal opportunities issues.

It can be an assumption easily made that those in a minority in a particular context (e.g. women or black staff) should have someone of the same minority as a mentor. 'The female headteachers ... were generally advocates for mentoring, *although* (my italics) half of them reported having been mentored by a man' (Coleman 2002b, p.143). In fact the evidence concerning cross-gender mentoring is mixed. Davidson and Cooper (1992, p.87) advocate same-gender mentoring because it can encourage development of female leaders. Megginson and Clutterbuck (1995) report on the successes of cross-gender mentoring. Both arguments in different ways also focus on the way these models affect the attitudes of men towards female leaders and managers.

Similarly with black or ethnic minority staff, Megginson and Clutterbuck (1995) describe projects in which both same-race and cross-race mentoring were effective, while Abrol (1999) describes how both English and Asian managers had been greatly supportive of her as an Asian female head in Birmingham, England, but her informal mentor and friend had been the woman who had been the first Asian secondary headteacher there.

All this points towards re-emphasising for leaders and managers the importance of their unique institutional contexts. If, for example, there is perceived to be a strong need to demonstrate overtly in a particular school or college that there is a shortage of the minority groups in certain positions, the allocation of a mentor as role model from that group may send out the signal that they are as capable as anyone else and be taken as encouragement to others. If that is not the case, the opposite view might be taken to show that all are treated equally, regardless of gender, race, etc. and the mentor may be of the same or different minority regardless.

The support of those staff with physical disability needs the same attention. One teacher in a wheelchair appointed to work in a primary school in Wales was allocated a mentor and reported that she felt that her mentor, whilst being friendly, undoubtedly patronised her by 'taking care' of her and 'looking after' her, something she felt her mentor would not have done for an able-bodied teacher and thus distorting the mentor/mentee relationships (Jenkins 2004). In this case, the issue is not one of same or different minority group as mentor, but likely to be either one of selecting a suitable person or of appropriate training.

Performance management and appraisal

A number of the issues here may be similar to those mentioned above in terms of who is the appraiser. A key difference may be that allocation of mentors is probably more often on a carefully selected individual basis, whereas if a school or college has a particular system of appraisal (e.g. by line management role), it can hardly be altered for one person without accusations of special treatment. Where the latter is not the case, attention may need to be given to the appraiser/appraisee pairings, with similar issues relevant as in the mentor/mentee. Wragg et al. (1996) noted that a number of female teachers in England preferred to be observed (as part of their appraisal process) by men rather than women, with some of them stating that they felt men would be more rigorous.

In terms of situations which may affect the performance of staff, Jenkins (2004) refers to some other interesting examples, all of which came from the actual experiences of her colleagues, and which pose potential dilemmas for leaders and managers:

- The woman returning from maternity leave and is now anxious for the next few weeks to leave school promptly. Should special allowance be made for her concerning after hours meetings for that period?
- The Muslim lecturer who, during the period of Ramadan, is weak and 'light-headed' by the evening because of fasting. Can she be expected to perform her normal duties then?
- The devout Muslim staff who need to offer prayers at certain times of the day. Should special arrangements be made, possibly at the expense of others' time?
- Should homosexual men or lesbian women be allowed to 'avoid' certain duties which might place them in a situation where false accusations might be made against them? (adapted from Jenkins 2004)

Even in the matter of dress, leaders and managers need to be sensitive as to whether equal opportunities refers to the culture of the institution and its country or to that of the ethnic origin of the individual. A German court ruled in 2003 that two Afghan-born Muslim teachers should be allowed to wear their traditional head covering at work, overruling the school's decision that these teachers should be treated the same as all other members of staff (Gentleman 2003).

Managing staff learning and development

Blandford (2000, p.7) places 'equality of opportunity' clearly in the contractual conditions of service which staff should be offered in terms of their professional development. This principle can be linked with what development is appropriate to each stage of an individual's career – from beginning through to near retirement. However, judgements may still need to be made in terms of situations where institutions may potentially be at odds with an individual's rights. For example, a member of staff with one year of service left before retirement should have as much opportunity to attend a training course as a younger colleague but issues of cost benefit to the institution may be considered by the manager responsible for training and development budgets, with the possible risk of seeming to discriminate between two motivated employees on grounds of age.

An equal opportunities culture in a school or college with staff from different ethnic origins may need to recognise inherent differences in approaches to learning and development. Irvine's (1990) study in USA found that the dominant cultures of countries of origin were the key aspects of students' approach to learning and there is no reason to suppose adults would be different (Ngcobo 2003) Thus, Irvine points out some of the contrasts between African and European approaches, acknowledging that these are stereotypical (see Table 7.2).

Table 7.2 Some contrasts between African and European approaches (based on Irvine 1990)

African	European
Event orientation	Clock orientation
Orally based	Print based
Uniqueness valued	Sameness valued

The implications for the management of staff learning and development may lie in attention being paid to the diversity of approaches to training needed so that those with a natural propensity to one approach (e.g. oral) are not penalised through an overreliance on another (e.g. print). It can be argued that this may be no different from ensuring that the different learning styles of staff are accounted for in their training (see Chapter 13 for a fuller discussion).

Implications for leaders and managers

If some of what has been described is to be achieved, Reeves (1993, p.262) suggests that equality of opportunity may need to be viewed as 'a central organisational goal, requiring management techniques – planning, resource allocation (costing), time scales for delivery, monitoring and performance indicators etc., for its achievement'.

It is also likely to require particular skills from the leaders and managers, including conflict management, negotiation and communication.

Conflict management
This skill may involve a number of strategies such as:

• arbitration
• separation – providing a 'cooling-off' period
• neglect – of trivial issues
• co-ordinating devices – marginalising the people concerned (based on Handy 1993, p.311–12).

Negotiation
This can be seen, according to Armstrong (1994) as having four operational stages:

• *Preparation*:   setting objectives, obtaining information and determining strategy.

- *Opening*:   revealing your bargaining position.
- *Bargaining*:   spotting weaknesses in the other person's case and convincing them of the need to 'move'.
- *Closing*:   recognising the impossibility of further compromise.

Communication

In contexts such as envisaged in this chapter, some of which are potentially extremely sensitive, the ability to maintain effective communications with interested parties is paramount. Armstrong (1994) argues that this can be done by:

- taking everyone's views into account (this includes those of minority groups)
- ensuring ideas are clearly articulated (language difficulties need to be anticipated)
- ensuring information is exchanged (those apparently advantaged *and disadvantaged both need to have all the known data)*
- encouraging synergy (collective creativity is greater than individual contributions).

The skilled leader may also see the need – in situations where emotions can destabilise the 'normal'- to utilise a neutral person, known, trusted and respected by the parties involved, as advocated by Slocombe (1995). In a situation where a member of staff felt that they had not been given equal opportunity, and this was due to race or gender, a neutral person could be extremely beneficial.

Conclusion

Effective leadership and management of an equal opportunities culture in any organisation will need both determination and sensitivity in managing the staff concerned. This is certainly true in educational organisations, but, as mentioned earlier, there are factors which make the desirability of achieving it even greater. Despite the difficulties, it is possible that schools and colleges have also at their disposal the greatest opportunity, what Tillotson (2001, p.6) calls 'the *unique* context' of schools, colleges and classrooms. As Wamahiu (1996) suggests, the way to achieve gender equality in Africa lies ultimately in the change in African classrooms from autocratic to democratic pedagogy. 'A change from an oppressive system to an empowering one' (p.57) will provide eventually the changes in the next generations which will make that equality a natural state. This is seen as the long-term solution; in the short term, leaders and managers have much to do but the first step lies in their inner convictions about equality of opportunity.

References

Abrol, S., with Ribbins, P. (1999), 'Pursuing equal opportunities: a passion for service, sharing and sacrifice', in Rayner, S. and Ribbins, P. *Headteachers and Leadership in Special Education*, London, Cassell.

Acker, S. (1994), *Gendered Education*, Buckingham, Open University Press.

Afshar, H. (1992), 'Women and work: ideology not adjustment at work in Iran', in

Afshar, H. and Dennis, C. (eds), *Women and the Adjustment Policies in the Third World,* Basingstoke, Macmillan, pp.205–229.

Al-Khalifa, E. (1992), 'Management by halves: women teachers and school management', in Bennett, N., Crawford, M. and Riches, C. (eds), *Managing Change in Education*, London, Paul Chapman Publishing and OUP, pp. 95–106.

Armstrong, M. (1994), *How to Be an Even Better Manager*, London, Kogan Page.

Begley, P. (2003), 'Western-centred perspectives on values and leadership', in Warner, M. and Joynt, P. (eds), *Managing Across Cultures*, London, Thomson Learning, pp 45–60.

Benn, S. (1974), 'The measurement of psychological androgyny', *Journal of Consulting and Clinical Psychology*, 42 (2), 155–162.

Blandford, S. (2000), *Managing Professional Development in Schools*, London, Routledge.

Bray, E. (1996), *The South African Bill of Rights and Its Impact on Education*, Suid-Afrikaanese Tydskeif Opovodekk, 16 (3), 158.

Bush, T. (1998), 'Organisational culture and strategic management', in Middlewood, D. and Lumby, J. (eds), *Strategic Management in Schools and Colleges*, London, Paul Chapman Publishing.

Coleman, M. (1994), 'Women in educational management', in Bush, T. and West-Burnham, J. (eds), *The Principles of Educational Management*, Harlow, Longman.

Coleman, M. (2002a), *Women as Headteachers: Striking the Balance*, Stoke-on-Trent, Trentham Books.

Coleman, M. (2002b), 'Managing for equal opportunities', in Bush, T. and Bell, L. (eds), *Principles and Practice of Educational Management*, London, Paul Chapman Publishing.

Davidson, M. and Cooper, C. (1992), *Shattering the Class Ceiling: The Women Manager*, London, Paul Chapman Publishing.

Debroux, P. (2003), 'The Japanese employment model revisited', in Warner, M. and Joynt, P. (eds), *Managing Across Cultures*, London, Thomson Learning.

Dimmock, C. (2002), 'Educational leadership: taking account of complex global and cultural contexts', in Walker, A. and Dimmock, C. (eds), *School Leadership and Administration: Adopting a Cultural Perspective*, London, Routledge Falmer, pp.33–44.

Foskett, N. and Lumby, J. (2003), *Leading and Managing Education: International Perspectives*, London, Paul Chapman Publishing.

Freeman, A. (1993), 'Women in education', *Educational Change and Development*, 13 (1), pp. 10–14.

Gardiner, G. (2004), 'Staff role models: it's not easy', *Headship Matters*, 26, London, Optimus Publishing.

Gentleman, A. (2003), 'French school bars girls for headscarves', *Guardian,* 25 September, p. 19.

Gold, R. (2001), 'The Human Rights Act in schools', *Leadership Focus*, 4, 51–52, Cambridge, Hobsons.

Gray, H. (1993), 'Gender issues in management training', in Ozga, J. (ed.), *Women in Educational Management*, Buckingham, Open University Press.

Handy, C. (1993), *Understanding Organisations,* 4th edition, Harmondsworth, Penguin.

Irvine, J. (1990), *Black Students and School Failure*, New York, Greenwood Press.

Jenkins, K. (2004), 'Can I help you, dear?', *Primary Headship*, (14), London, Optimus Publishing.

McElroy, W. (1992), 'Preferential treatment of women in employment', in Quest, C. (ed.), *Equal Opportunities: A Feminist Fallacy*, London, Institute of Economic Affairs.

Megginson, D. and Clutterbuck, D. (1995), *Mentoring in Action*, London, Kogan Page.

Middlewood, D. (1997), 'Managing recruitment and selection', in Bush, T. and Middlewood, D. (eds), *Managing People in Education*, London, Paul Chapman Publishing.

Middlewood, D. and Lumby, J. (1998), *Human Resource Management in Schools and Colleges*, London, Paul Chapman Publishing.

Ngcobo, T. (2003), 'Managing multi-cultural contexts', in Lumby, J., Middlewood, D. and Kaabwe, E. (eds), *Managing Human Resources in South African Schools*, London, Commonwealth Secretariat.

O'Neill, J., Middlewood, D. and Glover, D. (1994), *Managing Human Resources in Schools and Colleges*, Harlow, Longman.

Papps, I. (1992), 'Women, work and well-being', in Quest, C. (ed.), *Equal Opportunities: A Feminist Fallacy*, London, Institute of Economic Affairs.

Parker-Jenkins, R. (1994), 'Part-time staff recruitment: an equal opportunities dilemma', *Educational Management and Administration*, 8 (2), 3–4.

Reeves, F. (1993), 'Effects of 1988 Education Reform Act on racial equality of opportunity in FE Colleges', *British Educational Research Journal*, 19 (3), 259–273.

Shah, S. (1998) Roles and practices of college heads in AJK, Pakistan, unpublished PhD thesis, University of Nottingham.

Slocombe, L. (1995), 'Implementing redundancy: implications for school management', in Crawford, M., Kydd, L. and Parker, S. (eds), *Educational Management in Action*, London, Paul Chapman Publishing.

Summers, A. (2003), *The End of Equality*, Melbourne, Random House.

Tillotson, V. (2001), 'Equal opportunities policy: is it up to date?', *Headship Matters*, (8), 6–7, London, Optimus Publishing.

Walker, A. and Dimmock, C. (2002), 'Moving school leadership beyond its narrow boundaries: developing a cross-cultural approach', in Leithwood, K. and Hallinger, P. (eds), *International Handbook of Educational Leadership and Administration*, Boston, Kluwer Academic, pp. 167–202.

Wamahiu, S. (1996), 'The pedagogy of difference: an African perspective', in Murphy, P. and Gipps, C. (eds), *Equity in the Classroom*, London, Falmer Press for UNESCO.

Warwick, J. (1990*), Planning Human Resource Development through Equal Opportunities (Gender)*, London, Further Education Unit.

Wragg, E., Wikeley, F., Wragg, C. and Haynes, G. (1996), *Teacher Appraisal Observed*, London, Routledge.

Young, B. and Brooks, M. (2004), 'Part-time politics: the micropolitical world of part-time teaching', *Educational Management and Administration and Leadership*, 32, (2), 129–148.

8

Leading and managing
through teams

Introduction: the rationale for teams

Teamwork is widespread in schools and colleges in many countries. Teams are frequently advocated as an appropriate part of school and college structures. Katzenbach and Smith (1998) claim that teams are more effective than individuals:

> Teams outperform individuals acting alone or in larger groupings, especially when performance requires multiple skills, judgements, and experiences. Most people recognize the capabilities of teams; most have the common sense to make teams work ... real teams are deeply committed to their purpose, goals and approach. High-performance team members are also very committed to one another. (p.9)

Lashway (2003) links teamwork to the wider focus on shared or distributed leadership.

> The task of transforming schools is too complex to expect one person to accomplish single-handedly. Accordingly, leadership should be distributed throughout the school rather than vested in one position. (p.1)

Wallace (2001) elaborates on this view and advances five reasons for shared leadership:

- Shared leadership is morally just in a democratic country where individual rights are accorded high priority.
- Participating in shared leadership is a fulfilling experience for all involved.
- Team membership provides an opportunity for professional development.
- Co-operative relationships provide good models for children and students.
- Shared leadership is potentially more effective than principals acting alone, not least because staff 'own' the outcomes (adapted from Wallace 2001, pp.153–4).

Woods et al. (2004) link distributed leadership to teams, stating that

> the literature on teams, with its emphases on collaboration, multiple and complementary strengths and the need for all members to share a common view of both the purposes of the team and its means of working, has similarities to much of the discussion of distributed leadership. (p.447)

Democratic participation provides the rationale for teamwork in South African schools.

> The role of the senior management team is ... to share the management tasks more widely in the school. This is necessary if the management of schools is to become more democratic, inclusive and participatory. (Department of Education 2000, p.2)

Cardno (2002), drawing on experience in New Zealand, shows the importance of teamwork, and links it to the advent of site-based management:

> Teams abound in schools because they are structured in ways that allow teachers to work together to make curriculum and management related decisions. In settings where the implementation of education reform has increased the complexity of school management through devolution, principals have embraced the opportunity to share new tasks and decision-making with teams. (p.213)

It is evident that there is considerable support for the notion of teamwork in education. Indeed, their ubiquitous presence in primary and secondary schools, a 'grass roots response' (Wallace 2002, p.168), shows that they are widely believed to be an important feature of school organisation. However, such assumptions are by no means sufficient to ensure that teams are meaningful and effective. Developing successful teams can be problematic, as we shall see later in this chapter.

The composition of leadership and management teams

The shift in emphasis from 'management' to 'leadership' in education, noted in Chapter 1, is reflected in the language of teamwork, notably in English schools. The advent of the National College for School *Leadership*, and the introduction of a 'leadership' pay spine in England, have encouraged a change in nomenclature for the most senior teams in schools. Most now prefer to use the term 'senior leadership team (SLT)', rather than 'senior management team (SMT)', although the latter description is still widely used in other countries, including New Zealand and South Africa. The use of 'SLT' in England began in the twenty-first century so most of the research reported in this chapter refers to SMTs.

Leadership teams are not statutory in most countries, so their composition is a matter of institutional choice. In South Africa, the government does not prescribe the membership of the school management team but certain guidelines are indicated:

> The legislation does not define a school management team. The working definition being used by the provinces and the national department is that the SMT consists of the following members:
>
> • principal
> • deputy principal

- heads of departments.
  (Department of Education 2000, p.2)

Middlewood's (2003) research in the KwaZulu-Natal province confirms this assumption with SMTs 'normally consisting of principal, deputy principal and a small number of heads of departments' (p.173). This pattern also applies in many other countries.

Rutherford (2002) refers to a 'lack of consistency' in the composition of SMTs in English primary schools. His research in the Catholic sector demonstrates some agreement but also a measure of diversity in his five one-form entry primary schools (see Table 8.1).

Table 8.1 Composition of SMTs in five English Catholic schools (adapted from Rutherford 2002, pp.453–4)

School Co-ordinators		Headteacher	Deputy head
A	☞	☞	Religious education
B	☞	☞	Subject co-ordinators
C	☞	☞	Maths and English co-ordinators
D	☞	☞	Two key stage co-ordinators
E	☞	☞	None

Rutherford's case studies show that heads and deputies are generally included in SMTs but they vary in the number and roles of the other team members. Wallace (2001) confirms both the commonalities and the differences in structures, saying that SMTs in British primary schools typically 'consist of the head, deputy and other teachers with the most substantial management responsibility' (p.153).

Cardno (2002) shows that senior management teams are the most common permanent teams in New Zealand schools (see Table 8.2).

Table 8.2 Permanent teams in New Zealand schools (Cardno 2002)

Permanent teams	Percentage of schools
Senior management	81.8
Curriculum committee	63.8
Subject/department	61.4
Professional development	43.8
Student services	20.4

Team composition goes beyond these structural issues to consideration of the roles played by team members. There is a clear distinction between the members' position (e.g. deputy head) and the team role which they play, which 'refers to a tendency to behave, contribute and interrelate with others at work in certain distinctive ways' (Belbin 1993, p.25). Belbin's well-known classification identifies nine specific roles:

1 Company worker or implementor: translates ideas into practice.
2 Chair or co-ordinator: controls and co-ordinates.
3 Shaper: inspires and makes things happen.
4 Innovator: advances new ideas and synthesises knowledge.
5 Resource investigator: identifies ideas and resources from outside the team.
6 Monitor or evaluator: critical thinker and constantly reviews the team.
7 Team worker: socially oriented and promotes harmony.
8 Completer/finisher: drives for task completion.
9 Specialist: has pre-existing specialist skills and knowledge
  (adapted from Coleman and Bush 1994, p.269).

Teams are likely to be more effective if the selection of members has regard to these categories (Belbin 1993). In practice, however, given the legal responsibilities of heads and principals in most countries, formal status and hierarchy are likely to be more significant than Belbin's classification in determining team roles in schools and colleges.

An important variable in teamwork is the number of members in the team. If the team is too large, it is difficult for individuals to make a meaningful contribution and meetings are likely to be dominated by the chair and other senior members. Equally, small teams may be ineffective because they do not have sufficient collective expertise. 'In smaller teams it is more difficult to bring together the range of skills and approaches that lead to the significant enhancement of problem solving, creativity and enthusiasm' (Chaudhry-Lawton et al. 1992, p.137).

The four primary schools studied by Wallace (2001) all had between four and seven SMT members. The smallest was at 'Winton' where the head wanted to promote sharing and debate and was concerned about the viability of large teams.

> I have always stuck out against a larger team because I couldn't see how I could make it workable on a regular basis. I couldn't imagine how I could have regular and meaningful meetings with seven or eight people ... I don't think you can have genuine discussions in a group of that size. (quoted in Wallace 2001, p.159)

Wallace's (2001) research illustrates the importance of meetings both as 'symbols' of teamwork and in providing a regular framework for their operation. SLTs in England typically meet on a weekly basis and thus have a regular presence in the school timetable. Meetings provide much of the *raison d'être* for teams and those which do not meet regularly are likely to wither and die.

Size also influences the number and type of teams in schools. In New Zealand, for example, 98.8 per cent of large primary schools have senior management teams while only 75.6 per cent of small primary schools have them (Cardno 2002, p.214).

Developing effective teams

Teamwork is increasingly advocated, as we noted earlier, but the acid test of their practical value is whether they operate effectively and contribute to the development of successful schools and colleges. Teams form part of an essentially normative framework for school leadership and management, with several overlapping assumptions:

- Principals should develop and communicate a distinctive vision for the school or college.
- Leadership should be transformational so that staff and the wider school community can be inspired to share, and to implement, the principal's vision.
- Professional staff are encouraged to participate in teams, ostensibly on an equal basis, despite the hierarchical structures within which they all work.
- Teamwork is likely to lead to 'better' and more widely accepted decisions.

The reality is often rather different from this 'harmony' model. In England, and many other countries, governments are transfixed by 'standards', evidenced by test and examination scores. Teamwork and distributed leadership receive a measure of support because they are thought likely to contribute to the standards agenda. Yet the government's policies compromise the transformational model, for several reasons:

- The school's distinctive vision is subordinate to the government's target driven approach.
- Accountability pressures have intensified, making it 'risky' for heads to share power with their colleagues.
- Teamwork may be limited to implementing external priorities instead of formulating ideas to meet the specific needs of the school and its pupils.
- Team processes may be perceived as valuable but they are vulnerable if they do not lead to the outcomes desired by government.

Wallace (2001) summarises the tension facing English heads operating in this climate:

> Headteachers are confronted by a heightened dilemma: their greater dependence on colleagues disposes them towards sharing leadership. In a context of unprecedented accountability, however, they may be inhibited from sharing because it could backfire should empowered colleagues act in ways that generate poor standards of pupil achievement, alienate parents and governors, attract negative media attention or incur inspectors' criticism. (p.157)

These intensified external pressures have several implications for the nature of teamwork and for any assessment of its effectiveness. As Hoyle (1986) pointed out two decades ago, the extent and nature of teamwork and distributed leadership is a matter for the head, who has the power to increase, reduce or amend the level of shared decision-making. Glib assumptions of professional agreement, for example in South Africa where the Department of Education (2000, p.2) claims that 'most

SMTs work on the basis of consensus', have to give way to a more sober assessment of what is possible in a climate of enhanced accountability.

Wallace (2002) points out that leadership and management do impact on student learning but that the effect is indirect, or 'mediated', via classroom teaching. In smaller schools, where the principal is a full or part time teacher, there is the potential for direct effects but usually leadership exerts its influence on teachers who, in turn, seek to enhance pupil learning. Any single individual has a limited impact on outcomes but, if leadership is distributed widely, the potential effects are multiplied. 'It is as foolish to think that only principals provide leadership for school improvement as to believe that principals do not influence school effectiveness' (Hallinger and Heck 1999, p.186).

The beneficial effects of teamwork are assumed to arise from the interaction between people motivated to collaborate in order to achieve desired outcomes. In this sense, the combined effects of the team are potentially greater than the sum of its individual parts. The team process produces positive effects that could not be achieved by individuals acting alone. Wallace (2002) describes this effect as 'synergy'. Referring to his research in English primary schools, he shows that:

> Effectiveness of teamwork was related to the degree of synergy – harnessing team members' energies to attain joint goals, whereby more could be achieved by working together than the aggregate of what individual members could achieve alone. (p.169)

Nias et al. (1989), who also researched English primary schools, refer to the 'interdependence' of team members, who enjoyed working together and produced satisfying outcomes:

> Although group membership was affectively satisfying, this is not the whole story. At Greenfields, Lowmeadow and Sedgemoor the staff also felt a sense of collective responsibility for their work and saw themselves as a team ... To be a 'team' meant to recognize and value the unique contribution of each member, teachers and non-teachers alike, to a joint enterprise. Being a team did not necessarily mean doing the same job or working in the same teaching space, but it did mean working to the same ends. (p.60)

This example suggests that these schools had developed what Wallace (2001, p.162) describes as a 'culture of teamwork' which 'was sophisticated enough for contradictory beliefs and values to coexist without conflict, mutually empowering all members'.

Although teams are well established in schools and colleges, there is only limited evidence of any systematic evaluation of their effectiveness, although this aspect does form part of the Office for Standards in Education (Ofsted 2003) inspection framework for English schools. In the section of the framework devoted to leadership and management, inspectors are expected to assess 'how well the leadership team creates a climate for learning' (p.45) and the extent to which 'leaders create effective teams' (p.46).

These Ofsted requirements mean that school leaders should carry out regular assessments of the effectiveness of their teams. Middlewood and Lumby (1998, p.49) identify three criteria for team effectiveness:

1 The extent to which the quantity and quality of specified outcomes for the team has been achieved.
2 The extent to which the working of the team has enhanced its future capacity.
3 The extent to which the capacity of individual team members has been enhanced.

Middlewood (2003) refers to a survey of school principals in Durban. The 21 respondents mention six obstacles to team effectiveness in the new South Africa:

- some teachers are unqualified and lack skills
- personality clashes
- a frequently absent teacher
- intolerance by some team members
- shy staff dominated by others
- low morale and motivation, caused by increased workload.

In a different survey of 60 principals in the KwaZulu-Natal province, principals were asked to rate the performance of their senior management team on the basis of eight characteristics. The results are shown in Table 8.3.

Table 8.3 South African principals' rating of the performance of their senior management team (Middlewood 2003, p.179)

Characteristic	Good	Satisfactory	Weak	Poor
Clear purpose	43	10	7	0
Support/trust	7	24	18	4
Openness/candour	9	29	18	4
Agreed decision-making process	41	11	7	1
Leadership	44	11	5	0
Co-operation/conflict	4	16	27	13
Review needs	2	9	43	6
Review processes	0	2	37	21

These findings suggest that teams in South African schools require development if they are to become really effective. In particular, most principals experience conflict within their teams while a significant minority perceive support and trust to be weak or poor, and that there is a lack of candour and openness. Teams were relatively new in South Africa at the time of this survey (1997) and these problems demonstrate the need for team development. Developing effective teams requires a constructive approach to team learning, as we shall see in the next section.

Team development and learning

Leithwood (1998) claims that participatory decision-making is assumed in all forms of site-based management. This is generally achieved through 'the many task forces, groups, committees and teams that are responsible for enacting the bulk of non-classroom business in restructuring schools' (p.204). He adds that team learning is an important ingredient of effective teamwork and has two main dimensions:

1 A shared understanding of the team's purposes.
2 The actions permitted by the larger organisation for achieving those purposes.

These dimensions operate within a wider cultural framework which condition the ways in which teams function. The team's culture may be seen as a 'collective pro-gramming of the mind' (p.209) and often involves tacit rather than conscious knowledge. This creates problems for new team members 'who may have difficulty understanding the shared meanings held by their team colleagues' (p.209).

Leithwood (1998) adds that another learning challenge facing team members is 'what actions to take as individuals in order to contribute to the collective learning of the team' (p.210). This may take the form of 'mutual adaptation', where individuals adapt their contributions in response to the specific requirements of new tasks and also as a reaction to the perceived changes by other team members. Leithwood (1998) concludes that mutual adaptation is central to team learning: .

> The perspective on team learning which has been developed begins by locat-ing the collective team mind in the patterns of action undertaken by the team as a whole. Collective team learning entails change in these patterns of action through processes of mutual adaptation ... In this way the team's learning has the potential to both precede and to contribute to individual members' learn-ing. (p.214)

Cardno's (2002) research suggests that there is a low emphasis on team training and development despite the pervasive influence of teams in New Zealand schools. She adds that 'teams have considerable capacity to learn because they are units of action' (p.220) but such potential may be untapped because of certain barriers to learning. These barriers may involve an element of defensiveness:

> Defensiveness is evident in the kind of communication that takes place in organisations when issues surface that are likely to threaten or embarrass indi-viduals or teams ... For a team to learn (and to contribute to organisational

learning) it must overcome the barriers to learning that are ingrained in both individual and collective behaviour. (p.220)

Cardno (2002) also points to the need for strong leadership to promote team development and organisational learning. Such leadership could lead to productive rather than defensive communication and could release the 'unharnessed potential' of teams.

It is evident from this review that team learning is an important aspect of their effectiveness. Tuckman's (1965) classic model of team development assumes four stages of growth:

- forming
- storming
- norming
- performing.

Each of these stages has a potential learning dimension as members engage in mutual adaptation and the team moves from initial formation (or reformation in the case of changing membership) to successful operation or 'performance'. Cardno's (2002) point is that such learning should not be left to chance but should be built into the culture of teamwork, notably through leadership action.

Teamwork in action: co-principalship in New Zealand

One of the implicit assumptions of teamwork is that members operate as status equals. Their participation is assumed to be on the basis of specific expertise rather than formal positions in the school or college hierarchy. As we noted earlier, teams form part of a wider normative preference for collaborative work. However, the notion of *senior* management teams compromises this principle in that seniority is itself a qualification for membership. Given that shared leadership is in the gift of principals, there is always a balancing act between teamwork and hierarchy, as Wallace (2001, p.159) notes in respect of English primary schools: 'The extent to which headteachers shared leadership depended on the balance they sought between expressing belief in the management hierarchy and in equal contribution of team members in the SMT's operation.'

This contradiction between hierarchy and collaboration is explored in Court's (2004) study of a co-principalship in New Zealand. The board of a small primary school with three teachers needed to appoint a new principal. Two of the three teachers submitted a proposal for a co-principalship Their rationale was consistent with the team ethic:

They believed that collaborative planning and decision-making contributed to the development of better teaching and learning programmes ... they each thought that traditional management hierarchies were not the best model for school leadership ... they wanted shared leadership practices and collective responsibility to evolve in ways that would best suit the school and people's strengths. (p.180)

The school board was attracted to the proposal, and 'blown away' (p.180) by the quality of the applications, but met resistance when they consulted state officials; 'they were told that this was illegal – it would blur accountability lines' (p.174). Because New Zealand's schools are self-governing, the board was able to ignore this advice and made the collective appointment, beginning in 1993. The co-principals 'took a more inclusive, fluid and flexible approach to sharing the functions of leadership and management' (p.186). They acknowledged the pressures for legal accountability but were also 'committed to working within deeper forms of professional and personal accountability' (p.187).

Court (2004) concludes that the co-principalship contributed to a more democratic framework for school leadership and management, leading to genuine teamwork:

The strength of the co-principal approach ... is that its flat management structure was built on the prioritizing of open, honest communication and the sharing of information and decision-making both within the leadership team and between them and their support staff, board and parents in the school. (p.193)

Teamwork in action: Working Together for Success

The English National College for School Leadership (NCSL) has introduced many new leadership development programmes. One of these, Working Together for Success (WTfS), is targeted at senior leadership teams. Working Together for Success is an eight-day programme involving three events and four in-school interventions and concluding with a team learning event. The programme aims to 'improve personal and team performances' (NCSL 2003). It stresses the importance of teamwork but recognises that 'developing highly effective senior leadership teams is a complex undertaking requiring sustained support to develop skills and adapt behaviours' (NCSL 2003, p.3).

The early evaluation evidence (Bush et al. 2004) suggests that the programme has been successful in developing both teams and individuals. Participants in a small pilot study survey, with just 11 responses, recognised the value of leadership and team-building techniques that were clearly new to them. They were asked to outline the ways in which their leadership team had changed as a result of their involvement. The results are shown in Table 8.4.

Table 8.4 The impact of the WTFS experience on school leadership teams (Bush et al. 2004)

Impact on school leadership team	Number of mentions
Enhanced team coherence	7
Improved meetings	7
Development techniques	5
Improved planning procedures	4
Awareness of shared responsibility	4
Sense of sharing	4
Greater democracy	3
Awareness of different perspectives	3
Time management	2

Table 8.4 shows that this group of leaders perceived enhanced team coherence and improved team meetings as well as greater democracy and shared responsibility. It is important to be cautious in interpreting findings from such a small sample at this early stage of programme development but it does appear that carefully planned development can enhance team effectiveness. As Cardno (2002) suggests, team development should not be left to chance and this NCSL programme provides one example of the potential benefits of collaborative learning.

Advantages of teamwork

Teams have become widespread in schools and colleges in many different national contexts. This has occurred because leaders and staff feel that teamwork has advantages over individual activity. This is partly a normative position, a belief, rather than being grounded strongly in research evidence. Bell (1992, p.46), for example, claims 12 benefits for teamwork:

- agreeing aims
- clarifying roles
- sharing expertise and skills
- maximising use of resources
- motivating, supporting and encouraging members of the team
- improving relationships within the staff group
- encouraging decision-making
- increasing participation
- realising individual potential
- improving communication
- increasing knowledge and understanding
- reducing stress and anxiety.

These potential benefits are substantial but Coleman and Bush (1994, p.280) warn that 'these are ambitious claims and are not likely to be achieved without excellent leadership and a high level of commitment from all team members'.

Johnson's (2003) research in four schools in three Australian states provides some evidence to support the view that teamwork confers benefits on individuals and organisations. He identifies three advantages on the basis of this research:

1 *Moral support*: 89.7 per cent of respondents claim that they receive moral support from their colleagues 'to some extent' or 'to a great extent'. 'Teachers in this study reported important emotional and psychological benefits associated with working closely with colleagues in teams' (p.343).
2 *Morale*: Collegial support within teams was perceived to have improved teacher morale and reduced absenteeism and stress. 'The positive approach has led to strong staff participation and morale. Absenteeism and excessive negative stress levels are low' (Teacher, school B, p.343).
3 *Teacher learning*: Team work provided teachers with opportunities to learn from each other. 81.6 per cent of respondents reported feeling 'to some extent' or 'to a great extent' part of a learning community. This included breaking down some of the traditional subject barriers 'which previously inhibited learning and sharing of expertise across subjects' (p.344).

Such advantages do not accrue automatically as a result of teamwork. The school or college climate has a significant impact on whether teams succeed, as does the leadership of the team itself. Wallace (2002) argues that different levels of synergy are evident in teamwork. High SMT synergy is manifested in 'many ideas, willingness to compromise for consensus [and] outcomes acceptable to [the] head' (p.182). The presence of such factors provides the opportunity to reap the benefits of teamwork, as one of his case study schools demonstrates:

> Such potential appeared to be most fully realised at Winton through the relatively egalitarian way SMT members habitually operated, with greater commitment of time to a team approach and more scope for all members to contribute as much as they were capable of doing than in the other three teams. (p.180)

Disadvantages of teamwork

O'Neill (1997) identifies two fundamental limitations of teamwork in schools. First, teachers spend most of their working day physically isolated from their colleagues because teaching is overwhelmingly an individual activity. 'There is one historical "no-go" area in schools and colleges where team models have yet to make any real inroads; namely the classroom. Teaching is almost invariably a solitary activity' (p.83). He contrasts teaching, as an individual activity, with many sports, where the core activity involves working as a team.

Secondly, teachers value authority and the ability to exert control. In this view, team-work is used as a means of organising the delivery of the curriculum within a framework of control. 'Mandated' team approaches do not produce teacher collaboration:

> Despite an apparent move towards more collegial and collaborative forms of management in schools and colleges, the underlying, deeply entrenched occupational culture of teaching continues to value strongly the notion of 'control'. It is manifested most clearly ... in respect for formal status – most notably that of the headteacher or principal. (p.83)

Johnson (2003) refers to four disadvantages of team collaboration on the basis of his Australian research. Most of these mirror the perceived weaknesses of collegiality (Bush 2003).

1 *Work intensification*: a sizeable minority of teachers (41.2 per cent) say that team-work has not reduced their workload and many of these report added burdens, notably in attending team meetings. 'In many cases, the need to meet more frequently with colleagues to discuss and plan collaboratively placed an added work burden on teachers. Commenting on an "explosion of meeting commitments", one teacher at school B suggested that teachers needed "tenacity, stamina, and drive to work more in the same school time" ... many teachers find that changing their work practices leads ... to an intensification of their workloads' (Johnson 2003, pp.346–7).

2 *Loss of autonomy*: 21 per cent of teachers reported feeling constrained when working collaboratively while a similar number felt pressured to conform with the team. This provides a different slant on O'Neill's (1997) point about teaching as an individual activity and shows that teachers value professional autonomy. 'The loss of independence and autonomy by these teachers was seen as an inevitable consequence of having to conform with the implicit norms and explicit decisions of their working team' (Johnson 2003, p.347).

3 *Interpersonal conflict*: there was evidence of conflict between those who wanted to work collaboratively and teachers who preferred their autonomy. The former group were critical of these 'dissenters', 'resistors', 'back stabbers' and 'blockers'. 'The process of implementing collaborative practices in the four schools produced disputes between some staff' (p.348).

4 *Factionalism*: team collaboration produced some divisive competition between teams. 'Different groups within a school adopted different norms and set about defending them against the threat of other groups' (p.348). This point is similar to the findings of Wallace and Hall's (1994) research on senior management teams in English secondary schools. While the SMTs showed good internal coherence, they were perceived to be remote from other staff.

These limitations and disadvantages of teams show that even 'self evident "goods" like teacher collaboration' (Johnson 2003, p.349) may lead to contradictions and paradoxes.

Conclusion

Teams have become significant features of the organization and structure of schools and colleges in many countries. They are valuable in providing an apparently professional means of responding to the pace of change, notably that imposed by external bodies. They provide one example of shared or distributed leadership, which is increasingly advocated, notably by the English National College for School Leadeship. Teamwork can produce advantages in schools, for example in raising teacher morale and contributing to organisational learning. Yet, as we have seen, it may produce problems which can outweigh the benefits. 'Teams are not the solution to everyone's current and future organizational needs. They will not solve every problem ... nor help top management address every performance challenge. Moreover, when misapplied, they can be both wasteful and disruptive' (Katzenbach and Smith 1998, p.24).

Given the context-specific nature of school leadership and management, it is difficult and perhaps unwise to generalise about the factors most likely to lead to successful teamwork. This depends on the skills and attitudes of individual leaders and teachers more than the formal structures. Wallace (2001, p.165) proposes three 'context-dependent' prescriptions based on his extensive research on English senior management teams:

1 School leadership should be shared widely and equally to maximise the potential benefit for children's education and for teachers' job satisfaction and professional growth.
2 Headteachers have responsibility for promoting shared leadership but the right, because of their unique accountability for doing so, to delimit the boundaries of sharing and to have the final say where there is disagreement over leadership decisions.
3 Other teachers have the right to participate in school leadership but the responsibility, because of the headteacher's unique accountability for their work, to ensure that they operate within the boundaries set, including letting the headteacher have the final say where there is disagreement over leadership decisions.

This view is consistent with O'Neill's (1997) warning that teachers value control. It is also endorsed by Rutherford (2002), whose research with Catholic primary schools in Birmingham leads him to a similar conclusion:

> The headteachers demonstrate a values-driven, contingent approach to their leadership that balances the advantages and risks of shared leadership with their personal accountability for the success of their schools. It is clear that they retain the responsibility for making a final decision when there are irreconcilable differences in opinion. (p.457)

It is evident from these comments, based on empirical research, that teamwork has much to offer in dealing with school issues in a professional manner. However, unlike the New Zealand co-principalship discussed by Court (2004), they mostly operate within what seems to be an inescapable hierarchical framework. Teams are valuable in coping with increasing workloads, and in promoting professional collaboration, but they can always be 'trumped' by the principal acting alone. Singular leadership remains more powerful than the collective leadership of teams.

References

Belbin, M. (1993), *Team Roles at Work*, London, Butterworth-Heinemann.

Bell, L. (1992), *Managing Teams in Secondary Schools*, London, Routledge.

Bush, T. (2003), *Theories of Educational Leadership and Management: Third Edition*, London, Sage.

Bush, T., Glover, D. and Morrison, M. (2004), *Working Together for Success: First Interim Report*, Nottingham, NCSL.

Cardno, C. (2002), 'Team learning: opportunities and challenges for school leaders', *School Leadership and Management*, 22 (2), 211–223.

Chaudhry-Lawton, R., Murphy, K. and Terry, A. (1992), *Quality: Change Through Teamwork*, London, Century Business.

Coleman, M. and Bush, T. (1994), 'Managing with teams', in Bush, T. and West-Burnham, J. (eds), *The Principles of Educational Management*, Harlow, Longman.

Court, M. (2004), 'Talking back to new public management versions of accountability in education: a co-principalship's practices of mutual accountability', *Educational Management, Administration and Leadership*, 32 (2), 173–195.

Department of Education (2000), *School Management Teams: Introductory Guide*, Pretoria, Department of Education.

Hallinger, P. and Heck, R. (1999), 'Can leadership enhance school effectiveness?', in Bush, T., Bell, L, Bolam, R., Glatter, R. and Ribbins, P. (eds), *Educational Management: Redefining Theory, Policy and Practice*, London, Paul Chapman Publishing.

Hoyle, E. (1986), *The Politics of School Management*, Sevenoaks, Hodder and Stoughton.

Johnson, B. (2003), 'Teacher collaboration: good for some, not so good for others', *Educational Studies*, 29 (4), 337–350.

Katzenbach, J. and Smith, D. (1998), *The Wisdom of Teams*, London, McGraw-Hill.

Lashway, L. (2003), 'Distributed leadership', *Research Roundup*, 19 (4), 1–2.

Leithwood, K. (1998), 'Team learning processes', in Leithwood, K. and Seashore Louis, K. (eds), *Organizational Learning in Schools*, Lisse, Swets and Zeitlinger.

Middlewood, D. (2003), 'Managing through teams', in Lumby, J., Middlewood, D. and Kaabwe, E. (eds), *Managing Human Resources in South African Schools*, London, Commonwealth Secretariat.

Middlewood, D. and Lumby, J. (1998), *Human Resource Management in Schools and Colleges*, London, Paul Chapman Publishing.

National College for School Leadership (NCSL) (2003), *School Leadership Team-work-*

ing Programme, Nottingham, NCSL.

Nias, J., Southworth, G. and Yeomans, R. (1989), *Staff Relationships in the Primary School*, London, Cassell.

O'Neill, J. (1997), 'Managing through teams', in Bush, T. and Middlewood, D. (eds), *Managing People in Education*, London, Paul Chapman Publishing.

Office for Standards in Education (Ofsted) (2003), *Framework 2003 – Inspecting Schools*, London, Ofsted.

Rutherford, D. (2002), 'Changing times and changing roles: the perspectives of headteachers on their senior management teams', *Educational Management and Administration*, 30 (44), 447–460.

Tuckman, B. (1965), 'Developmental sequences in small groups', *Psychological Bulletin*, 63, 384–399.

Wallace, M. (2001), 'Sharing leadership of schools through teamwork: a justifiable risk?', *Educational Management and Administration*, 29 (2), 153–167.

Wallace, M. (2002), 'Modelling distributed leadership and management effectiveness: primary school management teams in England and Wales', *School Effectiveness and School Improvement*, 13 (2), 163–186.

Wallace, M. and Hall, V. (1994), *Inside the SMT: Teamwork in Secondary School Management*, London, Paul Chapman Publishing.

Woods, P., Bennett, N., Harvey, J. and Wise, C. (2004), 'Variabilities and dualities in distributed leadership: findings from a systematic literative review', *Educational Management, Administration and Leadership*, 32 (4), 439–457.

PART III

Leading and Managing Key Processes

9

Staff recruitment and selection

Introduction

As this whole volume is based upon the assumption that it is people who are the most important resources in an effective school or college, it is axiomatic that having the best possible staff in place is highly desirable. In strictly chronological terms, recruiting and selecting effectively is therefore the highest priority. In reality, most leaders will take up their roles and manage the staff who are already in post. They will have occasion to arrange for some to depart and to appoint others. Whatever the numbers, the importance of getting recruitment and selection right is paramount. Certainly a wrong appointment can be disastrous and costly.

This chapter examines some recent developments in recruitment and selection in education. Developments in psychology continue to underline the point that eliminating subjectivity from this process is impossible and, indeed, the importance of the values context within which staff are appointed may make this undesirable. Even in periods of acute shortages of staff, there is an argument for leaders to maintain the key principles of effective recruitment and selection, and considerable risks in abandoning them for short-term reasons. There is also a case for monitoring staff performance in employment which may encourage leaders and managers to review regularly their procedures in recruiting and selecting staff.

Strategic context

Recruitment and selection need to be considered, not in the specific context of finding someone to do a particular job, but in the overall context of planning the human resource needs of the organisation. Hall (1997, p.149) suggests these should include consideration of:

- How many and what types of people are needed.
- Which of these needs can be satisfied by transfer and development of existing staff and where staff need to be recruited externally.

- Anticipated problems in recruitment (for example, due to the school's location or the higher wages offered by other local employers).
- The need for a recruitment timetable, so that posts do not remain vacant unnecessarily.

This strategic overview sets the context for trying to ensure that the organisation is consistently staffed by the appropriate people to enable it to achieve both its immediate and longer-term goals. Neglecting effective recruitment and selection in this context, and simply reacting to an employee's departure by automatically replacing the person with another of the same type, can have risks which may not become immediately apparent. For example, poor recruitment and selection can raise the possibility of high staff turnover. This is not only damaging in terms of the constant process of obtaining new employees, but may lead to staff demotivation and low morale, and of course to 'client dissatisfaction' (Mullins 1989).

In this context, recruitment, selection and the actual appointment are best perceived as one continuous process as far as their management is concerned, although each clearly involves a different stage:

- Recruitment is the process by which people are encouraged to apply for employment at the school or college.
- Selection is the process through which the best person for the particular post is chosen and offered employment.
- Appointment is the final agreement in which employer and employee commit themselves to the contract of employment.

Factors affecting recruitment

External authority

The scope for leaders and managers at individual context level may be considerably constrained by the fact that staff are nominated or appointed to their organisations by education authorities. In China, for example, Washington's (1991, p.4) research suggested that 'principals have no role in deciding who gets hired or fired'. Lewin et al. (1994) confirmed this but Bush et al. (1998, p.190) found a school principal who claimed to have appointed at least 60 per cent of his staff.

In countries such as Greece, all qualified teachers are allocated to a particular area of the country, with a small amount of discretion given to local principals as to which particular schools they are employed in (Ifanti 1995).

In the Republic of South Africa, Thurlow (2003, p.61) describes how

> recruitment typically is carried out 'centrally' through the provincial education departments. Schools notify the employing department of existing vacancies, together with some basic specification of the posts. In turn, the

employing department is responsible for advertising all vacant posts in a gazette, bulletin or circular and prospective applicants apply directly to the department, using departmentally determined application forms and standard forms for curricula vitae. Furthermore, it is the employing department which handles the initial sifting of applicants for all posts in order to eliminate applications which do not comply with the basic requirements of the post(s) as stated in advertisements. Once this process, which is highly standardised, is completed, the employing department passes the remaining applications to schools, which are responsible for final selections.

Labour market

Clearly, the number of those available for work will be affected by a variety of factors such as:

- the general economic climate of the country
- the perceived status of jobs in education, compared with those in other areas of employment
- population and demographic trends, e.g. the number of people of a certain age available, the gender balance
- the number of entrants into professions such as teaching and the numbers of those returning after career breaks of various kinds.

Legislation

Management of recruitment and selection has to be carried out within the framework of the relevant legislation. This can involve legislation concerning discrimination and the issue of applying equal opportunities in education, as dealt with in Chapter 7. Another example might be legislation which deals with the holding of data about people who apply for posts, whether or not they are appointed. In the UK, the Data Protection Act means that those seeking to appoint staff can only hold data which is sufficient to allow the process of selection to be undertaken and that the data cannot be used for any other unrelated purpose. In practical terms, this means that all copies of application forms, references and other documents of unsuccessful applicants must be destroyed after the allowed brief period, as must any notes made by selectors after they have been retained for a period allowing for any legal appeal against their decision.

Local conditions

The particular circumstances of the school or college (Is it expanding or contracting? What is its local reputation?) and of its local environment will affect potential applicants in their decision as to whether to apply. The cost and availability of housing in the vicinity can be a key factor, as is the accessibility of the school or college by road or public transport.

Effective recruitment

Within the strategic context described, managers of recruitment need to consider all possibilities before automatically deciding to appoint a new employee, for example:

- whether it needs to be filled or whether the work can be reorganised, relocated or redistributed
- the nature of the job to be filled and the kind of person wanted
- whether someone should be recruited from inside the school or outside
- whether the incentives (e.g. pay, promotion, support in post) are appropriate for the kind of person sought (from Hall 1997, p.150).

Having made a decision that a new person should be appointed, effective leaders and managers are likely to have a clear picture overall of the kind of staff they wish to have in place to achieve their goals. This may involve a list of skills, capabilities and qualities that, ideally, employees should have, but the most important thing to be remembered here is that all appointments are primarily on the basis of *potential*. Until someone is actually doing the work involved in the post, the actuality is uncertain. In that sense, recruitment and selection is essentially 'a prediction of performance' (Morgan 1997, p.128).

International schools provide an interesting example of how a particular kind of staff is desired:

> Staff should be carefully recruited so as to represent ... the major culture areas of the world, and as many nationalities as possible ... to give students a variety of racial, ethnic and national role models. (Blaney 1991, p.74)

In reality, however idealistic the aspirations, leaders and managers have to deal with who actually applies. Hardman (2001) suggests that there were four categories of teachers applying for posts at international schools – local teachers, childless career professionals, career professionals with families, and 'mavericks'. Each of these has different motives for applying, ranging from a genuine quest for new teaching opportunities to, in the case of some 'mavericks', a desire for global travel, exploration and a possible escape route from their own national system. As Cambridge (2000) has pointed out, childless career professionals may be the easiest to employ because they are the cheapest to recruit, transport and provide accommodation for, further illustrating the difficulties for selectors in striving to appoint the best people for the jobs.

Few organisations appear to possess a written policy on their overall recruitment and selection strategy. Leaders and managers who consider this should probably include in it statements about:

- purpose of the strategy
- equal opportunities commitment
- commitment to keeping all applicants informed about the processes involved and the current state of their application
- a commitment about the use of data
- a statement about approaches to assessment used to measure applicants against job requirements
- a commitment to confidentiality, objectivity and professionalism applied in the process.

There would also need to be a caveat concerning the use of resources in carrying out the policy.

Stages in recruitment

Mullins (1989, p.175) suggests that these are:

- The need to know about the job to be filled.
- The need to know about the type of person and qualities required to perform the job effectively.
- The need to know the likely means of best attracting a range of suitable applicants.

The first two are normally dealt with by a job description and a person specification. Some writers, such as Thomson (1993), advocate an 'exit interview' (i.e. interviewing the person who is leaving to create the vacancy) as the best means of ascertaining what the job actually has involved.

In constructing a job description, leaders and managers may need to ensure that it accurately reflects, not only the nature of the job itself, but the general approach taken by the organisation. Plachy (1987) drew a distinction between 'Duty-oriented' and 'Results-oriented' job descriptions. Thus, a receptionist may:

> 'Greet visitors and refer them to the appropriate person' (Duty oriented)

> or 'Help visitors by greeting them and referring them to the appropriate person' (Result oriented)

> 'Answer visitors' questions and maintain an orderly reception area' (Duty oriented)

> or 'Reassure visitors, by making them feel welcome, answering questions and maintaining an orderly reception area' (Results oriented) (based on Plachy 1987).

The differences are subtle but significant, indicating to the possible employee something of the nature of the organisation and its approach to its work.

The tasks for those constructing the person specification is to identify the skills, knowledge, attitudes and values necessary to do the job effectively. Acknowledging the point made earlier about appointing on potential, Hackett (1992, p.35) argues for a focus on the behaviour expected of the person when they are actually appointed:

> A more direct approach to establishing just what you need to look for is to consider what the job-holder must be able to do – that is, what *abilities* he [sic] needs. If you can match these against the *demands* which the job will make, you are less likely to find that you have recruited someone who is incapable of performing to the required standard. If you also give some thought to the *rewards* which the job offers, in terms of pay and benefits, relationships and job satisfaction, you can then work out what individual *needs* these are likely to satisfy. If you recruit someone whose needs are met by the rewards the job offers, he [sic] is much more likely to stay and work hard.

Leaders and managers may wish to appoint people who will fit, both with the team within which they will be working and the culture and ethos of the organisation as a whole. Teams are dealt with elsewhere in this volume, but the integration of newly appointed members of staff into the school or college will be easier if they have a clear idea of what kind of organisation they may wish to apply to. Accurate details of the organisation, including those reflecting its culture, provide an opportunity for unsuitable candidates to deselect themselves, thus saving both parties time and expense.

As far as the 'fitting' of new employees to the organisation's culture is concerned, Law and Glover (2000, p.191) suggest that a tension exists

> between traditional, reactive perspectives where staff are recuited to 'fit' existing plans (e.g. where recruitment is linked to an audit of forecast needs for specific skills, numbers and expertise) and a more proactive perspective where the (existing and potential) skills of current staff are recognised and developed, thus avoiding 'reactive' and potentially unstable recruitment strategies.

Their earlier research (Glover and Law 1996) found that too few schools were willing to analyse the institutional context closely enough 'perhaps because (of) taken-for-granted assumptions that skills and competencies are shared potentially by everyone' (p.192). In the fast-changing context of educational organisations in the twenty-first century, it could well be argued that the 'proactive perspective' is highly desirable for effectiveness.

Who should be involved?

The perceptions of stakeholders other than professionals as to what constitutes effectiveness in a person to be appointed, and as to how the prevailing culture of the school or college is perceived, becomes important here. In any case, of course, the involvement of lay personnel in recruitment and selection of staff is statutory in several countries (e.g. UK, Australia, New Zealand), notably those where self-governance of schools and colleges has become a major feature of the education system. The main influence of lay personnel is that of parents, and of governors representing community, business and other interests; some of these are likely to have experience of recruitment and selection outside education. Research by Bush et al. (1993) into the first grant-maintained schools in England and Wales (i.e. funded directly by money from central government) showed that governors exerted a powerful influence in this area of school management.

Training for those involved

There is a strong case for ensuring that those leading and managing recruitment and selection are trained to carry out this process. The key argument for training is in the need for *consistency* both across all the people (a mixture of professional and lay) involved in appointing any individual and across the number of different occasions when appointments are to be made. Apart from the need for as much objectivity as possible, which consistency of approach will aid, it is a help to the school or college if a clearly understood operation comes into action each time a vacancy occurs, again saving in unnecessary time and expense. Norris (1993, p.27) indicated, for example, that by 1980, through research studies outside education, 'interviewer bias was also found to be significantly reduced by using trained interviewers'.

In school staff procedures, parents can play a critical role. Principals such as Van Halen (1995, p.15), having stated that it took him ten years – with 'significant' training – to feel confident about selecting teachers and middle managers, believed that training for parents involved in the process was essential.

> Parents on selection panels fall into one of three categories: those who leave the decisions to the professionals; a group that have their minds made up beforehand and do not come clean about the hidden agendas; and finally, the minority who are trained in the selection processes or who are open about the process and stay with the assessment criteria all along.

Morgan's (1997, p.127) study of selection panels in action in England and Wales led him to examine the roles of professional and lay members and conclude that there can be a dilemma in relations between these roles. His recommendation was that the professional and lay roles should be visibly differentiated and be placed

> on a complementary rather than competitive basis in contexts where 'lay controllers' participate in the selection of staff, complementary roles would mean that heads or other 'professionals' would lead the systematic determination of the job criteria; deploy multiple means of deriving evidence on the key competency requirements; and assemble and accumulate the evidence of candidates' strengths and weaknesses in the form of complete profiles which would be used by the lay members for their final decision.

Factors affecting selection management

The quality of the applicants

As noted earlier, selectors can only make a choice from those who actually apply and it is at this stage that the care taken in job descriptions and person specifications will pay dividends. If none of the applicants reaches the minimum requirements, it is much easier and reassuring to be able to decide to re-advertise, rather than be tempted to 'have a look at what we've got anyway', running the real risk of choosing someone who does not meet the needs. When the pressure is on to fill a post, this temptation can be significant, but the long-term consequences of appointing an employee who may turn out to be less than competent can be very damaging.

Quality of selectors

The issue of personnel and training has already been discussed, but leaders and managers could consider the development of middle managers in this field by offering them an involvement in the actual process, without them having any authority or responsibility in that specific appointment, e.g. observing at an interview (with candidates' permission), or reading applications.

Fallibility of selectors

Research both inside and outside education has indicated the large number of prejudices that can distort a selection process. These can include:

- basing judgements upon intuition rather than facts
- making 'snap' judgements

- insisting on a personal stereotype of what is a 'good' candidate
- comparing candidates with the previous post holder or with other candidates rather than the agreed criteria
- preferring a candidate in one's own image.

The most human interactive part of the selection process, the interview, is particularly prone to these prejudices, and research by Norris (1993), Riches (1992), Morgan (1997) and Morgan et al. (1983), among others, have shown shortcomings such as:

- Interviewers often make up their minds about a candidate within the first five minutes of the interview and – consciously or unconsciously – spend the rest of the interview trying to justify their judgement.
- Interviewers' judgement of candidates can be affected by their appearance, speech, gender and race either positively or negatively; people tend to favour others whom they perceive to be like themselves.
- Physically attractive candidates are more likely to be appointed.
- An average candidate who follows several poor candidates is seen as particularly good.
- Research on memory shows that we remember information we hear at the beginning and end of an interview and, thus, tend to forget vital details and facts given in the middle.
- It is impossible for the human brain to concentrate at the same level over a prolonged period; thus if you are interviewing several candidates on the same date, they may not receive equal amounts of your attention.

For these reasons, the British Psychological Society reported that even well-conducted interviews were only 25 per cent better than choosing someone by sticking a pin in a list of candidates (Thomson 1993, p.30)!

However, the picture is not totally negative as Hinton (1993) points out. Despite errors occurring, these do not prove that people are inaccurate in their selections. Both Hinton (1993) and Morgan (1997) point to the large number of social, psychological and micropolitical factors at work during selection, with Hinton warning that sometimes a group of people agreeing on a selection at the end of interviews will often mistake the warm glow of relief and satisfaction of having agreed on *a* choice for the actually important one of agreeing that an accurate choice had been made. Despite this, Hinton (1993, p.137) concludes that the selection panel is significantly better than one person and 'despite differences in their judgements they could well perform their function successfully and select a suitable candidate for the job'. The counterbalancing of individual prejudices is a crucial element of this.

Effective management of selection

With the need for consistency and objectivity being paramount, a structured approach to the process of managing the actual process of selection is advocated by Middlewood and Lumby (1998). They suggest that the key issues for leaders and managers to consider are:

1 Personnel: who will be involved – and the extent and nature of that involvement?
2 Criteria: against which standards will candidates be assessed?
3 Weighting: what should be the relative importance of the criteria?
4 Instruments: how will the candidates' performance be assessed?
5 Matching: making a decision on which person is best suited to the post.

Personnel

The involvement of both professional and lay people has already been discussed but further interesting issues and examples are developing. In South Africa, a teacher union representative is entitled to be present at the selection of all teachers and, in some schools and colleges in the USA and the UK, a representative of external stakeholders may be part of the selection process. Where the job involves greeting visitors, for example, a parent or 'client' representative may be used as they will be well placed to assess what is needed.

An increasing trend in some countries is the involvement of pupils and students in the process of selecting their own teachers or headteachers. Hardi (2002) reports that in all Lithuania secondary schools, there is an entitlement for students to be involved, while Downes (1996) describes a typical case of student shrewdness in assessing teacher potential in an English school.

Involvement of course covers a range of actions, from conducting applicants around a school or college on a 'guided tour', to forming student panels to question all candidates, through to being on the final selection panel.

If the current holder of the post is still there, some managers believe it useful for applicants to have an opportunity to talk with them, or be shown the area for work by them. They should not be involved in the actual selection (indeed, in some countries this is prohibited by legislation), if for no other reason than that there would be a temptation to seek someone similar to replace them.

Criteria and weighting

Criteria are likely to include biographical data (especially qualifications and experience), skills, knowledge, attitudes and values (such as personal ambition or commitment), and it is in the weighting of the relative importance of the various criteria that the analysis of the job requirements and person specification enables a checklist to be made for all selectors to use consistently. Middlewood and Lumby (1998, p.70) comment that the devising of weightings is 'difficult because of the need to rank elements of the work – it is easy to say that one task is more important than another but rather more difficult to give it a value. However, this is one way in which we can overcome some of the inconsistencies in the selection process'.

Instruments for assessing candidates

In several developed countries (the UK, the USA, Hong Kong, Singapore, Australia, Canada), methods of assessing candidates during a selection process have become increasingly sophisticated since the late 1980s. This is especially true at leadership level. In some countries, these are conducted centrally through assessment centres of various kinds, so that those who are successful can be nominated as having reached the required standard. Such assessment exercises can include, as well as psychometric tests:

- *In-tray exercise*: candidates are asked to sift and prioritise and decide upon action for a sample of documents.
- *Written report*: having been given certain information, candidates are asked to write a report for a particular audience.
- *Role play simulation*: candidates are asked to enact the job applied for in a particular situation.
- *Oral presentation*: candidates are asked to present formally to the interviewers a brief (usually five or ten minutes) synthesis of their views or approach to a particular issue. Usually, candidates may use visual aids in support of their oral presentation, e.g. slides or overhead projections.
- *Leaderless group discussion*: candidates are grouped together to discuss a topic or reach a decision on a question. Selectors are involved only as observers of individuals' performances with the group's processes. Situations in which the groups are placed are usually co-operative (e.g. the group must come to a consensus on an issue), but operate within a competitive framework (adapted from Middlewood and Lumby 1998, p.71).

All assessment processes still appear to involve a face-to-face interview. At an assessment centre, this is likely to be with one or more trained professional assessors. However, in some countries which award candidates notification of having reached a required standard (e.g. the National Professional Qualification for Headship [NPQH] in England), applicants still have to apply for headship posts in individual schools, where they may encounter similar assessment methods in different circumstances. They will certainly encounter an interview.

Some of the potential inadequacies of interviews have already been referred to, but perhaps the most important thing for selectors to remember is that interviewing is a two-way process, enabling both interviewers and interviewees to be clear about whether they are suitable for the post. This approach reduces the risk of a situation which can be tense, stressful and even confrontational for candidates, which blurs the ability of selectors to see the true ability of the candidates. McPherson's (1999) study of the selection of secondary school principals in KwaZulu-Natal, South Africa, identified 'The atmosphere in selection interviews is very tense and candidates are not made to feel at ease', among their problems, as well as bias of some committee members towards certain candidates, and the time allowed as being too short to enable candidates to do themselves justice (cited in Thurlow 2003, p.66). Questioning is a specific skill in which interviewers can be trained, but in any case managers need to be clear about what it is they are trying to find out. Williams et al. (2001, p.55) offer a case study of a school committed to appointing the best quality staff:

> At all job interviews candidates are asked: 'Tell us about the worst day and the best day you have had in the classroom.' This is designed to explore their capacity to reflect on themselves, their classroom practice and their ability to learn from both success and failure. Staff are therefore encouraged to use their initiative, to risk failure and develop confidence in their own ability.

In another school, questions are asked 'designed to tease out the candidate's resilience and her/his capacity to deal with difficult situations in class' (Williams et al. 2001, p.41).

It seems logical also to include observation in methods of assessing candidates' suitability for a post, since managers can see them actually carrying out a task which they are being appointed to do, albeit in a somewhat artificial situation (i.e. selected class, selected topic, etc.). Again, an example from Williams et al. (2001, p.41) is typical:

> All short-listed candidates are asked to teach 'their best lesson' to a particular class, and they are observed by the head, the senior teacher responsible for staff development and a governor. Questions are then asked at the interview about the lesson.

Although less common than with teachers, examples also occur of classroom assistants being observed working with pupils with special educational needs (Lorenz 1999) and receptionist/clerical staff being observed while 'working in the office' for a period (Williams et al. 2001).

Matching

The crucial point in managing the final part of the recruitment and selection process is that *all* the evidence available needs to be reviewed by those selecting. The weakness of many processes has been the overemphasis placed on the interview, which is almost always the final part of the process (Morgan 1997; McPherson 1999). The whole evidence should include the original applications, the references (where applicable), feedback from panels, observations, other assessment methods *and* the interview. Southworth (1990) stresses the importance of applying three criteria to the total evidence:

- adequacy (i.e. how sufficient is it?)
- integrity (i.e. how truthful and reliable is it?)
- appropriateness (i.e. how relevant is it?).

It is worth noting, that where some selectors, especially lay people such as governors or parents, are brought into the process only at the final stage of the interview, it would be difficult for leaders and managers to criticise them for seeing the interview as the most important part of the whole selection process. Although Morgan (1997, p.127) does argue that one model for clarifying professional/lay roles is that: 'it is therefore the role of the professional to assemble the evidence with as much selection expertise as possible and the role of the lay members to decide upon it in similar manner to the role of a jury', he is referring to the whole of the evidence, not merely evidence from the interview.

Monitoring the effectiveness of recruitment and selection processes

Ultimately, the test of how effectively the recruitment and selection processes have been managed lies in the quality and performance of the staff appointed. Performance and its review is discussed in full in Chapter 12 but making a link between an employee's subsequent performance and the way that person performs is acknowledged as being difficult (Middlewood 1997; Morgan 1997). Miles (2000) carried out research on this topic in three secondary schools in England and found there was not a single case where school leaders, in dealing with ineffective or only adequate performance of staff, had even considered whether the way those staff had been selected had any bearing on this. The leaders tended to hold the view that as the selection process had resulted in some good performers, it was not worth changing it – a view that they probably would not have found acceptable in other parts of their management! Both Middlewood and Morgan advocate follow-up discussion, both informal and formal, as the best process available.

Leading and managing in difficult contexts

In times of severe shortages of available staff, there is a temptation for leaders to cut back on normal rigorous procedures of recruitment and selection in order to obtain staff quickly. Not only are there legal risks in this, but there is also the danger of appointing staff who will eventually turn out to be more of a disadvantage than a benefit. When the shortage is acknowledged, national governments may introduce schemes by which, for example, entry into the teaching profession can be easier and faster. Woodward (2003) describes 'Teach First', a fast-track system to get graduates into teaching in schools in London quickly. The scheme acknowledges that these teachers will not necessarily do more than two years, but 'it could be that this is the price teaching has to pay in today's recruitment market'.

Ultimately, in such situations, leaders may have to continue to acknowledge that contexts change and, as Gerry (2002, p.8) argues:

> There is a structural problem then with teacher recruitment. It is likely to get much worse, not better. What then should we do? I don't believe that scouring the world for teachers is either ethical or desirable. Instead we have to re-engineer what we do and switch education from being as teacher intensive as it is currently.

Whatever the models of staffing schools and colleges that leaders believe will exist in the future, the need will remain for ensuring that managing of recruitment and selection of staff is as rigorous and effective as ever.

References

Blaney, J. (1991), 'The international school system', in Janietz, P. and Harris, D. (eds), *World Year Book of Education 1991: International Schools and International Education*, London, Kogan Page.

Brown, P. and Lauder, H. (1996), 'Education, globalization and economic development', in Halsey, A., Lauder, H., Brown, P. and Wells, A. (eds), *Education: Culture, Economy and Society*, Oxford, Oxford University Press.

Bush, T., Coleman, M. and Glover, D. (1993), *Managing Autonomous Schools: The Grant-Maintained Experience*, London, Paul Chapman Publishing.

Bush, T., Coleman, M. and Xiaohong, S. (1998), 'Managing secondary schools in China', *Compare*, 28 (2), 183–195.

Cambridge, J. (2000), 'International schools, globalization and the seven cultures of capitalism', in Kayden, M. and Thompson, J. (eds), *International Schools and International Education*, London, Kogan Page.

Downes, P. (1996), 'Students and their choice of head', *Managing Schools Today*, 9 (3), 16–17.

Gerry, C. (2002), 'Thinking differently: life in interesting times', *Headship Matters*, (17), 8–9, London, Optimus Publishing.

Gleeson, D. and Gunter, H. (2001), 'The performing school and the modernization of teachers', in Gleeson, D. and Husbands, C. (eds), *The Performing School*, London, Routledge.

Glover, D. and Law, S. (1996), *Managing Professional Development in Education*, London, Kogan Page.

Hackett, P. (1992), *Success in Management: Personnel*, 3rd edition, London, John Murray.

Hall, V. (1997), 'Managing staff', in Fidler, B., Russell, S. and Simkins, T. (eds), *Choices for Self-Managing Schools*, London, Paul Chapman Publishing.

Hardi, S. (2002), Students and teachers: mutual assessment, paper presented to International Education Conference, Athens.

Hardman, J. (2001), 'Improving recruitment and retention of quality overseas teachers', in Blandford, S. and Shaw, M. (eds), *Managing International Schools*, London, RoutledgeFalmer.

Hinton, P. (1993), *The Psychology of Interpersonal Perception*, London, Routledge.

Ifanti, A. (1995), 'Policy making, politics and administration in education in Greece', *Educational Management and Administration*, 23 (4), 217–278.

Law, S. and Glover, D. (2000) *Educational Leadership and Learning*, Buckingham, Open University Press.

Lewin, K., Xu, H., Little, A. and Zheng, J. (1994), *Educational Innovation in China: Tracing the Impact of the 1985 Reforms*, Harlow, Longman.

Lorenz, S. (1999), *Effective In-Class Support: The Management of Support Staff in Mainstream and Special Schools*, London, David Fulton.

McPherson, J. (1999), Selection of schools principals, unpublished dissertation for M.Ed. in Educational Management, University of Natal.

Middlewood, D. (1997), 'Managing recruitment and selection', in Bush, T. and Middlewood, D. (eds), *Managing People in Education*, London, Paul Chapman Publishing.

Middlewood, D. and Lumby, J. (1998), *Human Resource Management in Schools and Colleges*, London, Paul Chapman Publishing.

Miles, E. (2000), Selection and performance, unpublished MBA dissertation, University of Leicester.

Morgan, C. (1997), 'Selection: predicting effective performance', in Kydd, L., Crawford, M. and Riches, C. (eds), *Professional Development for Educational Management*, Buckingham, Open University Press.

Morgan, C., Hall, V. and Kackay, A. (1983), *The Selection of Secondary School Headteachers*, Milton Keynes, Open University Press.

Mullins, L. (1989), *Management and Organisational Behaviour*, 2nd edition, London, Paul Chapman Publishing.

Norris, K. (1993), 'Avoidable inequalities?', *Management in Education*, 7 (2), 27–30.

Plachy, R. (1987), 'Writing job descriptions that get results', *Personnel*, 64 (10), New

York, American Management Association.

Riches, C. (1992), 'Developing communication skills in interviewing', in Bennett, N., Crawford, M. and Riches, C. (eds), *Managing Change in Education*, Milton Keynes, Open University Press.

Southworth, G. (1990), *Staff Selection in the Primary School*, London, Blackwell.

Strathern, M. (2000), 'The tyranny of transparency', in *British Educational Research Journal*, 26 (3), 309–321.

Thomson, R. (1993), *Managing People*, London, Butterworth-Heinemann.

Thurlow, M. (2003), 'Recruitment and selection', in Lumby, J., Middlewood, D. and Kaabwe, S. (eds), *Managing Human Resources in South African Schools*, London, Commonwealth Secretariat.

Van Halen, B. (1995), 'We can do it better', *Principal Matters*, 7 (3), 14–15.

Washington, K. (1991), 'School administration in China: a look at the principal's role', *International Journal of Educational Management*, 5, 4–5.

Williams, S., MacAlpine, A. and McCall, C. (2001), *Leading and Managing Staff through Challenging Times*, London, The Stationery Office.

Woodward, W. (2003), 'Quick fix', *Educational Guardian*, 29 July, pp.1–2.

10

Induction and retention

Introduction

Effective leaders and managers of people in individual schools and colleges need to ensure that their employees' potential is maximised at all stages of their development during their time at the institution. This obviously covers the period from the moment they are appointed and take up their posts to the time they leave, either for another post elsewhere or because they retire from their professional careers. If staff depart too readily from the organisation before full potential – at whatever level – is realised, this can be a serious loss to the organisation's performance capacity and can also be very cost-ineffective.

This chapter links two important aspects of this leadership and management issue. It explores the importance of induction for all employees as the crucial first phase of employment, and illustrates how effective induction can make a significant difference to a new member of staff's performance. It also examines some of the ways in which organisations attempt to retain effective employees, especially in the context of external situations affecting the staff's professional concerns. Some of these ways are more successful than others, especially when taking into consideration the longer-term future of the school or college.

Links between induction and retention

It is difficult to ascertain whether there is a causal link between an effective induction process and the consequent ability of the organisation to retain the employee's services, but it is probably easier to suggest the opposite, i.e. if a person is given a poor start in a school or college, there may be a very good chance that he or she will not stay very long. Hicks and Tilby (2004) surveyed 11 teachers who had left three schools in Hertfordshire, England, after only one year. Eight out of the 11 felt they had 'not been made to feel welcome' or 'not felt supported' when they began at the schools. Grace and Lawn (1991) described how poor induction programmes for newly qualified teachers (NQTs) in a London borough had been a 'very serious'

141

reason for them leaving their schools after one year or less. Outside education, 'numerous studies have shown that the induction method affects both the rate of turn-over in the first six months and the rate of integration' (Hunt, 1986, p.213).

Common sense would suggest that the favourable impressions about their new school or college formed by a new member of staff would have an influence on how long they wished to continue working there. In Department of Education and Science (DES 1992) guidance on probationary teachers, it was suggested that only in the third year of a post did an NQT begin to give back to the school more than they were taking from it. In times of staff shortages it becomes even more important to retain effective employees, thus increasing the significance of effective management of induction.

What is induction?

Induction is formally seen as important in the effective management of staff in many countries. The Commonwealth Secretariat and World Bank (1992) included 'agreed procedures on induction' in its framework for effective management of staff within educational organisations and recognised it as a practice which was very much the business of site-based leaders and managers. The main purposes of induction may be seen as:

- Socialisation – enabling the new employee to become part of the organisation.
- Achieving competent performance – enabling the new person to contribute to the organisation through the way he or she carries out their job.
- Understanding the organisational culture – enabling the new colleague to appreciate the core values and beliefs of the institution.

Socialisation

Schein (1978, pp.36–7) identified five elements in this process of the inductee being assimilated into the organisation.

1 Accepting the reality of the organisation (i.e. the constraints governing individual behaviour).
2 Dealing with resistance to change (i.e. the problems involved in getting personal views and ideas accepted by others).
3 Learning how to work realistically in the new job, in terms of coping with too much or too little organisation and too much or too little job definition (i.e. the amount of autonomy and feedback available).
4 Dealing with the boss and understanding the reward system (i.e. the amount of independence given and what the organisation defines as high performance).
5 Locating one's place in the organisation and developing an identity (i.e. understanding how an individual fits into the organisation).

The first four of Schein's elements all contain reference to, or an assumption about, induction including coming to terms with what the *real* job is like in the organisation. No matter how thorough the process of recruitment and selection has been, it is only when the actual work begins that the realities of the nature of the work, the responsibilities and the organisation are fully recognised. What was allowable and even encouraged in a previous place of work may be frowned upon in the new place. Routines may be different. New headteachers, for example, (Weindling and Earley 1987; MacBeath 1998), have complained of lack of management when they took up their post but, as MacBeath found, this often means 'different' management from the approach they are used to and wish to employ.

The notion of establishing one's place in the school or college for more junior staff is also something that takes time. A post may have *status* on paper, but it is possible for the inductee holding the post to discover that others have more *stature* and that colleagues go to them automatically instead of to themselves, e.g. for decisions. Similarly, a new post-holder may be told to get on with the job, only to do so and then be asked why they did not check first, simply because the degree of autonomy is different from that experienced elsewhere.

Achieving competent performance

Although leaders and managers will always want their new appointees to perform very effectively from the first day, it is likely that those in their first posts in particular will take a little time to achieve this. Kakabadse et al. (1987, p.8) suggest there may be three stages to reaching high performance.

1 *Getting used to the place*, i.e. overcoming the initial shock and immobilisation of the new organisation and job demands.
2 *Relearning*, i.e. recognising that new skills have to be learned or how learned skills have to be reapplied.
3 *Becoming effective*, i.e. consolidating one's position in the organisation by applying new behaviours and skills or integrating newly formed attitudes with ones held from the past.

This suggests that the key element for the inductees is learning, both about themselves and the organisation.

Understanding organisation culture

Hunt (1986, p.213) calls this simply the 'transfer of loyalties to the new organisation', stressing that until this happens, the new employee will never become committed to the success of the new place of employment and therefore performance will never be at optimum level.

Whom is induction for?

In England and Wales, the School Management Task Force (1990) recommended that all new members of staff in schools should have an entitlement to induction but this remains an aspiration in many schools and colleges. In developed countries, there is considerable emphasis on the need for effective induction for teachers beginning their professional careers and, since 1990, for new principals/headteachers. Much less emphasis has been given to the needs of middle managers (Blandford 2000) and to other teachers joining school or college staffs. In developing countries, 'there has been little educational research regarding the entry-year needs and critical skills for beginning principals' (Kitan and Van der Westhuizen 1997, p.127).

As far as other staff in schools and colleges are concerned, the situation is weaker. Thomson (1993, p.110) suggests that temporary and part-time staff can often be ignored in induction processes 'in the misguided belief that they will not care much about the organisation and that they are just there to do the job'. Similarly, as noted in Chapter 3 support staff are often put in the position of having to organise their own induction (Balshaw and Farrell 2002) because school leaders do not provide it, confirming the findings of Mortimore et al. (1994).

Finally, it can be argued that even when someone takes up a new post within the same organisation, e.g. through internal promotion, some form of induction is needed for that person. Dean (2001) reflects how, on being promoted from deputy to head within the same school, it was assumed that he knew all there was to know about the school and the post, whereas when he had been appointed as deputy, he had been inducted carefully.

What is involved in effective induction?

Whatever form the induction process takes, the central issue is that it should 'meet the needs both of the inductee and the organisation,' (Blandford 2000, p.178). Managing the induction of newly appointed staff may well include the following:

- Arranging preparatory visits to the school or college prior to starting.
- Giving information about the organisation.
- Offering guidance and support over personal (e.g. accommodation) issues related to taking up the new appointment.
- (In larger institutions) arranging off-site programmes for all new employees together.
- Allocating a specific person as mentor to support the new employee during induction. (This is an important and widely used practice and is dealt with fully in Chapter 11.)

It is easy for leaders and managers to devise lists, especially of the information that they feel inductees need. These lists can be formidable, covering everything from the physical layout of the site, through every organisation policy, to details of individual students. However, such lists if presented merely as lists, can be daunting, especially for people in their very first posts.

Induction programmes

One of the commonest ways in which leaders and managers support new members of staff is by devising a formal induction programme. In addition to the preparatory visits mentioned earlier, these normally consist of a series of meetings, seminars or workshops which familiarise the inductee with the school or college and its personnel, and usually include the opportunity to raise queries or problems found in the earlier stages of employment in the new post. Sometimes, such programmes are arranged exclusively for NQTs, sometimes for all those newly appointed to the organisation.

Emphasising the importance of induction

There is evidence that, unless leaders and managers show their belief in the importance of induction, it may be ineffective. In the vocational post-compulsory sector of education, many so called 'technical teachers' felt that their qualification was in their former occupation and felt no need for induction (Holloway 1994), the consequence being in many cases 'an alienating experience for the students' (p.47). The organisation's leaders and managers need to show an active interest in the induction process, however removed they might be in a larger school or college from the day-to-day management of it. Andrews (1998, pp.79–85) identified five different paradigms of teacher induction:

- the laissez-faire
- the collegial
- the formalised mentor–protégé
- the statutory competency based
- the self-directing professional

and there are elements in all but the first of these which the manager may feel are relevant for all induction. The leader may feel the need to get directly involved sometimes simply to demonstrate the organisation's care for its employees and also its insistence on high standards. Middlewood (2003) quotes the following example from South Africa:

> The principal of a primary school near Pietermaritzberg related how he had appointed a new teacher who lived a long way from the school. After a few

weeks he began to arrive late and as he did this began to become unpopular with other staff. The principal discussed the reasons for his lateness with him and was convinced that the alleged transport problems were not the real reason. The principal then drove to the teacher's house each morning although it was forty miles out of his way, to bring the teacher in. This meant the teacher had to be up even earlier as the principal was in school by 7.15am, whereas the teacher was not expected until 8.00am. After just over a week, the teacher declined the lift and began to arrive at school regularly on time. As he became accepted as a loyal member of staff, he became contented and lateness was no longer a problem. The problem had been identified and solved at an early stage. The drives in together, although only for a week, also enabled the principal to develop a helpful relationship with the teacher, facilitating the induction period.

Seeing induction as part of a continuous process

Experience and research support the notion that 'effective induction should be systematic, planned and part of a school-wide approach to supporting *all* staff' (Bines and Boydell 1996, p.7). Jones and Stammers (1997) and Bubb et al. (2002) see effective induction as the bridge which enables beginners to move smoothly into the second and third years of their professional work, enabling such arrangements as those for performance management to become a natural part of the employees' working life. In that sense, it can be argued that resources for induction 'should be seen as an investment' (Jones and Stammers 1997, p.82).

Effectiveness in induction

It is suggested that induction is most likely to be effective where both managers and inductees see the process as something to which they *both* contribute, a principle common in people management. A newly appointed member of staff can be at their most vulnerable in the early period and can easily feel isolated when everyone else seems comfortable, e.g. with routines and procedures. Although it is a period for reflection for the newcomer, those early days can make this difficult (see Hall 1997, p.172).

Induction therefore needs to involve a significant element of being self-directed and, as far as managers are concerned, viewed as a two-way process. Induction programmes and the whole induction process require this perception. There would be a great danger for managers in assuming all was going well with a new member of staff, when this was not the case, since a simple matter such as the difference in status deterred the beginner from being outspoken.

Research carried out by Sehlare et al. (1994) in high schools in the former Bophuthatswana found several discrepancies between the views of principals and those of 'beginner' teachers regarding the induction process for the latter. (There were also, it should be noted, several areas of agreement.) Differences in perception of the support of being given to the teacher were found in the following areas:

- classroom organisation and management
- the referral system in the school
- the teaching load of beginner teachers
- interaction with parents
- feedback from the principal
- effectiveness of formal meetings in the school.

In clarifying the aims and objectives of the school, an important aspect of early experience in the school community if the newcomer is to integrate his/her own practice and values, 100 per cent of principals felt they did this for the beginner teacher 'always' or 'often'. In contrast, almost exactly half (50.7 per cent) of the teachers in the same school felt their principals did this 'always' or 'often'. In fact, 32.5 per cent said it was done 'sometimes' and 16.2 per cent said 'never'! Other marked discrepancies are shown in Table 10.1.

Table 10.1 The views of principals and beginner teachers regarding the induction process of the latter *Source*: Sehlare et al. 1994

Area	Always/often		Sometimes/never	
Interaction with parents	Principals	82.9%	Principals	14.6%
	Beginner teachers	64.3%	Beginner teachers	35.1%
Effectiveness of formal meetings	Principals	95.1%	Principals	4.9%
	Beginner teachers	57.2%	Beginner teachers	42.2%
Referral system	Principals	85.3%	Principals	9.7%
	Beginner teachers	55.8%	Beginner teachers	39.6%
Classroom management and organisation	Principals	71.5%	Principals	24.4%
	Beginner teachers	54.6%	Beginner teachers	41.1%

It is the manager, of course, who has the responsibility, and if the beginner teacher has the perception that he/she is not being helped enough in dealings with parents, then it *is* an issue.

Careful monitoring of the induction process could lead to feedback on an aspect so apparently quantifiable as the teaching load of beginner teachers. In the above research, 43.5 per cent of teachers felt their teaching load was too heavy a burden, whereas 78 per cent of principals were satisfied that they did not put too much pressure in this way on their beginners.

The researchers drew conclusions from their work that many of the differences could be ascribed to communication problems between the two partners. They believed this was affected by, on the one hand, a lack of confidence of beginner teachers to communicate freely with the principal and on the other the failure of the principal to be proactive in helping teachers in formal situations such as in-school meetings or meeting parents. They identified time and a conducive atmosphere as being the key elements in narrowing 'the gap between what the principal thinks he is doing to help, and what the beginner teacher actually experiences' (Sehlare et al. 1994, p.77).

In short, although induction is for the new provided by the experienced, the induction process will be most effective where the experienced acknowledge that they have things to learn from it also.

The importance of retention of staff

There is a reasonable amount of evidence (NCE 1996; Mortimore and MacBeath 2003), to suggest that an effective school or college is most likely to have a staff which has a 'balanced mix' of younger and newer employees, those who have significant professional experience and those who are mature people in the later years of their careers. Common sense would suggest that this is likely to be the case, offering in theory a mixture of enthusiasm and new ideas, confidence in practice and wisdom of long experience. It must be stressed of course that these qualities by no means necessarily relate to the implied age groups, but it does indicate to leaders and managers the importance of retaining the services of a reasonable proportion of staff so that the organisations can benefit from their knowledge of the place of employment, its culture and practices. Of course, it is important that good quality staff do leave, moving on to a promotion elsewhere for example, when the time is right, but if too many staff leave, especially after only a year or two in post, the age and experience profile of the staff becomes unbalanced. Moreover, a momentum of staff exodus can be started and a high turnover rate of staff is often a key element in failing or poorly performing schools (Stoll and Myers 1998).

Career cycles

If induction, as mentioned earlier, is ideally managed as a 'bridge' between the very early stages in post and the subsequent development of a professional career, then the issue of retention may not arise until later in a person's career. If we examine models of life and career cycles, it can be helpful for analysing when retention may become an issue. Leithwood (1992) suggested four key career stages for teachers:

1 Developing the ability to teach and manage classrooms.
2 Developing classroom confidence and flexibility.
3 Developing greater subject leadership and responsibility.
4 Developing management skills across the institution.

Others, such as Day (1996, p.124), suggest that teachers need to be led and managed with a focus on their development as 'whole persons throughout their careers … recognising that teachers are not technicians but that teaching is bound up with their lives, their histories, the kind of persons they have been and have become'.

In such contexts, leaders and managers need to recognise not only the skills levels reached by staff and the responsibilities they are capable of taking on, but also the attitudes, aspirations and personal relationships developed which can all influence decisions about whether they should leave or remain at a school or college.

A particularly challenging stage for leaders and managers to retain effective employees is the one which follows the induction, settling in or 'coming to terms with reality' stage. Since the school or college will have given much to developing these staff, much will be lost if they leave at that point, just when, it can be argued, a positive return is being made for the organisation's investment. In England a worrying feature for the teaching profession has been the exodus of 16 per cent of teachers after three or four years' experience (Johnson 2003).

Draper's (2002) research into teachers' career plans in Scotland found that they could be divided into four categories:

- stayers – those who plan to stay in the classroom
- starters – those who will be applying for promotion
- stoppers – those who have sought promotion but do not intend to do so in the future
- movers – those who have sought and will continue to seek promotion.

She concludes that leaders and managers of staff need to be constantly aware of staff's career plans; ignoring them is a 'risky strategy' which could have a serious impact on retention.

Retention at a national level

Some aspects of retention relate to the whole issue of whether employees wish to remain in the education profession anyway, and are therefore to some extent beyond the influence of individual leaders and managers. For example, in some developed countries, a benign economic climate can make retention difficult. As Hallgarten (2001) points out, in England 'The creative industries have flourished and many barriers to female graduate employment have been eroded (leading to) … teaching too often being compared unfavourably with the growing range of alternative careers' (p.15). He goes on to report how the number of teachers who left the profession for employment outside education rose by about 30 per cent between 1998 and 1999, and the number of returners continued to decline.

Conversely in a number of developing countries, as economies improve, education becomes more important, pay rises and fewer people are likely to leave the profession (Foskett and Lumby 2003).

As discussed in Chapter 6, when morale and motivation are low because of national factors, leaders and managers have extra pressures on them to retain good quality staff who may be dispirited and beginning to consider alternative career options.

While 'retention' is the key issue for leaders and managers at institutional level, Bush (2002) makes a useful distinction between three terms:

Retention means keeping teachers within the profession or in a particular school.
Attrition means loss of teachers from the profession.
Turnover relates to the movement of teachers from a particular school. This involves people moving to other schools as well as those leaving the profession. (Bush 2002, p.1)

Retention during periods of shortage

Apart from those regions or countries where staff movement is managed centrally, i.e. allocating people to different schools after a fixed period of years, the issue of retaining effective staff is particularly challenging during periods of labour shortages in the education profession. In such circumstances, individual schools and colleges may become even more conscious of the need to hold on to the staff they have for fear of there being no replacements available, or only very inferior ones.

In such times of acute staff recruitment difficulties, leaders at all levels sometimes adopt specific strategies to hold on to key staff (these examples are all drawn from England where an acute shortage of teachers has existed since at least 2001).

Golden handcuffs

At national level, the government has offered cash incentives of specific sums to those entrants who guarantee to remain in the profession for at least three years, with mention of a further cash bonus if a further two years of service is given.

At district level, one local education authority which was reorganising all its school system (from first, middle and upper schools to primary and secondary ones) feared that many teachers would leave the area because of the turbulence and the enforced changes to jobs and schools. It offered in 2003 and 2004 'golden handcuffs' of lump sums to those who would guarantee to stay at least three years in their new post.

At individual school level, Hicks and Tilby (2004) found three headteachers of large secondary schools – in three separate areas – who stated that they had negotiated individual one-year contractual 'deals' with key staff (all were heads of subject departments) which involved special 'cash bonuses' or 'incentives to remain' for a further year at their schools. These staff were seen as highly effective, hard to replace and needed in their schools and departments at a crucial time. One head commented that the cost of recruiting, appointing and training a new head of department would cost almost as much as the 'handcuff' payment, so he considered it well worth the money, especially as he was not guaranteed to get a replacement at all. These deals were not secret in the schools and appeared to be readily accepted by other staff. Although they were technically linked with achievement targets, all three headteachers admitted that they were the same targets that would have been set anyway, regardless of the additional money.

Internal promotions

Hicks and Tilby's (2004) research showed that the commonest strategy used by school leaders to retain key staff was to offer them promotion within the school. In one school, out of a teaching staff of 82, 17 were offered and accepted a promotion in 2002, 14 of whom had been actively considering applying for a post elsewhere. Three of these admitted that they had specifically approached the headteacher 'to see what might be offered' even though they had not been anxious to leave!

All the promotions involved additional responsibilities, some of which were felt to be genuine, others more contrived. Eight of the 14 felt that the promotion and additional money attached would retain them for only a year at the most and several of the 17 believed that other staff were 'wary' of the strategy.

As far as support staff in the same schools were concerned, the strategy did not apply as the headteachers made it clear that these were easy to replace, because of a plentiful supply, and promotion would be earned in the normal way.

The weakness of both of the above strategies is that they are essentially short-term, retaining staff for a year or two at most. This is not likely to be a sufficient period for the supply of replacements to have improved significantly. There is also the risk of an even bigger exodus at the end of the short-term period, leaving the staff in an even more exposed staffing position. They may be effective, however, in helping an organisation through a period of turbulence or pressure where staff stability is deemed essential. The other risk is that when staff have differential salary rates, as Hardman (2001) found in international schools, inequalities in pay and conditions of service can lead to feelings of resentment.

Other strategies

Because of concern about teachers leaving urban areas, Chicago established a Teacher Retention Unit. Its main features are:

• regular meetings with teachers and principals
• commissioning research on the teacher retention issue
• investigating the reasons why teachers leave teaching

- conducting exit interviews with departing teachers
- assisting teachers to find new positions within Chicago
- facilitating networking to support Chicago teachers (Chicago Public Schools Rentention Unit 2002).

Retaining temporary and part-time staff

There is a particular irony during periods of staff shortage that schools and colleges need to call upon the services of many temporary, agency or supply staff as replacements, and also make more use of part-time staff. The quality of these staff is critical in ensuring continuity of effective learning and therefore retaining the best of these temporary staff is a key requirement of leaders and managers. In further education colleges, especially in vocational areas, a traditional reliance on part-time and temporary staff has often meant their neglect in terms of effective management (Lumby 2001). In mainstream schools, given disruption because of failure to fill a vacancy, leaders and managers need to develop strategies to ensure that the best of the temporary staff wish to return to their schools. Cole (2001, p.7) points out that 'supply teachers are a unique and valuable group without whom a school could not function effectively'. She focuses on the need for the students to understand that constant new faces in the classroom means little progress is made and that they should understand that 'disrespectful behaviour at the expense of the supply teacher simply means they will not return, and another new face will appear the next day' (p.7).

Cole's research (2001) showed that supply teachers valued most of all 'friendly and supportive staff' as by far the main reason why they were willing to return to a school. 'Good information' and 'student discipline support' were also important but the emphasis on the staff relationships was clear, helping them 'feel a sense of security and belonging during their time at the school' (p.7), thus motivating them to return.

Retention: long-term strategies

The following strategies are more qualitative in nature than the short-term more quantitative measures described above.

Offering high-quality professional development

A school or college's commitment to provision of effective professional development on site which meets the individual and career needs of staff can have a powerful influence on their own willingness to commit themselves to that organisation. Taylor's (2003) study of a college-based Masters degree programme showed that the majority of those undertaking the programme were determined to stay until they completed the whole course and obtained their qualifications. She quotes the principal as saying: 'It has become a conscious ploy of mine to get key staff on the programme so that they will feel committed to completing it, thus keeping them here for at least three years' (p.94). Taylor further points out that these staff would not apply for posts elsewhere which did not offer a comparable opportunity.

Writers such as Bolam (1993), Hargreaves (1994) and Leithwood (1992) acknowledge the way in which regular opportunities for professional development play a part in retaining high-quality staff. The staff concerned see these opportunities not only as developing their skills, but also as enhancing their career profiles, thus enabling them to make better decisions about the correct timing of a move to another institution, helping them as it does to be at the right stage for a different or more senior post.

Developing an attractive culture

Although culture is written about in more detail elsewhere in this book, there are some aspects which leaders and managers may note are of significance in encouraging employees to feel that theirs is a place in which they wish to continue to work.

Praise and recognition
- A brief, informal note to an employee.
- Taking time in regular meetings or informal gatherings to recognise the work of employees.
- Providing positive feedback in the presence of more senior staff.
- Utilising the performance management process to comment on good performance.
- Presenting employees with plaques, certificates, formal letters or the like.
- Running an employee or team of the month programme, say, in the in-house magazine.

Career opportunities
- Providing formal or informal training opportunities.
- Supporting an individual or team to take on new initiatives or additional responsibilities.
- Allowing a valued employee greater autonomy in his/her work.
- Providing opportunities to attend external or overseas training programmes, seminars, or conferences.
- Instigating career breaks or sabbaticals to recognise key contributors to the organisations.
- Offering valued employees the opportunity to rotate in higher positions or to lead key projects in the organisation (based on Mercer 2001).

Sensitivity on the part of leaders and managers is essential. Praise and recognition are effective aspects of management style but the praise and opportunities need to be individualised. For instance, in a department where teamwork is encouraged, recognition for any one individual while ignoring the team may provoke dissatisfaction, embarrassment and one-upmanship. Individual preferences need to be kept in mind. The opportunity to attend an overseas conference may prove to be more of an inconvenience than a benefit to an employee with a dependent child. Instead, a management development programme at a local institute might be more welcome.

Conclusion

The more seamless the whole process of induction, following on from appointment, and the associated programme of support and development, the more likely it is that valued employees will stay at the school or college. The time will come for many when it is appropriate for them to leave, but the nature and quality of leadership and management may make them feel that they wish to remain until that appropriate time arrives. They may also be willing to support their organisation through any difficult times that may occur in the meantime.

References

Andrews, I. (1998), 'The mentor and beginning teacher's differing relationships within five paradigms', in Gray, W. and Gray, M. (eds), *Mentoring: Aid to Excellence in Education, the Family and the Community*, Vancouver, International Association for Mentoring.

Balshaw, M. and Farrell, P. (2002), *Teaching Assistants: Practical Strategies for Effective Classroom Support*, London, David Fulton.

Bines, H. and Boydell, D. (1996), 'Leading primary school induction', *Management in Education*, 10 (3), 6–7.

Blandford, S. (2000), *Managing Professional Development in Schools*, London, Routledge.

Bolam, R. (1993), 'Recent development and emerging issues', in GTC Trust, (ed.), *The Continuing Professional Development of Teachers*, London, GTC Trust.

Bubb, S., Hilbourn. R., James, C., Totteredell, M. and Bailey, M. (2002), *Improving Induction*, London, RoutledgeFalmer.

Bush, T. (2002), Teacher retention: research evidence, paper for Education and Lifelong Learning Scrutiny Panel, London Borough of Greenwich.

Chicago Public Schools Retention Unit (2002), *What Is the Teacher Retention Unit?* available at http//www.cps-humanresources.org.initiatives.

Cole, O. (2001), 'Motivating and retaining your supply staff', *Headship Matters*, (13), 5–7, London, Optimus Publishing.

Commonwealth Secretariat and World Bank (1992), *Priorities for Improving Teacher Management and Support in Sub-Saharan Africa*, London, Commonwealth Secretariat.

Day, C. (1996), 'Leadership and Professional Development: developing reflective practice', in Busher, H. and Saran, R. (eds), *Managing Teachers as Professionals in Schools*, London, Kogan Page.

Dean, C. (2001), 'Internal promotion to headship', *Headship Matters*, (11), London, Optimus Publishing.

Department of Education and Science (DES) (1992), *The Induction and Probation of New Teachers*, London, HMSO.

Draper, J. (2002), 'Should I stay or should I go?', *Primary Headship*, (2), London, Optimus Publishing.

Foskett, N. and Lumby, J. (2003), *Leading and Managing Education: International Dimensions*, London, Paul Chapman Publishing.

Grace, G. and Lawn, M. (1991), *Teacher Supply and Teacher Quality: Issues for the 1990s*, London, Multilingual Matters.

Hall, D. (1997), 'Professional development portfolios', in Kydd, L., Crawford, M. and Riches, C. (eds), *Professional Development for Educational Management*, Buckingham, Open University Press.

Hallgarten, J. (2001), 'Making teacher supply boom-proof', *School Leadership*, (3), 9–11.

Hardman, J. (2001), 'Improving recruitment and retention of quality overseas teachers', in Blandford, S. and Shaw, M. (eds), *Managing International Schools*, London, RoutledgeFalmer.

Hargreaves, A. (1994), *Changing Teachers, Changing Times*, London, Cassell.

Hicks, G. and Tilby, J. (2004), 'Holding on to key staff', *Headship Matters*, (25), 7–8, London, Optimus Publishing.

Holloway, D. (1994), 'Further education teachers' development: a post-technocratic model', *Journal of Teacher Development*, 3 (1), 46–57.

Hunt, J. (1986), *Managing People at Work*, Maidenhead, McGraw-Hill.

Johnson, M. (2003), 'From victims of change to agents of change', *Professional Development Today*, 6 (1), 63–68.

Jones, K. and Stammers, P. (1997), 'The early years of the teacher's career', in Tomlinson, H. (ed.) *Managing Continuous Professional Development in Schools*, London, Paul Chapman Publishing.

Kakabadse, A., Ludlow, R. and Vinnicombe, S. (1987), *Working in Organisations*, Aldershot, Gower Press.

Kitan, M. and Van der Westhuizen, P. (1987), 'Critical skills for beginning principals in developing countires: a case from Kenya', *International Studies in Educational Administration*, 25 (2), 126–137.

Leithwood, K. (1992), *Teacher Development and Educational Change*, Lewes, Falmer Press.

Lumby, J. (2001), *Managing Further Education: Learning Enterprise*, London, Paul Chapman Publishing.

MacBeath, J. (ed.) (1998), *Effective School Leadership: Responding to Change*, London, Paul Chapman Publishing.

Mercer, W. (2001), *Retaining your Star Performers*, Birmingham, Headstart.

Middlewood, D. (2003), 'Managing induction', in Lumby, J., Middlewood, D. and Kaabwe, S., *Human Resource Management in South African Schools*, London, Commonwealth Secretariat.

Mortimore, P. and MacBeath, J. (2003), 'School effectiveness and improvement: the story so far', in Preedy, M., Glatter, R. and Wise, C. (eds), *Strategic Leadership and Educational Improvement*, London, Paul Chapman Publishing.

Mortimore, P., Mortimore, J. and Thomas, H. (1994), *Managing Associate Staff*, London, Paul Chapman Publishing.

National Commission for Education (NCE) (1996), *Success Against the Odds*, London, Routledge.

Schein, E. (1978), *Career Dynamics*, New York, Addison-Wesley.

School Management Task Force (1990), *School management: the way ahead*, London, HMSO.

Sehlare, B., Mentz, P. and Mentz, E. (1994), 'Differences in perceptions of principals and beginner teachers on the induction of the latter', *South Africa Journal of Education*, 14 (2), 73–77.

Stoll, L. and Myers, K. (1998), *No Quick Fixes: Perspectives on Schools in Difficulty*, London, Falmer Press.

Taylor, J. (2003), The impact of a college-based Masters programme on school culture and its effectiveness, unpublished MBA dissertation, University of Leicester.

Thomson, R. (1993), *Managing People*, Oxford, Butterworth-Heineman.

Weindling. R. and Earley, P. (1987), *Secondary Headship: The First Years*, Windsor, NFER/Nelson.

11

Mentoring and coaching

Introduction: what do we mean by mentoring?

Mentoring has become increasingly significant as a mode of professional development in many countries, including Australia, England and Wales, Hong Kong, Singapore and the USA. It is regarded as an important dimension in the preparation and ongoing development of teachers and leaders. It is also a significant part of the socialisation process for educators learning a new role. Crow (2001) distinguishes between two forms of socialisation:

- professional – preparing to take on an occupational role, such as teacher or principal
- organisational – focusing on the specific context where the role is being performed.

Socialisation includes three types of new learning (p.3):

- skills to perform the job, e.g. classroom observations
- adjustment to the specific work environment, e.g. who to trust for information
- internalisation of values, e.g. the importance of collaboration and collegiality.

Adjustment to the school or college context may be eased by an effective induction programme (see Chapter 10). Support and development are important in the leadership and management of all staff, not just those new in post, and mentoring and coaching are two of several approaches used to facilitate socialisation. Another example is 'critical friendship'. Day (1995) defines critical friendships as practical partnerships entered into voluntarily and based on a relationship of equals. These are informal modes of support which may be vital in helping new staff to adjust and established colleagues to develop:

> Critical friendship … can serve to decrease isolation and increase the possibilities of moving through stages of reflection to confrontation of thinking and practice … In terms of the appraisal of classroom practice, for example, a critical friend may establish and sustain a responsive, mutually acceptable dia-

logue through which situations will be created in which the teacher is obliged to reflect systematically on practice. (Day 1995, p.123)

While critical friendship is usually a relationship of equals, the concept of mentoring refers to a process whereby a more experienced person assists someone who is less experienced. Although Roberts (2000) and Samier (1999) claim that the notion is ambiguous, there are many similar definitions. Daresh (1995, p.8), for example, in reviewing the literature from an American perspective, points to 'the experienced professional as a mentor, serving as a wise guide to a younger protege'. While this model is common, Crow (2001) also refers to co-mentoring where the process is mutual. This peer-mentoring model may be regarded as being akin to critical friendship in that neither party is seen to have more expertise or experience than the other. Daresh and Playko (1992) show that mentoring may be interpreted in different ways:

Mentoring is an ongoing process wherein individuals in an organisation provide support and guidance to others so that it is possible for them to become effective contributors to the goals of the organisation. Unlike many other views of mentoring, we do not necessarily believe that a mentor must be an older person who is ready, willing and able to provide 'all the answers' to those who are newcomers. (p.3)

Research with headteachers in England concluded that the most appropriate mode was that of peer-mentoring. Unlike new teachers, principals are all senior professionals with substantial experience, leading to the view that mentors and mentees have 'equal standing'. This perspective was adopted by all mentors in the research although some mentees favoured an 'expert-novice' model, recognising the mentor's greater experience of the headship role (Bush et al. 1996, pp.135–6).

The nature of mentoring is inevitably influenced by the context where the process takes place. While it is often regarded as a Western concept, Leung and Bush (2003) suggest that it has a long history within Chinese culture:

Lifelong mentoring, which is embedded in the Chinese culture and heritage, is the passing of the ancestor's knowledge, values, attitudes and ethics to the successive generation … the best relationship between a mentor and a mentee is like water, a natural element that ultimately changes the shape of whatever it touches. (p.263)

Mentoring and coaching

Rajan's (1996) study of leadership in 500 organisations showed that 'coaching and mentoring' were ranked as the most valuable means of promoting leadership development. Bassett (2001) distinguishes coaching from mentoring by stressing the skills development dimension of the former:

Mentoring has more to do with career and life development and cannot be successfully entered into between a learner and their manager or assessor. Whereas coaching is considered to be about enabling the individual to improve their performance in their chosen field and is commonly used in the sports and skills development arena. (p.3)

Davies (1996, p15) argues that 'coaching and supporting can be seen as the most effective management approach'. He endorses the definition of Kinlaw (1989). Coaching is:

A mutual conversation between manager and employee that follows a predictable process and leads to superior performance, commitment to sustained improvement, and positive relationships. (p.15)

Davies (1996) joins with Durcan and Oates (1994) to identify five stages of the coaching process:

1 Setting out the purpose of the coaching in terms of the skill to be developed or the experience to be gained.
2 Delegating authority to make decisions which, by definition, encompass risk.
3 Individuals need practice at the task they are being coached in.
4 Coaching involves ongoing evaluation by the employee.
5 Building in time for reflection.

West and Milan (2001), writing from a general leadership perspective, differentiate coaching for development from skills and performance coaching:

The development coaching task is to create the conditions for reflective learning. A coach does this by first creating a psychological space, which allows the executive to stand back from the workplace, and then providing a supportive, yet challenging, relationship and dialogue in which the executive can gain perspective on his or her experiences and self, and on his or her leadership task within the organization. (pp.7–8)

They link the coaching process to Kolb's (1984) learning cycle:

1 Concrete experience.
2 Observation/reflection.
3 Conceptualisation.
4 Active experimentation (p.8).

Development coaching has three dimensions:

• Professionalism: maintaining neutrality and explicit standards of conduct, guaranteeing confidentiality, committed to ongoing personal and professional development.
• Purpose: helping the individual to adapt congruently and therefore creatively and innovatively to the challenges involved.

- The relationship: a collaboration between two people with the goal of a growth in self-awareness and functioning of the client; power is equal.

These authors regard coaching as a marriage between consulting and counselling (see Table 11.1).

Table 11.1 The coaching continuum (West and Milan 2001, p.70)

Consulting	Counselling
Hard	Soft
Head	Heart
Cerebral	Emotional
Analytical	Experiential

Mentoring may also include an element of counselling. Finn (1993), for example, regards it as an appropriate metaphor for the mentor relationship. This view received some empirical support from research in the English East Midlands:

Mentoring does have elements of counselling, notably in listening and empathising with the mentee (mentor).

The mentor's work is like that of a counsellor, she listens and makes me reflect (new principal).
(Bush 1995, p.11)

West and Milan (2001, p.191) conclude that coaching has much to offer in developing leaders:

Professional coaching for leadership development has a substantial contribution to make to business and, in particular, to the leaders running businesses. Through providing a partnership of equals, development coaches can support leaders in addressing the challenges they face. Development coaching can assist leaders to learn by standing back from their context; it can help them develop leadership competence for that context: and, finally, it can help them to achieve balance in their often unbalanced lives.

Mentoring and coaching are among the processes used in the National College for School Leadership's (NCSL's) New Visions programme for early headship. A survey of the programme leaders, 'consultant heads', shows mixed results from these approaches as Table 11.2 suggests.

These findings show that coaching, 'peer coaching' and mentoring have been used effectively in some of the regional groups but less so in others, and not utilised at all in some groups. Mentoring has the potential to foster leadership development for new heads despite the mixed response from the New Visions consultant heads. Where used, mentoring was often informal and involved either group leaders mentoring the new heads or a co-mentoring model where the new heads provided mutual support and challenge. Coaching and 'peer coaching' were successful aspects of the New Visions programme, as can be seen from Table 11.2. This involved either leaders coaching participants or 'co-coaching' between the new heads themselves.

Table 11.2 Assessment of specific approaches used in New Visions (consultant heads) (Bush and Glover forthcoming)

Mode	Used effectively	Limited effect	Not used
Action learning sets	12	0	0
Reflection	11	1	0
Case study	11	1	0
Action enquiry	10	2	0
Problem-based learning groups	9	2	1
Inter-visitation	8	2	2
Coaching	7	4	1
Peer coaching	6	5	1
Mentoring	4	4	4
Diagnostic instruments	3	6	3
Leadership portfolios	3	5	4
Study visits	2	3	7
Networked learning communities	1	8	4
E-learning	1	9	2

Mentoring in practice

The mentoring process is used in many countries and for several different groups. This section provides an overview of some of these categories.

Student mentoring in Hong Kong

Mentoring for students in Hong Kong is motivated by concern about attrition rates, not least because student numbers partly determine university funding levels. Two universities have adopted mentoring so that 'student retention can be increased and academic achievement can be promoted' (Leung and Bush 2003, p.264). The Hong Kong Baptist University has a formal and compulsory programme which deliberately matches mentors (academic staff) and mentees (students). The objectives of this programme are:

1 To help students to adjust to the changes during their transition to the university setting.
2 To help students understand the field of study.

3 To share experiences and views on different issues.

4 To assist students to achieve their own goals by providing information, opportunities, guidance and suggestions in problem solving and learning techniques
(Leung and Bush 2003, p.265).

Large-scale research with mentors and students shows that there were several
problems in implementing this programme:

• There were too few women staff to meet the demand for same-sex mentoring.
• Mentoring is not regarded as a formal part of staff workload so it tended to be
  conducted whenever there was 'spare time'.
• There was no training for mentors.
• Mentoring was not part of the reward system of the university so it often had a
  low priority
  (Leung and Bush 2003, pp.267 and 269).

Mentoring of newly qualified teachers in England

Newly qualified teachers are regarded as competent to teach but their skills are
immature and need to be nurtured. Mentoring is an important part of their induction. Bush et al. (1996) conducted research with six schools in the East Midlands of
England and found that, in most schools, 'there was no identifiable structure or
continuity to mentoring provision' (p.123). Mentoring was usually informal and
mentees were often left to ask for advice as problems arose. This approach has limitations, as one mentee notes:

> I feel like it's sink or swim at times ... I think I could have done with some
> more structured support ... You can't rely on ad hoc meetings because they
> disappear. You've no time. (quoted in Bush et al. 1996, p.125)

This lack of time for mentoring emerged as one of the main limitations of the
process although the allocation of a manager, typically a head of department or
deputy head, as mentor also created some problems because they were perceived as
'less approachable' and mentees were reluctant to admit to difficulties with their
'line manager'. Despite these limitations, many mentees and mentors gained benefits from the process and also claimed that it helped the school through improved
teaching and learning (Bush et al. 1996).

Mentoring for aspiring principals in Singapore

Training for prospective school principals in Singapore was introduced as early as
1984, well ahead of most other countries. The Ministry of Education and the
National Institute of Education (NIE) collaborated to develop the Diploma in Educational Administration (DEA) which had an annual intake of 50 vice-principals
from primary and secondary schools. The programme was full-time for one year
and participants were selected by the Ministry.

Mentoring is an integral part of the training programme and occurs largely when participants are attached to a mentor principal's school on a full-time basis for eight weeks. Mentees practise a range of leadership skills negotiated with their mentors. Participants are coached, reinforcing the links between mentoring and coaching noted earlier, and given feedback on how they have handled their tasks. Mentors also model leadership behaviour through their own daily work. The mentoring pairs are supported by an NIE facilitator whose role is to ensure that learning objectives are clearly understood and pursued. Bush and Chew (1999, p.46) conclude that 'the Singapore model of mentoring is ... working reasonably well, judging by ... feedback obtained from yearly cohorts of DEA participants, many of whom have assumed principalships after their training'. The DEA was replaced by the Leaders in Education programme in 2002 but this also includes a mentoring component.

Mentoring for school leaders in the USA

Daresh (1995) reports that mentoring is a critical component of pre-service leadership development programmes in many American universities and notes that more than 20 states have mandated mentoring programmes for beginning administrators. He claims that this development is one aspect of the move to prepare school leaders for the 'real world'.

Daresh (1995) reviews the American research on mentoring for school leaders and reaches the following broad conclusions:

- The main rationale for mentoring is that 'the role of the leader is a lonely effort, and that having the ability to relate to peers concerning personal and professional concerns is a way to reduce that sense of isolation' (p.14).
- Mentoring enhances university-based programmes by linking participants with colleagues in the real world who can provide practical solutions to problems faced in the field.
- There is a lack of clarity about the purposes and definitions of mentoring.
- Both participants *and* mentors appear to benefit from mentoring (Daresh 1995, p.14).

Barnett (1995, p.54) claims that 'mentors hold the key novices need to unlock their professional expertise', Hibert (2000, p.1), an assistant principal in the USA, echoes this view, saying that 'this mentoring process has helped me apply the theories of leadership ... I have become more reflective and thoughtful about why I do what I do and how I go about doing it'.

Mentoring for new principals in England and Wales

Mentoring became a significant part of headship development from 1991 following the work of the School Management Task Force. This initiative was introduced at a time when there was no formal requirement for heads to be trained for their management role. Bush (1995, p.3) described this in-service model of professional development 'as a substitute for training rather than forming part of it'.

This model of mentoring has been subject to significant research and comment (Bolam et al. 1995; Bush and Coleman 1995; Southworth 1995; Bush et al. 1996). These all point to the supportive nature of the scheme, as mentors in East Anglia suggest:

- A mentor is a sympathetic, trusted colleague or friend available to respond in confidence to the new head's needs by listening, observing and offering support in a non-judgemental way.
- A mentor is able to listen and observe within a sensitive, non-judgemental, confidential relationship, being a sounding board as necessary to enable the mentee to find his or her own solutions and directions.
- A mentor is someone outside the immediate situation who is non-judgemental and is a listener, sounding-board and confidante.
- Mentoring is the art of listening without judging, enabling without guiding, exploring without directing. The art is in the relationship
  (Southworth 1995, pp.19–20).

Bolam et al.'s (1995, p.33) research in Wales reaches a similar conclusion, with mentors and new heads both saying that 'establishing mutual trust and confidence' is a key element of the process. Bush and Coleman's (1995) work in the English East Midlands suggests that 'effective mentoring reduces professional isolation, provides support and feedback on performance and gives confidence to new heads during a period of change and uncertainty' (p.72).

The benefits of mentoring

Mentoring has the potential to produce significant benefits for mentees, mentors and the education system. 'Mentoring needs to produce benefits for both mentor and protégé if it is to be a mutually rewarding experience and provide motivation for both partners. Ideally, these benefits should extend to the schools involved in the relationship' (Bush 1995, p.7). Luck's (2003) research for the NCSL shows that the process had a positive impact on both mentors and mentees.

Benefits for mentees

Mentoring programmes have been widely welcomed as a contribution to the professional development of staff at entry points to new or promoted posts. Southworth (1995, p.21), for example, states that 'the evidence from evaluation and research reports suggests that there is an overwhelmingly positive response from participants in the process'. Hobson (2003, p.2) adds that 'all major studies of formal mentoring programmes for new headteachers have concluded that such mentoring work was effective'. The main benefits for headteachers are perceived to be:

- Peer support, notably in mentoring for new headteachers (Bush et al. 1996).
- Enabling heads to gain in confidence in their new role (Bush and Coleman 1995).
- A reduction in the isolation experienced by many heads through the 'sounding-board' provided by mentors (Coleman et al. 1996). Mentoring is one element in a process of networking designed to reduce professional isolation (Daresh and Playko 1992).
- Learning about the new role through interaction with the mentor (Coleman et al. 1996).
- Developing their expertise in a range of areas, including staff management and motivation, and conflict resolution (Luck 2003).

Research in the English East Midlands shows that heads value the opportunity to reflect on practice with a senior colleague away from the immediate pressures of their new post:

> Being free from the shackles of the job and being able to take time with a respected professional equal.

> Knowing that there is somebody in the background I can turn to is a great source of comfort.
> (Bush 1995, p.8)

Some of these benefits also apply to newly qualified teachers. Bush et al. (1996) refer to four main gains for this group of mentees. Participants welcome mentors who:

- Listen and act as a sounding-board.
- Offered guidance and reassurance.
- Were non-judgmental.
- Could admit that they were also fallible (p.127).

Pocklington and Weindling (1996) explore the use of mentoring as a leadership development strategy. They argue that 'mentoring offers a way of speeding up the process of transition' (p.189) and claim that it is a powerful strategy:

> As part of their organizational socialization, new heads are attempting to make sense of their role and to gain a clear understanding of what it is to be a headteacher. They also have to learn the complex task of managing change and reshaping the school culture to improve teaching and learning. We believe that mentoring, that holds up a mirror for self-reflection, offers a powerful means of assisting this process. (p.190)

Mentoring may not always form part of a formal scheme and there can be benefits from informal support. Petzko et al. (2002) surveyed 1,400 middle school principals in the USA. Most of them had no specific preparation to lead middle schools, being trained for either secondary or elementary schools. When asked to identify the person who influenced them most during their first year as principal, 44 per cent indicated another principal while 22 per cent said it was a central office administrator. These authors note that a high proportion of these principals engage in professional development and recommend that internships and other field experience should be reviewed to become important parts of leadership development programmes. They also advocate the provision of trained mentors for new principals.

Training is an important dimension of successful mentoring programmes and the quality of the mentoring experience for participants is likely to vary according to the level and nature of training provided for mentors. Playko (1995), drawing on extensive experience of mentoring for school leaders in the USA, stresses that experience as a principal is not sufficient to ensure quality mentoring processes:

> Where I have seen effective mentoring programmes taking place, there has been a recognition that designation as a mentor is not simply a kind of 'long service reward' … Instead, there are some critical skills and abilities that must be demonstrated … those who are identified as having the basic qualities of effective mentors [should receive] … specialised training in such areas as human relations skills, instructional leadership skills and basic understandings of what mentoring is as a form of instruction. (p.91)

Benefits for mentors

There is significant evidence from a range of contexts about the many benefits for mentors. Research on student mentoring in Hong Kong (Leung and Bush 2003) found that most of the mentors enjoyed the process, as one respondent illustrates:

> I got great satisfaction mentoring students. We talked about many things, his studies, his social life and what he wants to do in his career. Although there were many difficulties, we have developed understanding and [a] close relationship after one year. (p.268)

Mentors of newly qualified teachers also derived benefits from the process, describing it as 'a learning partnership', 'a two way interaction', 'for mutual support' and 'of benefit to both of us' (Bush et al. 1996, p.128).

Comparative research on mentoring for new principals in England and Singapore demonstrates the satisfaction often gained by mentors:

> It offers me the satisfaction of helping a colleague's professional development and also prompts me to reflect on my leadership role. (English mentor)

> It is enriching and satisfying to know that someone is learning from you. (Singapore mentor)
> (Coleman et al. 1996, p.8)

The benefits for headteacher mentors in England are reinforced by Southworth (1995, p.22), who describes the process as 'stimulating, sometimes even rejuvenating', and by Bolam et al. (1995, p.38), who suggest that it is 'a novel and valued professional development experience'. Luck's (2003) research confirms these benefits: 'The data clearly show that mentors benefited from the experience as well as mentees, thereby achieving a double whammy for professional development' (p.31).

Playko's (1995) reflections as a mentor in the USA show that the gains cross national boundaries. 'Perhaps the greatest benefit derived by mentors is the fact that relationships with proteges cause greater reflection to take place on one's own behaviours, attitudes and values' (p.86).

The benefits for mentors might be regarded as one of the unintended consequences of a process which is designed to produce gains for participants. Similar advantages are evident from the NCSL's New Visions programme for early headship, where the consultant heads report many benefits for themselves and their schools (Glover and Bush forthcoming).

Benefits for schools and the education system

Mentoring has been encouraged or sponsored by governments because of its perceived benefits for the education system. Research in Singapore and England points to these advantages:

> The relationship proliferates organisational norms and cultures, ensures hard-learned knowledge and skill are transferred to younger colleagues, improves the overall performance of the work group, and provides a steady supply of trained personnel. (Chong et al. 1990, p.21)

> The mentoring process benefits the educational system by helping new heads to become more effective at an earlier stage in their careers, and by the espousal of a culture of mutual support and development among the wider community of heads. (Bush and Coleman 1995, p.67)

Playko (1995, p.89), referring to the USA, points to two main benefits for schools and the wider educational system:

- Mentoring programmes are an important way to ensure that a 'culture of collegiality' begins to emerge in a school or district.
- Mentoring provides the potential to identify future generations of potentially effective school leaders.

Limitations of mentoring

Crow (2001), in a detailed review of internship and mentoring, stresses four potential pitfalls:

- Mentors may have their own agendas.

- Mentoring can create dependency.
- Some mentors attempt to clone mentees.
- Mentoring runs the risk of perpetuating the status quo (p.13).

Research in England and Singapore (Bush and Chew 1999) shows that the main problems of mentoring are:

- lack of time for the mentor to perform the role effectively
- the risk of mentees becoming dependent on the mentor
- an overemphasis on the notion of support leading to a lack of challenge and 'rigour'
- the risk of an inappropriate 'match' between mentor and mentee (pp.49–50).

Southworth (1995, p.23) also refers to the problematic nature of pairing: 'a tricky and imprecise part of the process ... which sometimes breaks down when partnerships fail to function effectively'. Roberts (2000) and Samier (1999) both point to the importance of the 'chemistry' between mentor and mentee and suggest that this is less likely to occur within formal mentoring programmes, where matching is determined by a third party using 'objective' criteria.

The gender aspects of matching may be particularly problematic. Most of the students at Hong Kong Baptist University preferred same-sex mentoring but this was not possible for many female students because of the under-representation of women staff. Only 95 out of 310 female students (30.6 per cent) had women mentors. This had negative consequences for mentees, mentors and the quality of the programme:

> Some female students had complained that they were embarrassed to talk to their male mentors about their personal problems (female mentor).

> The reason that I prefer to have a mentee of the same sex is to avoid destructive gossip and discrediting innuendoes (male mentor).
> (Leung and Bush 2003, pp.267–8)

Ehrich (1994) refers to the dangers of 'institutionalised' mentoring where it is a compulsory component of staff development programmes. As the author notes, the Singapore DEA programme has an institutionalised mentoring dimension. Ehrich (1994) points to two problems with such a compulsory programme:

- There may be unwilling participation, leading to 'a low level of productivity'.
- It may be perceived as threatening because it is imposed on staff (p.16).

Despite these potential problems, research in several countries (Bolam et al. 1995; Daresh 1995; Bush and Chew 1999) shows that they are outweighed by the advantages and that mentoring is often highly successful in promoting the development of students, teachers, and practising and aspiring leaders. However, they provide helpful cautions for school and college leaders planning to introduce, or to develop, mentoring or coaching programmes.

Conclusion: towards a model of mentoring

There is little doubt that mentoring has the potential to foster the development of participants, whether these are students, new teachers or school leaders. Bolam et al. (1995), for example, report that most people involved in headship mentoring in Wales, as mentees or mentors, consider that the process had been successful. These respondents identified ten features of successful mentoring:

- confidentiality between partners
- a positive and supportive mentor
- mutual trust
- the mentor acting as a 'sounding-board'
- compatible personalities
- a mentor who is experienced
- an open and frank relationship between mentor and mentee
- availability of time for mentoring
- mutual respect
- a structured mentoring process
  (adapted from Bolam et al. 1995, pp.38–9).

Southworth (1995) acknowledges such requirements but also casts doubt on the 'idealised' advantages of mentoring. 'Maybe the rhetoric of mentoring is a little too distant from the actual reality' (p.26). He expresses concern that the process may support participants to 'survive' headship but not to equip them to 'develop and improve the quality of learning for pupils, staff and themselves' (p.27).

Southworth's (1995) caution is sensible but mentoring is certainly flexible enough to respond to such concerns. The key requirement is to ensure that mentors are selected carefully, matched with appropriate mentees and, above all, trained to work towards the objectives of the specific mentoring scheme to which they are contributing. If these desiderata are met, mentoring can continue to make a powerful contribution to the learning of students, teachers and leaders.

References

Barnett, B. (1995), 'Developing reflection and expertise: can mentors make the difference?', *Journal of Educational Administration*, 33 (5), 45–59.

Bassett, S. (2001), The use of phenomenology in management research: an exploration of the learners' experience of coach-mentoring in the workplace, paper presented at the Qualitative Evidence-Based Practice Conference, Coventry, May.

Bolam, R., McMahon, A., Pocklington, K. and Weindling, D. (1995), 'Mentoring for new headteachers: recent British experience', *Journal of Educational Administration*, 33 (5), 29–44.

Bush, T. (1995), 'Mentoring for principals: pre-service and in-service models', *Singapore Journal of Education*, 15 (1), 1–13.

Bush, T. and Chew, J. (1999), 'Developing human capital: training and mentoring for principals', *Compare*, 29 (1), 41–52.

Bush, T. and Coleman, M. (1995), 'Professional development for heads: the role of mentoring', *Journal of Educational Administration*, 33 (5), 60–73.

Bush, T. and Glover, D. (forthcoming), 'Leadership development for early headship: the New Visions experience', *School Leadership and Management*.

Bush, T., Coleman, M., Wall, D. and West-Burnham, J. (1996), 'Mentoring and continuing professional development', in McIntyre, D. and Hagger, H. (eds), *Mentors in Schools: Developing the Profession of Teaching*, London, David Fulton.

Chong, K.C., Low, G.T. and Walker, A. (1990), *Mentoring: A Singapore Contribution*, Singapore, Singapore Educational Administration Society.

Coleman, M., Low, G.T., Bush, T. and Chew, J. (1996), Rethinking training for principals: the role of mentoring, paper presented at the AERA Conference, New York, April.

Crow, G. (2001), School leader preparation: a short review of the knowledge base, NCSL Research Archive, available at http://www.ncsl.org.uk

Daresh, J. (1995), 'Research base on mentoring for educational leaders: what do we know?', *Journal of Educational Administration*, 33 (5), 7–16.

Daresh, J. and Playko, M. (1992), 'Mentoring for headteachers: a review of major issues', *School Organisation*, 12 (2), 145–152.

Davies, B. (1996), 'Re-engineering school leadership', *International Journal of Educational Management*, 10 (2), 145–152.

Day, C. (1995), 'Leadership and professional development', in Busher, H. and Saran, R. (eds), *Managing Teachers as Professionals in Schools*, London, Kogan Page.

Durcan, J. and Oates, D. (1994), *The Manager as Coach: Developing Your Team for Maximum Performance*, London Pitman.

Ehrich, L. (1994), 'A mentoring programme for women educators', *School Organisation*, 14 (1), 11–20.

Finn, R. (1993), 'Mentoring – the effective route to school-based development', in Green, H. (ed.), *The School Management Handbook*, London, Kogan Page.

Glover, D. and Bush, T. (forthcoming) The experience of consultant leaders involved in leading the New Visions programme for newly-appointed headteachers in England: recognition of a developing role, *Westminster Studies in Education*.

Hibert, K. (2000), 'Mentoring leadership', *Phi Delta Kappan*, 82 (1), 16–18.

Hobson, A. (2003), *Mentoring and Coaching for New Leaders*, Nottingham, NCSL.

Kinlaw, D. (1989), *Coaching for Commitment*, San Francisco, CA, Pfeiffer.

Kolb, D. (1984), *Experimental Learning: Experience as the Source of Learning and Development*, Hemel Hempstead, Prentice Hall.

Leung, M.L. and Bush, T. (2003), 'Student mentoring in higher education: Hong Kong Baptist University', *Mentoring and Tutoring*, 11 (3), 263–272.

Luck, C. (2003), *It's Good to Talk: An Enquiry into the Value of Mentoring as an Aspect of Professional Development for New Headteachers*, Nottingham, NCSL.

Petzko, V., Clark, D., Valentine, G., Hackmann, D., Nori, J. and Lucas, S. (2002),

'Leaders and leadership in middle level schools', *NASSP Bulletin*, 86, 631.

Playko, M. (1995), 'Mentoring for educational leaders: a practitioner's perspective', *Journal of Educational Administration*, 33 (5), 84–92.

Pocklington, K. and Weindling, D. (1996), 'Promoting reflection on headship through the mentoring mirror', *Educational Management and Administration*, 24 (2), 175–191.

Rajan, A. (1996), *Leading People*, Tunbridge Wells, CREATE.

Roberts, A. (2000), 'Mentoring revisited: a phenomenological reading of the literature', *Mentoring and Tutoring*, 8 (2), 146–169.

Samier, E. (2001) 'Public administration mentorship: conceptual and pragmatic considerations', *Journal of Educational Administration*, 38 (1), 83–101.

Southworth, G. (1995), 'Reflections on mentoring for school leaders', *Journal of Educational Administration*, 33 (5), 17–28.

West, L. and Milan, M. (2001), *The Reflecting Glass: Professional Coaching for Leadership Development*, London, Palgrave MacMillan.

12

Performance appraisal and review

Introduction

The educational performance of institutions, teachers and learners in many countries has been increasingly significant as economic prosperity has been perceived to be closely linked with the quality of an educated and skilled workforce. Brown and Lauder (1996, p.23) state that 'the increasing importance attached to education in the global economy is not misplaced in the sense that nations will increasingly have to define the wealth of nations in terms of the quality of human resources among the population'. This chapter is concerned with the task facing the leaders and managers in individual schools and colleges, of enabling their staff to perform as effectively as possible. Only through that will the educational goals of the organisation be achieved, and this is the real significance of performance management for these people. At national level, 'performance management' is also a term used by governments for particular systems of monitoring and assessing staff performance in public services. Such systems are often imposed or proposed by central agencies whose agendas can conflict with those at institutional level.

This chapter discusses how the purposes and implications of such schemes may be perceived according to their different contexts. It then examines the principles underpinning the leadership and management of effective performance and its review at institutional level and the significance of such related issues as performance related pay. It proposes that performance management is not a separate issue to be managed but an integral part of employee management as a whole, central to the success of the organisation. Only this kind of approach is likely to be effective in a fast-changing world where notions of effectiveness in learning are evolving rapidly.

Purposes of performance management

Background

The management of employees' performance and the consequent need to assess that performance has its origins in business and industry. McGregor (1957) is generally recognised as having linked the appraisal of performance with management by objectives (MBO) which involved the setting of specific goals and periodic review of their achievement. Regular evaluation of teaching in a formalised way was well established in the USA in the 1970s, and Wood and Pohland (1983, p.178) found that the results were 'suitable as a basis for administrative/organisational decision-making in the areas of staffing and compensation instead of ... efforts to improve teaching practices'.

The perceived need of national governments of developed countries (e.g. the UK, New Zealand, Australia, Canada) for accountability for the resources expended on education led them to develop ways of appraising teachers' performance. Its use was also developing quickly too in business and industry, with Townley (1989) arguing that, as the 'production line' approach disappeared, the greater emphasis on employees' autonomy and discretion led to demands for them to be monitored more closely. The 1990s' new management of the public services means that, according to Mahoney and Hextall (2001, p.175): 'In England we now find that there are performance management systems at work in almost all areas of the public service, for example, health, housing, tax collection, employment services, local authority provision, etc.'

In the late 1980s and early 1990s there were various attempts to introduce appraisal of the performance of teachers and headteachers, for example in England and Wales. The scheme for England and Wales, from 1993 to 1995, had a focus on professional development but because of its essentially 'added-on' nature, it became less of a priority for schools (Middlewood 2001a) and was eventually perceived as 'discredited' by the national government. Valuable lessons had been learned from that experience (Middlewood 2001a, pp.127–31) and by the late 1990s countries such as England and Wales, New Zealand, Australia and Canada were using the term 'performance management', with appraisal being seen as part of that whole process.

Perceptions of purpose

It can be argued that it is managers' and employees' perceptions of the real purposes of the managing and appraisal of performance that may dictate how effective it actually is. Newton and Findlay (1998, p.136) suggest that the terms 'will be written in a manner that is broadly convenient to management' and Holloway (1991), arguing that performance appraisal should serve the supposedly common interest of employer and employee, says that this cannot work unless the employee is active, not passive. Leaders and managers clearly need to be sensitive to the fact that, if there are suspicions on the part of staff that the real purposes of performance management are different from those overtly stated, there will be difficulties, no matter how efficient the process is. As Long (1986, p.62) puts it:

> There is no such thing as the perfect performance review system. None are infallible, although some are more fallible than others ... The relative success

or failure of performance review, as with any other organizational system, depends very much upon the attitudinal response it arouses.

The criticism that is most often directed at specific national schemes of performance management is that they are for purposes of control. Fitzgerald et al. (2003) raise the same questions for schools and teaching in New Zealand as Smyth and Shacklock (1998) have for Australia, and Sikes (2001) for England and Wales, i.e. whether the underlying purpose is to increase the managerialist control of the teaching profession, thus de-professionalising teachers and reducing their role to that of functionaries (Ozga 1995). This topic is discussed later in this chapter.

South Africa provides a clear example of the mistrust of the purposes of appraisal and teacher performance, as Thurlow (2001) makes clear. Prior to the removal of apartheid, the conviction held by most teachers in South Africa was that the performance management and appraisal system was secretive, top-down and for the purposes of control, especially of non-white teachers (Chetty et al. 1993). By 1996 in the post-apartheid republic, Jantjes (1996, p.53) was still able to point to a 'lack of common understanding between teachers and administration as to the real purposes of teacher appraisal' and suggested that it would continue to be 'regarded with mistrust', until this was rectified.

This 'legacy of mistrust coming from previous experience is the biggest obstacle for the school manager to overcome in developing some form of effective performance management' (Middlewood 2003, p.131), and whichever model evolves in South Africa, there is an attempt in the public documentation to be open and clear about purposes. (Mokgalene et al. 1997)

Basic purposes

The evidence from leadership and management of people in organisations leads us to believe that, to work effectively, employees need:

- to know what it is they have to do
- to receive help, support, advice etc when they need it
- to get regular feedback on how they are performing
- to receive recognition for what they have done.

These basic tenets receive support from those concerned with support staff (Lorenz 1999) as well as teachers (West-Burnham 1993) but, in agreeing about purposes, it is important not to omit the underpinning function which is a *formative* one – 'feedback which can be used by practitioners to further develop their practice' (Elliott 2001, p.208). This formative nature does seem to imply a developmental approach but critics of specific nationally imposed schemes of performance management tend to see them as essentially anti-professional, and therefore at odds with the true purpose of managing staff performance, which they see as enabling the employees to identify their own improvement needs.

Middlewood (2001a) and Cardno and Piggott-Irvine (1997) have argued that it is certainly possible to achieve the dual purposes of performance management, i.e. accountability and professional development. However, they argue that this has to be done in a context of professionalism, of openness, and of both managers and staff being involved in developing the process. Clearly, this does not happen where schemes are imposed from outside the organisation, e.g. by national governments. Jennings and Lomas (2003) found that the new scheme of performance management for secondary school headteachers in England was received favourably by those head-teachers. However, this reception is in the context of a clear emphasis on pupil performance targets, something which the headteachers themselves are responsible for only through the work of other staff. The favourable response of these headteachers may be of little significance unless a similar attitude is held by those staff.

The importance of context for performance management

The performance of employees in education as in other employment areas is deeply influenced by the culture within which the employee operates. The intensity of the focus upon the teacher, for example, is strongly affected by the attitude taken towards teachers in a particular society or culture. Furukawa (1989, p.54) suggests that 'Japan's strong tradition of group importance' would not allow a heavy emphasis on assessment of the individual, a view supported by Hampden-Turner and Trompenaars (1997) who see the way that Western managers can be competitive, individualistic and concerned with achieved status as being alien to the Japanese outlook. In Islam, the teacher is respected 'like one's father' (Shah 1998), so that duties and respect owed to the father are transferred to the professional site, making a detailed or challenging assessment of performance not only difficult and unlikely, but possibly anti-Islamic. In Pakistan Madrasas (i.e. educational institutions with religious affiliations), religious discourse dominates all HRM functions so that all judgements of teaching are of a higher authority.

Hampden-Turner and Trompenaars (2003, p.51) support the view that, in many Asian counties, the 'teacher is life-time father', turning the whole context for examining teacher performance on its head, 'performance' here being perceived in an entirely different context from Western ones. In China, Bush et al. (1998, p.191) describe the process of teacher performance evaluation as complex.

> Given frequent peer observation and joint preparation, Chinese teachers are well informed about the teaching quality of their colleagues in the whole school and able to make comments on colleagues' teaching style, subject knowledge level, capacity for managing class discipline, strength and weak-

ness in teaching, and reputation among students. As a result of this familiarity, teachers are evaluated by a committee of their peers as well as by the principal (Washington 1991). This process is frequent and iterative rather than occasional and 'top-down'.

According to Child (1994, p. 81) Western approaches to performance, 'touch sensitive fields in China, and Western functionalism is farthest removed from the collective norms of Chinese traditions and socialist ideology'.

The influence of aspects of religious belief upon reviewing performance is not confined to Asian or Eastern contexts. In some Church schools in Western countries, the leaders are clear that the values expressed through the faith must be fully integrated and indeed dominate the process of performance management. Thus the Diocese of Sheffield (2000) quotes 'challenge, evaluation, consolidation, celebration and *prayerful* reflection will be important characteristics to our approach in this school and will be an accepted part of the process' (quoted in Sikes 2001, p.96). Robertson (2001) describes how actual performance objectives of staff need to reflect closely what a church school exists for in its provision for pupils and employees, including greater insight into their spiritual being.

The importance of contexts illustrates how closely attitudes to, and the effectiveness of, performance management are allied to what intrinsic view and value of education exists in the particular context within which performance management is implemented.

Specific performance management schemes

Certain specific schemes, such as those introduced in England and Wales and in New Zealand, are based on a rational model of goal-setting and reviewing, and have the aim of connecting organisational and individual planning. The feedback and development arising from the review process lead to improvement of the individual practitioner, thus contributing to raising organisational achievement. The twin purposes of accountability (through the goals achieved) and motivating the employee to greater improvement should be achieved, especially where some notion of reward is attached to the achievement.

Serious concerns exist, however, about the narrowness of this kind of model, reflecting as it apparently does a particular view of education. The language of those proposing effective implementation of the scheme in England and Wales is revealing. Hobby (2001, p.79), a member of the group that researched and proposed much of the scheme, suggests that success depends upon, as first priority, 'a rigorous understanding of the link between their (teachers') behaviour and their objectives – if I do X then Y will occur' and then he advises teachers to: 'Input the two or three main priorities identified by the feedback into objective setting for performance management'.

This language reflects what Sikes (2001, p.97) describes as the 'technicist, managerialist, and mechanistic' nature of the system. This approach is seen, by Sikes (2001) and Gleeson and Gunter (2001) for example, as exclusive and ignoring the fact that effectiveness in education is based on relationships and that development and improvement depend upon recognition of employees as people with individual lives and experiences and not as automatons. For Bassey (1999, p.14), any such narrowness, involving focus on measurement of indicators of performance, can be 'dangerous' because it 'denies education is, first, the experience and nurture of personal and social development of the whole person towards worthwhile living and, second, the acquisition, development, transmission, conservation, discovery, and renewal of worthwhile culture'.

Essentially therefore, such performance management schemes are seen as reflecting and further encouraging a functionalist view of education, and not one which develops people, either staff or learners, as questioning, self-critical and self-motivated. Gleeson and Gunter (2001, p.151) suggest that such schemes will only 'reward outcomes that are not grounded in authentic learning or professional practice'.

Problems associated with assessing performance of educational staff

Difficulty of measuring outcomes

As Preedy (2001, p.94) has explained, outcomes in education can be 'multidimensional, complex and long term'. While defining what to count as an outcome is difficult enough 'finding indices which adequately capture these outcomes is yet more difficult, and developing devices with which to appraise achievement of these outcomes is of yet another order' (Mahoney and Hextall 2001, p.184). The 'judgementalism' of the specific outcomes of, for example, teaching can also be unhelpful to those working in the face of difficulties (Thompson 2001). This relates to the extreme difficulty of making comparisons between those who will need to operate in one way in one context and others operating in a different way in a quite different context. Thrupp's (1999) comparison of teachers' effectiveness in prosperous and deprived schools in New Zealand illustrates the quite different notions of effectiveness that emerge.

A further factor is the issue of attribution. There is a problem in attempting to identify the particular contribution made to a learner's performance by any individual teacher, rather than by a whole history of teachers and 'there are also real issues about the significance of external factors which are quite literally beyond the control of any school or teacher' (Mahoney and Hextall 2001, p.184).

Another criticism of the focus on assessing performance of individual staff is that it encourages the idea that achieving outcomes is the only desirable aim for staff and this is at the expense of reflection, an essential part of the development process.

Preoccupation with performance to achieve outcomes can lead to performance cultures which are in Elliott's (2001, p.198) words 'intolerant of time … People within the organisation therefore have to be kept in a continuous state of activation'. This implies changes to the way in which the teacher's 'professional self' is conceptualised, to 'promote the auditable, competitive and ever active performer' in the place of the 'inspiring teacher' (Strathern 2000, p.49).

This 'anti-reflection' aspect of the England and Wales performance management scheme may in itself be a reflection of the work culture of Northern European nations where staff in general work the longest hours. Senge (1993) describes the Japanese manager who, when he is sitting quietly at his desk, will not be interrupted by his staff as they know he is working hardest then. When he moves around his office, they know it is safe to disturb him. He contrasts this with the Western notion of the exact opposite being the case. Humphrey and Oxtoby (1995) also point out that the notion of a thrusting, energetic middle manager is alien to Egyptian colleges, whereas the quiet person who gets on with his job is seen as the ideal. In such contexts, notions of performance and therefore of assessing outcomes are completely different, as discussed earlier.

The issue of rewards

Whatever the format of performance management, there is an acknowledgement that recognition or rewards are an important part of the process. Whilst material rewards are eschewed as alien in some cultures, in Western countries, there is debate about the merits of value pay schemes or what is commonly known as performance related pay (PRP). Motivation was explored in detail in an earlier chapter, but national governments appear convinced that additional money is a valuable means of extrinsic motivation of educational professionals.

Evidence from outside education is not encouraging. Poster and Poster (1997) point to the overwhelming evidence from researchers in the USA 'who are unanimous in stating categorically' that PRP simply does not work. Cutler and Waine (1999, p.67) in recounting the poor record of PRP in the business and health employment sectors, point out that, even where it has some supporters, 'the underlying model of causation in a PRP scheme is in itself uncertain'. Evans (2001, p.110) points out that, while recognition is a motivator, it is only so by being repeated regularly, whereas PRP is concerned with one-off rewards. Moreover, she argues that, if PRP does bring about change in some professionals' practice, it would be merely in the functionalist area of development.

One of the biggest concerns about PRP in its present forms is its potential divisiveness. Middlewood's (2001a, p.137) research found 'the importance attached by the teachers to a team ethos, a sense of unity and recognition that teachers work most effectively in a strong, mutually supportive framework', all of which would be threatened by schemes to pay some teachers at the expense of others. Bassey (1999, p.22) draws on comparisons with other public sector employees to point out that 'individual performance related pay is perceived as rarely helping teamwork'. Indeed, Storey and Sisson (1998) see the whole drive towards individual PRP as being reflective of a wider move towards individualism and away from collegiality. This potential dilemma is illustrated in the key question of 'what about the attitude of those who achieve reasonably well, but are *not* rewarded?' Wragg et al. (2004) found in their research into the application of PRP to teachers in England and Wales that there was bitter resentment from those teachers who had not received awards, as well as complaints about bureaucracy and form-filling. That research also supported Evans's contention that little changed in the classroom.

One of the biggest arguments in favour of PRP is that its very existence indicates to its employees that the organisation does value performance highly, and the absence of it may show the opposite (Murphy and Cleveland 1995). Furthermore, proponents of PRP, such as Tomlinson (1999), argue that it is a definite *dis*incentive to effective staff in education when they see moderate colleagues who achieve less than themselves receiving the same payment. He sees pay as one of the means of 'positive reinforcement' for effective professionals, and suggests that however collegial an educational organisation is, the differences (i.e. improvements) are ultimately 'made by the individual teacher in the individual classroom' (p.12).

However, certain practical difficulties exist. Parry (1995) describes how, in the USA, teachers are increasingly challenging performance appraisal outcomes through litigation and, where performance payments are attached, the consequences of a successful legal challenge are even more threatening to the school or college. Where material consequences are an outcome of performance management, there is an even greater need for spending time and other resources, additional administration, etc. on ensuring the accuracy of the assessment, although, of course, accuracy itself does not guarantee perceptions of fairness, as Longenecker and Ludwig's (1995, p.68) research showed. They found that a school or college could establish a performance management scheme which was thoroughly efficient but that 'a procedurally sound system alone will not necessarily produce effective, accurate, ethical performance ratings'. Perceptions of staff whose performance is being managed and reviewed are crucial.

Managing performance at individual site level

If the reservations put forward so far in this chapter appear unduly negative, this is because the schemes described are either:

- imposed in a top-down way with little ownership by the staff affected or
- transferred from one setting to another which, as Long (1986, p.62) warned after studying over 300 performance appraisal systems, 'rarely function satisfactorily. The failure is due ... to cultural differences'.

The positive aspect of all this is that there is considerable scope for leaders and managers at individual school or college level to develop schemes which are customised to the specific organisation. Knowledge and understanding of the staff, what motivates them, and the organisation's own vision and goals, give leaders and managers opportunities for this. Although good organisation of any scheme is essential, the emphasis for them is also on the broader context of commitment and development within which the performance occurs. Without these, any scheme, however well organised and intentioned, can become 'a ritualistic version to satisfy (DES) requirements' (Hall 1997, p.53), or a kind of tokenistic rating of performance, such as found in Egyptian schools (Humphreys and Oxtoby 1995) or as described by Middlewood (2001b) in Greece.

Features of performance management schemes

Whatever the scheme, leaders and managers need to address issues and manage them in the way most appropriate to their school or college:

Collection of data about performance

The issues here are:

- What data should be collected?
- From what sources should it be collected?
- How should it be collected?

What data?

The crucial point here is that the information collected should be both quantitative and qualitative. As performance management in education followed that in business and industry, it was ironic to find in the 1990s a huge emphasis in assessing educational employee performance on quantitative data (primarily test and examination results) at a time when what Eccles (1995) described as a 'revolution' had taken place in industry, i.e. the realisation of the prime importance of qualitative data in a 'new philosophy of performance measurement' (p.14). The increasing and more sophisticated use of ICT makes compiling the data easier, especially quantitative data, but it also increases the risk of simply collecting too much data, adding complication to any scheme.

To decrease the emphasis on test results and scores, data representing feedback from stakeholders in the teachers' or lecturers' performance is valuable. Such data are 'more sensitive to the complexities of connecting ... processes causally to outcomes. These would include elements of self, peer, student and parent evaluation, in addition to support from external agencies ... These indicators of effectiveness become things to be empirically verified, refined and discovered in particular contexts of practice (Elliott 2001, p.208).

From what sources?

Feedback from students, parents, etc. seem, eventually to be certain to become an essential source of data, in addition to colleagues, line managers and others so often seen as the automatic assessors of performance. Advocates of what is known as '360 degree feedback' support this notion of an increasing range of relevant sources. Tomlinson (2000, p.94) describes it as a way of genuinely evaluating individual performance and supporting development, and points to the time needed between collection and action required, reducing the pressure for hasty action and allowing reflection, a point referred to earlier.

However, the leaders' and managers' knowledge of the sources, and their relationships to and within the community of the institution, is crucial if trust is to be developed and maintained. In South Africa, the involvement of the people from local villages in the committees for new arrangements for performance appraisal, although laudable in its democratic intentions, led to women feeling threatened and disempowered by the male dominance in those communities (Sebakwane and Mahlare 1994), thereby undoing the positive professional benefits that the women may have felt through being in educational employment at all. In New Zealand, minority ethnic men and women are questioning the male white dominance of the system, according to Foskett and Lumby (2003, p.81). Leaders and managers need to consider how those who are to supply evidence are chosen, whether these have been agreed with the employee, or who to negotiate with if there is disagreement over this.

How to collect the data?

A wide range of instruments is available and in the USA, where there has been an emphasis on accumulating large amounts of data, Parry (1995, p.22) refers to 'classroom reports, evaluation interviews, supervisors' ratings and rankings, checklists, annual ratings, peer or colleague evaluation, self-evaluations, narrative or anecdotal reports, work portfolios, occasionally even pupil evaluation or ratings, and even pupil test scores'. A contrasting approach operates in some parts of India where teachers need to keep diaries in which they record their achievements as well as occasions when they fall short of targets (Rajpu and Walia 1998).

For leaders and managers in each individual school or college, the issue is again one of sensitivity, it being necessary not only to agree the source but the suitability of the method of collection for its intended purpose. For example, a questionnaire to parents (which needs to be constructed carefully anyway) may only elicit responses from those who are enthusiastic about the employee, or indeed hostile, and these responses are likely to be based on limited experience.

Disengaging the whole process of data collection from a variety of stakeholders from the micropolitics involved may be virtually impossible, so it is likely that the skills of the managers of the process will be needed to ensure the perception of trust and fairness essential for its effectiveness.

Discussion between manager and employee

At the heart of any performance management process lies the discussion (variously called 'interview', 'dialogue', 'review meeting') between the member of staff and the manager responsible for their performance. This part of the process has been seen as valuable even when other parts have been discredited and Middlewood (2001a) reports that these were highly valued in the original UK scheme, sometimes providing the first opportunities for some members of staff to sit down and review their development with a senior colleague. It is here that the reports from whatever sources are reviewed, importantly including self-appraisal, and agreement about further goals and opportunities are negotiated. Some form of report of what has been agreed is also necessary and the balance between a degree of confidentiality and openness needs to be struck. Individual confidentiality revealed at the discussion must be respected but this has to be balanced with the need to have an overview of the employee's performance and future, so that it can be seen as allied to the organisation's vision and goals.

Effectiveness in performance management – the future

Changing scenario

In developed countries, at the beginning of the twenty-first century, there is evidence of a shift away from a narrow focus on functionalist teaching and learning for reasons including the following:

- understanding of how the human brain works
- recognition of the existence of different learning styles and different learning personalities
- acceptance of the importance of emotional intelligence
- recognition that different factors (e.g. diet, environment) affect the learning quality of individuals have helped towards a rethinking about the purpose of teaching and its relationship with learners.

These factors can be set in the context of:

- the increasing use and influence of ICT in access to and adaptation of learning
- recognition that learning is a lifelong process, to which statutory education and 'formal' learning contribute.

The 'new learning paradigm' of Law and Glover (2000, p.165) includes:

- Learning is a journey – not a destination.
- Inner experience is valued – not just visible outcomes.
- Teacher learns also – from students.

In this new context of learning the role of the educationalist becomes that of a 'manager of learning' (as opposed to transmitter of knowledge in the 'old' context of teaching). It is in this role that the question of how we can best assess the effectiveness of educational employees becomes crucial and much less simplistic than the outcomes-based model. If the task of the educationalist is to manage learning, with the emphasis therefore on the process of learning, there are a number of difficulties that appear to present themselves:

- If the ultimate progress in learning is *internal* – can it be 'seen'?
- If the teacher's influence, for example, is *indirect* – can it be isolated?
- If the employee provides only opportunities for learning, what happens if learners do not take them?

These are difficult questions and ones to which many current schemes of performance management are ill-suited. Effective leaders and managers are in any case those who think strategically, looking ahead to changing contexts within which their organisations operate and will need to address such issues. Furthermore, as learning patterns change in the twenty-first century, there will be more learning situations away from the physical presence of staff, thus reducing the emphasis on controlled artificial contexts on which assessment is based (Middlewood 2001b, p.187). This may also lead to more formal recognition of the role played by others (especially parents perhaps) in the learning process.

Research carried out by the present writer into the views of young teachers about teacher performance assessment in the future (Middlewood 2002) found that these professionals were hostile to the present outcomes-focused climate, claiming that it even encouraged cheating. The view of the majority was that teaching is about relationships, and that these were damaged by the current process. Some felt that it protected weaker teachers because they could 'teach to the exam' and this was poor preparation for the students' adult life. These teachers believed that the following were essential for effective performance appraisal:

- Extensive use of qualitative data, and only limited use of quantitative.
- Involving learners in the assessment of teachers' performance.
- Involving parents and other groups also.

They were also cautionary about the need to keep feedback within limits, one teacher remarking:

> If we have pupil evaluation forms at the end of every lesson, we will end up no better than we are now – loaded with paper and it will be the same as every other assessment – the kind we hate now. I mean, managers will just add up all the evaluations and produce a score – back to square one! (Middlewood 2002, p.8)

Key principles for effectiveness

From the evidence of research in England and Wales (Middlewood 2001), New Zealand (Cardno and Piggott-Irvine 1997) and South Africa (Thurlow 2001), it is possible to suggest the following as appropriate action for leaders and managers.

- Develop an ethos of trust. Only within this will the best performance be drawn from all staff who need to feel ownership of the process of how their performance is managed and viewed.
- This trust and openness involves equity of treatment across all employees of the school or college, including leaders and managers. Although contributions will be different, the performance of each individual needs to be felt and seen as being important to the success of the organisation.
- Be aware of the changing nature of roles within the school or college e.g. of teachers and support staff. What was relevant to their performance at one time can quickly become less so.
- Develop the use of 360 degree feedback. Leaders and managers would be well advised to begin this process with their own performance, as is happening in England and Wales, New Zealand and some states of Australia.
- Apply team appraisal. Not only is this concept a comfortable one in, for example, Japan, but the young teachers whose views were examined by Middlewood (2002) believe that this *is* the way ahead, fairer and less threatening to both the best and moderate employees. Individual action plans can be developed within this process, fitting well with the notion of individual teachers' professional portfolios (Draper 2000), a concept which is developing in various countries. Caldwell (1997) also points out that rewards can be readily given to recognise team efforts and that these have the advantage of not relating to levels of hierarchy.
- Above all, managing performance will never be effective if it is managed as an 'add-on', something extra to be done alongside other 'people issues'. Middlewood (1997), Hellawell (1997), Cardno and Piggot-Irvine (1997) and Draper and Gwynne (2003) have, with others, pointed out that performance management should be at the centre of all that leaders and managers do in their schools and colleges. The need to get performance management right is crucial to the success of the educational organisation. Draper and Gwynne (2003, p.7) state that managed performance of both personal and professional need, which 'stretches way beyond the current process of performance management, will have a profound and central influence' on the culture and success of educational organisations.

References

Bassey, M. (1999), 'Performance related pay for teachers: research is needed', *Professional Development Today*, 2 (3), 15–28.

Brown, P. and Lauder, H. (1996) 'Education, Globalization and Economic Development', in Halsey, A., Lauder, H., Brown, P. and Wells, A. (eds), *Education: Culture, Economy, Society*, Oxford, Oxford University Press.

Bush, T., Coleman, M. and Ziaohong, S. (1998), 'Managing secondary schools in China', *Compare*, 28 (2), 83–195.

Caldwell, B. (1997), 'The impact of self-management and self-government on professional cultures of teaching: a strategic analysis for the twenty-first century', in Hargreaves, A. and Evans, R. (eds), *Beyond Educational Reform*, Buckingham, Open University Press.

Cardno, C. and Piggott-Irvine, E. (1997), *Effective Performance Appraisal: Integrating Accountability and Development in Staff Appraisal*, Auckland, Addison Wesley Longman.

Chetty, D., Chisholm, L., Gardner, M., Mcgan, N. and Vinjevold, P. (1993), *Rethinking Teacher Appraisal, South Africa: Policy Options and Strategies*, Johannesburg, University of Witterand.

Child, J. (1994), *Management in China during the Age of Reform*, Cambridge, Cambridge University Press.

Cutler, T. and Waine, B. (1999), 'Rewarding better teachers', *Educational Management and Administration*, 27 (1), 55–70.

Diocese of Sheffield (2000), *Model Policy for Performance Management for Roman Catholic Schools in Hallam and Church of England Schools in Diocese of Sheffield*, Sheffield, Sheffield Hallam Pastoral Centre.

Draper, I. (2000), 'From appraisal to performance management', *Professional Development Today*, 3 (2), 11–22.

Draper, I. and Gwynne, R. (2003), 'Predicaments in performance management', *Headship Matters*, (24), 5–7, London, Optimus Publishing.

Eccles, R. (1995), 'The performance measurement manifesto', in Holloway, J., Lewis, J. and Mallory, G. (eds), *Performance Measurement and Evaluation*, Milton Keynes, Open University Press.

Elliott, J. (2001), 'Characteristics of performative cultures', in Gleeson, D. and Husbands, G. (eds), *The Performing School*, London, RoutledgeFalmer.

Evans, L. (2001), 'Developing teachers in a performing culture. Is PRP the answer?', in Gleeson, D. and Husbands, C. (eds), *The Performing School*, London, RoutledgeFalmer.

Fitzgerald, T., Yangs, H. and Grootenbauer, P. (2003), 'Bureaucratic control or professional autonomy: performance management in New Zealand schools', *School Leadership and Management*, 2 (1), 74–80.

Foskett, N. and Lumby, J. (2003), *Leading and Managing Education: International Dimensions*, London, Paul Chapman Publishing.

Furukawa, H. (1989), 'Motivation to work', in Riches, C. and Morgan, C. (eds), *Human Resource Management in Education*, Milton Keynes, Open University Press.

Gleeson, D. and Gunter, H. (2001), 'The performing school and the modernisation of teachers', in Gleeson, D. and Husbands, C. (eds), *The Performing School*, London, RoutledgeFalmer.

Hall, V. (1997), 'Managing staff', in Fidler, B., Russell, S. and Simkins, T. (eds), *Choices for Self-Managing Schools*, London, Paul Chapman Publishing.

Hampden-Turner, C. and Trompenaars, F. (1997), *Mastering the Infinite Game: How East Asian Values Are Transforming Business Practices*, Oxford, Capstone.

Hampden-Turner, C. and Trompenaars, F. (2003), 'A mirror-image of the world: doing business in Asia', in Warren, C. and Jaynt, E. (eds), *Doing Business With New Markets*, London, Nicholas Brealey.

Hellawell, D. (1997) 'Teacher appraisal', in Professional Development Today, 3, pp.46–50.

Hobby, R. (2001), 'Virtuous circles', in *Professional Development Today*, 5 (1), pp.71–80.

Holloway, J. (1991), 'The building blocks of performance measurement', in Holloway, J., Lewis, J. and Malloy, G. (eds), *Performance Measurement and Evaluation*, London, Sage Publications.

Humphreys, S. and Oxtoby, M. (1995), 'Improving technical education in Eygpt: management development, international assistance and cultural values', *The Vocational Aspect of Education*, 47 (3), 274–287.

Jantjes, E. (1996), 'Performance based teacher appraisal: from judgement to development', *South African Journal in Education*, 16 (1), 50–57.

Jennings, K. and Lomas, L. (2003), 'Implementing performance management for headteachers in English secondary schools: a case study', *Educational Management and Administration*, 31 (4), 369–383.

Law, S. and Glover, D. (2000), *Educational Leadership and Learning*, Buckingham, Open University Press.

Long, P. (1986), *Performance Appraisal Revisited*, London, Institute of Personnel Management.

Longenecker, G. and Ludwig, D. (1995), 'Ethical dilemmas in performance appraisal revisited', in Holloway, J., Lewis, J. and Mallory, G. (eds), *Performance, Measurement and Evaluation*, London, Sage Publications.

Lorenz, S. (1999), *Effective In-Class Support: The Management of Support Staff in Mainstream and Special Schools*, London, David Fulton.

McGregor, D. (1957), 'An uneasy look at performance appraisal', *Harvard Business Review*, 35, pp.89–94.

Mahoney, P. and Hextall, I. (2001), 'Performing and conforming', in Gleeson, D. and Husbands, C. (eds), *The Performing School*, London RoutledgeFalmer.

Middlewood, D. (1997), 'Managing appraisal', in Bush, T. and Middlewood, D. (eds), *Managing People in Education*, London, Paul Chapman Publishing.

Middlewood, D. (2001a), 'Appraisal and performance in the UK', in Middlewood, D. and Cardno, C. (eds), *Managing Teacher Appraisal and Performance: A Comparative Approach*, London, RoutledgeFalmer.

Middlewood, D. (2001b), 'The future of managing teacher performance and its appraisal', in Middlewood, D. and Cardno, C. (eds), *Managing Teacher Appraisal and Performance: A Comparative Approach*, London, Paul Chapman Publishing. pp.180–195.

Middlewood, D. (2002), Developing teacher assessment in the changing context of the twenty first century, paper presented to the 4th International Education Conference, Athens, May.

Middlewood, D. (2003), 'Managing teacher performance and its appraisal', in Lumby, J., Middlewood, D. and Kaabwe, S. (eds), *Managing Human Resources in South Africa*, London, Commonwealth Secretariat.

Mokgalane, E., Carrim, N. Gardiner, M. and Chisholm, L. (1997), *National Teacher Appraisal Pilot Project Report*, Johannesburg, University of Witterand.

Murphy, K. and Cleveland, J. (1995), *Understanding Performance Appraisal*, London, Sage Publications.

Newton, T. and Findlay, P. (1998), 'Playing God? the performance of appraisal', in Mabey, C. Salaman, G. and Storey, J. (eds), *Strategic Human Resource Management*, London, Sage Publications.

Ozga, J. (1995), 'Deskilling as a profession: professionalism, deprofessionalsm and the new managerialism', in Busher, H. and Saran, R. (eds), *Managing Teachers as Professionals in Schools*, London, Kogan Page.

Parry, G. (1995), 'Concerns and issues related to teacher appraisal in the USA', *Education and the Law*, 7 (1), 17–29.

Poster, C. and Poster, D. (1997), 'The nature of appraisal', in Kydd, L., Crawford, M. and Riches, C. (eds), *Professional Development for Educational Management*, Buckingham, Open University Press.

Preedy, M. (2001), 'Evaluation: measuring what we value', in Middlewood, D. and Burton, N. (eds), *Managing the Curriculum*, London, Paul Chapman Publishing.

Rajpu, J. and Walia, K. (1998), 'Assessing teacher effectiveness in India: overview and critical appraisal', *Prospects*, 28 (1), 137–150.

Robertson, M. (2001), 'Performance management and performance objectives in church schools', *Education Today*, 51 (1). 41–44.

Sebakwane-Mahlare, S. (1994), 'Women teachers and community control in Lebowa secondary schools', *Multicultural Teaching*, 12 (3), 31–41.

Senge, P. (1993), *The Fifth Discipline*, London, Century Business.

Shah, S. (1998), Gender perspectives on principalship in Pakistan, unpublished PhD thesis, University of Nottingham.

Sikes, P. (2001), 'Teachers' lives and teaching performance', in Gleeson, D. and Husbands, C. (eds), *The Performing School*, London, RoutledgeFalmer.

Smyth, J. and Shacklock, G. (1998), *Re-making Teaching: Ideology, Policy and Practice*, London, Routledge.

Storey, J. and Sisson, K. (1998), 'Performance related pay', in Mabey C., Solaman, G. and Storey, J. (eds), *Strategic Human Resource Management*, London, Sage Publications.

Strathern, M. (2000), 'The tyranny of transparency', in *British Educational Research Journal*, 26 (3), 309–321.

Thrupp, M. (1999), 'Schools making a difference: let's be realistic!', Buckingham, Open University Press.

Thurlow, M., with Ramnarain, S. (2001), 'Transforming educator appraisal in South Africa', in Middlewood, D. and Cardno, C. (eds), *Managing Teacher Appraisal and Performance: A comparative approach*, London, RoutledgeFalmer. pp. 90–111.

Tomlinson, H. (2000), '360 Degree feedback – how does it work?', *Professional Development Today*, 5 (2), 93–98.

Townley, B. (1989), 'Selection and appraisal: reconstituting social relations', in Storey, J. (ed.), *New perspectives on Human Resource Management*, London, Routledge.

Washington, K. (1991), 'School administration in China: a look at the principal's role', *International Journal of Educational Management*, 5, 4–5.

West-Burnham, J. (1993), *Appraisal Training Resource Manual*, Harlow, Longman.

Wood, C. and Pohland, P. (1983), 'Teacher evaluation and the "hand of history"', *Journal of Educational Administration*, 21 (2), 169–181.

Wragg, E., Haynes, G., Wragg, C. and Chamberlain, R. (2004), *Performance Pay for Teachers*, London, Routledge.

13

Staff and organisational learning

Introduction

This chapter examines the way in which staff development within a school or college is most effective when it is placed within the context of an organisation which is focused primarily on learning. The development and learning of the people and thereby the organisation, ideally, became inextricably integrated. While accepting that this may not be a realistic aspiration for places where resources, including human resources, are scarce, it is argued that staff learning how to learn is crucial for achieving the aims of educational organisations. In this chapter, the features of a learning school or college are described and types and contexts of staff learning are examined. Finally, the roles of leaders and managers in developing schools or colleges as learning organisations are discussed.

The significance of a focus on learning

Educational organisations, whether they be kindergartens, schools, colleges or universities, exist to facilitate learning in one form or another. The people who are employed to work in them have learning as their key purpose, however removed their daily tasks may seem to be from this. The staff who clean and maintain buildings, playgrounds or fields do this so that the pupils or students can learn effectively in the best possible environment, just as the clerical staff's ultimate focus in dealing with paperwork is for the same purpose – the systems they administer have the same function.

The staff for whom this is most obviously and visibly true are the teachers and lecturers, although increasingly, as noted in Chapter 3, numbers of support staff work directly with learners and are contributing to pupils' or students' learning. Much educational literature and research substantiate the view that the most effective teachers are those who themselves are good learners, and who continue to learn. (Day et al. 1987; Hopkins et al. 1994; Middlewood et al. 1998; Stoll et al. 2003). Therefore, a school or college which is able to encourage its teachers, support staff and, ideally, all its employees to learn and continue to learn should be the one that is most effective in helping its pupils or students to learn. This is the simple premise underpinning the link between staff learning and the notion of a learning school or learning college. However, this simplicity disguises a number of issues which are likely to affect the realisation of such an organisation.

In many developing countries, where resources are scarce, the focus in staff development remains firmly on more conventional training and development of teachers. In the study by Dalin (1994) of educational improvement projects in Ethiopia, Bangladesh and Colombia, high priorities included reducing the large number of unqualified and untrained teachers in schools through training and staff development which focused on basic classroom skills, writing and updating schemes of work for pupils and making resources for their pupils' use. As both Coleman (2003) and Middlewood (2003) point out in research on South African schools, the struggle to put in place an appropriate culture of learning and teaching depends first and foremost on establishing the idea that learning is important and in those contexts where teachers themselves have not even accepted the significance of arriving on time, this larger task remains daunting (Chisholm and Vally 1996).

In developed countries, where scarcity of resources is less of an issue, assumptions cannot be made that teachers are necessarily effective learners (Baud 1995). The emphasis in the 1990s in many of these countries on quantitative outcomes, more tests and examinations, and assessment of performance in such terms has narrowed the focus in schools and colleges towards achievement of set targets 'rather than the double loop learning which questions and reconsiders the targets themselves, adjusting accordingly' (Lumby 2001, p.14). The challenge here therefore remains.

Features of a learning school or college

The concept of a 'learning organisation' originated in the business world, since Revans (1982) proposed the equation that the rate of learning in an organisation must be equal to or greater than the rate of change. As educational organisations also became aware of the need for constant change, and that relying on current principles and processes would lead to dysfunctioning or stagnation, so the importance of committing all those in the school or college to continuous learning and development has become for many of them the key to continuing success.

Essentially, the main features of such schools and colleges are that they:

- focus their energies and activities on learning
- regard the needs of the learner as central
- establish and develop an ethos and ethic of enquiry
- recognise that learning exists in many forms and comes from many sources, including external networks and stakeholders
- acknowledge that learning is a lifelong process and that the organisation's role is

in making a contribution to this process
- are in a continuous transformational state.

This list gives the impression that, for employees, these are not peaceful places in which to work! As Dale (1994, p.27) says, being a member of a learning organisation is not easy, and can even be uncomfortable, because many people desire stability and contentment, and they have a right to this. She proposes the idea of a 'dynamic conservatism' as being relevant to them, with the ideal state being one 'in which learning and working are actually synonymous' (p.24).

A learning organisation may be seen more realistically by leaders and managers as an aspiration, working towards which will help a school or college achieve the conditions within which many of the features of a learning organisation can be brought about.

Any school or college has to exist within the context of its time, even if that context continually changes. It needs therefore to meet the demands of that time and this will often include statutory requirements of national governments as well as those of, for example, employers and other stakeholders. As such the learning that it facilitates will ideally incorporate:

- learning as a means to an end
- learning as a process, learning how to learn
- learning which provides knowledge which is worth pursuing for its own sake.

Learning as a means to an end is where learning is perceived by the learner as being worthwhile because it leads to something specific and tangible. Often this will be acquiring a skill which enables the learner to perform a new task, or, most commonly in formal education, a qualification or certification which leads to better employment prospects and thereby a better standard of living. This inevitably is a view of learning taken by many people in developing countries where educational attainment is seen as the 'passport' to economic success, e.g. in South Africa 'to build youths' self-confidence, teach them basic skills and prepare them for employment,' (Reeves 1994, p.106). This is not restricted to such contexts however. Sugimine (1998, p.121) describes the desperate competition in Japan to get children into the right streams so that 'schools have become fact-grinding and knowledge based institutions even at elementary level', all to try to ensure entry to schools and colleges which would 'guarantee' success in the 'prosperity stakes'. In some European countries, such as Greece (Middlewood 2001), extra classes are seen as essential for children to pass examinations for the same reason.

Learning as a process, a journey rather than a destination (Ferguson 1982), includes a focus on enabling the learner to take from formal education into life beyond this knowledge of themselves as a learner which they can apply effectively in all future contexts. Learning to give knowledge for its own sake embraces the intellectual curiosity which is enjoyed by those who learn a particular topic and are fascinated and feel enriched by what they learn in, say, history or science. Those who suggest that effective teachers are passionate about *what* they teach (the subject) would see this kind of learning as an essential component in the learning school or college.

All these kinds of learning need to exist because all are essential to the development of people as a whole, although the emphasis on one kind at the expense of another will inevitably occur over time and according to place or national policies. Similarly, just as it is suggested that there are different levels of learning (shallow, deep and profound), so learning at each of these levels will exist in the organisation, because they all exist as part of everyday life and learning.

The range of types and levels of learning fits well with the developing notions of multiple intelligences (Gardner 1983) and variety of learning styles (e.g. Honey and Mumford 1988), but it is the overall or collective capacities that an organisation has which makes it a learning school or college. MacGilchrist et al. (1997, p.105), writing about schools in particular, refer to the concept of the 'intelligent school' which has the capacity to 'read their overall context in a way that they are neither overwhelmed by it nor distanced from it but are in a healthy relationship with it and know they need to respond to both its positive and negative aspects'.

Staff learning and development

Any organisation where the staff are neglected as adult learners, will reduce its potential to be effective for those who attend it. The words 'training and development' are the most commonly used ones in the context of staff learning but learning by training has the connotations 'of highly specific, content-driven and targeted programmes geared to knowledge acquisition and information-giving' (Law and Glover 2000, p.247). As such, it relates very much to a functionalist view of education, one which sees it essentially as a means to an end. As discussed in the previous chapter, this can have the effect of treating teachers, lecturers and all staff involved in education as functionaries, carrying out the requirements of higher authority. This particularly is the case where the curriculum is 'assessment led' with a focus on outcomes, usually owing to pressures from state and parents as described by Pell (1998) in rural South Africa.

The word 'development', on the other hand, implies concern for the staff *as people* in their learning, either professional or personal or both. 'Professional' originally implied certain qualities inherent in the occupation (especially a degree of autonomy) and not 'the value of the service offered by the members of that occupation' (Ozga 1995, p.22). As such, professional learning and development implies that the employee will have a degree of ownership in determining what training is needed for them to improve. In that context, it is closely linked with personal development, because the engagement of the feelings, attitudes and motivation of the individual are seen as essential if they are to improve. Several writers on teacher development, such as Day (1999, p.124), argue that development relates to individual history as well as present circumstance, that the work that educational staff do 'is bound up with their lives, their histories, the kind of person they have been, and have become'.

The need for both training and development, in these senses, can be illustrated with reference to implementation of management schemes. Glover (1994) describes a case study concerning the implementation of a scheme of appraisal. While it is clear that carrying out appraisal requires specific skills, such as observation, that managers can be trained in, it became obvious that the managers' main problems lay in overcoming teachers' reluctance, even hostility, to the scheme. What the managers therefore needed to learn was how to build positive relations with their staff, to negotiate, to listen and develop 'counselling skills' (p.183). Extreme proficiency in the skills for mechanistic delivery of the scheme were useless without the personal skills needed to persuade the staff to accept the scheme in the first place.

Similarly, in their study of managers of subject areas in schools in England and Wales, Harris et al. (2001) found that these were often provided with training which might make them proficient in subject knowledge, use of resources etc., but there was no guidance as to the leadership abilities required to help the subject departments operate as a team, which needed an understanding of each individual, a relationship with them to enable them to improve.

As Waters (1998, p.34) explains 'simply telling someone how to feed back critical observations to colleagues isn't sufficient if the teacher needs to develop assertiveness skills to make the feedback behaviour feel congruent, and high level of personal self-esteem to underpin the skills'.

Effectiveness in staff learning

The following are some of the more important factors which influence staff learning:

Understanding of adult learning

The recognition of factors specific to adults is crucial in how staff learning is managed. These include:

* adults bring a wide range of previous knowledge and skills to the learning
* adults may feel anxiety and fear of judgement in coming to new learning
* adults may resist what they believe may be an attack on their competence
* adults need to see the results of their learning and have accurate feedback (adapted from Brookfield 1986).

The experience that adults bring to new learning may be in conflict with what they, as staff of a school or college, are expected to know and, as Taylor and Bishop (1994) point out, 'unlearning' is extremely difficult.

Acknowledgement of the institutional context

Traditionally, formal training for educational employees has been away from where they work, provided via formal programmes. In a number of developed countries, particularly where self-management and self-governance have become the key features of educational organisation, there has been a significant move to site-based training and development. This is an acknowledgement that staff need to internalise the knowledge and experience gained through training in the real context within which it will be applied. Haq's (1998) survey of educational provision in South Asia showed the inadequate quality (as well as quantity) of even basic training for serving teachers but Khan (2000, p.65) acknowledges the weakness of training in Pakistan which is 'totally external' and leaves the trainees 'poorly prepared for adapting this externally created knowledge and utilising it in their environment'. He points out that in such situations training becomes 'more of a formality to fulfil than an opportunity to learn and to contribute to learning' (p.65).

The contextualisation of staff learning also needs to take account of the very specialised roles that members of staff have. Whether the role be teacher, lecturer, head of subject department, librarian, teaching assistant, clerical officer, etc., some of the learning needs to give the role holder greater insight into those skills and knowledge specific to the role. Thus, Balshaw and Farrell (2002), in describing the training necessary for assistants supporting children with severe learning difficulties, refer to the uniqueness of the role and how important it is in training to differentiate it from the teacher's or care worker's, however closely they need to work as a team. Similarly, Best (2000), in a large-scale survey of deputy headteachers' perceptions of their training, found that a substantial majority most valued the training aimed specifically at deputy headship, compared with more generic training about leadership and management.

One of the significant points of ensuring that role-focused learning exists as part of overall staff learning is that it contributes to the value which the role holder perceives as being placed on the work done. So Burton's (1994) study of the role of the reprographics supervisor, and Foreman-Peck and Middlewood's (2002) interviews with teaching assistants, all showed that these people felt training in their role had raised their esteem in the eyes of others. This in itself no doubt contributed to the subsequent value placed on the training by these employees.

Recognition of how staff learn in different ways

The different means by which the learning of members of staff can occur can be divided into four broad categories, as shown in Figure 13.1.

- Studying and analysing one's work includes not only reflecting in both single-loop and double-loop terms upon one's own practice, but sometimes undertaking a systematic analysis of a process undertaken, as advocated by Brighouse (1991) who speculates why this micro-analysis is so little used in education compared with training in medicine, sports or the arts (Brighouse 1991, p.84). It will also of course include feedback received from the pupils or students themselves, and in many cases personal reading.

- Learning from other staff includes all everyday opportunities to talk with other colleagues, both more and less experienced than oneself. It also includes informal observations both in one's own school or college and when visiting, for whatever reason, other organisations.

- Specific provision will be all the processes and structures provided by the school or college, ranging from being mentored, appraised or formally observed to being given the opportunity to participate in decision-making or understudying a particular post for a period. This is in addition to seminars, workshops, conferences or structured visits which may be provided.

- External provision. Despite the emphasis on site-based provision in some countries, it is still important for staff to meet and discuss with staff from other schools or colleges, so that an insular attitude is avoided and the widest possible pool of ideas is accessed.

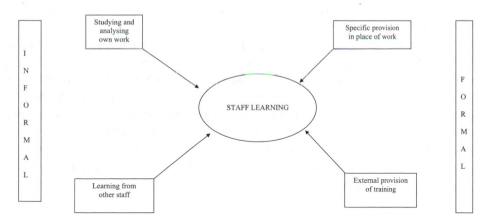

Figure 13.1 Different means by which staff learn

The link between staff learning and the learning organisation

As mentioned previously, effective teachers are also effective learners and there is evidence that staff learning has a direct influence on the learning of the people for whom the school or college actually exists, i.e. the pupils or students. If students are surrounded and supported by adults who are clearly committed to and enthusiastic about their own learning, much of this will 'rub off' on the pupils and students.

Barth (1990, p.31), describing the importance of staff sharing their experiences for development, says that there is 'evidence that when adults share and co-operate, students do the same'. Hughes (2001, p.11) found that not only other colleagues, including kitchen staff, showed 'respect' for those who were undertaking a high-level course. She also refers to the pupils noticing the 'excitement and enthusiasm' displayed by the staff involved.

In an extended piece of research into the impact of a site-based programme on the participants and the host school, Middlewood (1999, p.88) found that the link between staff and student learning showed in three ways:

(i)   by *what* they found out about students i.e. knowledge obtained through content of the investigation

(ii) by what they found out from doing research *with* the students i.e. understanding of students through the process and

(iii) what they found out by *being* students themselves i.e. identifying through empathising.

The third of these is the most powerful in staff learning having an influence on student or pupil learning. Not only are some of the skills needed by staff in formal study of this kind similar in kind to those needed by students at various levels in schools and colleges, such as carrying out investigations, analysing evidence, etc. (see Terrell et al. 1998, p.16), but the empathy of learners meant that a significant majority of staff felt their relationships with students had improved. Examples included staff helping students with homework at break time, rather than lecturing them for not doing it at home! Both Hughes (2001) and Middlewood (1999) refer to staff and students or pupils openly sharing their different learning experiences. Hughes (2001, p.12) quotes one adult: 'It's only through struggling with your own learning that you gain a greater understanding of the child's viewpoint.'

This empathy with and sharing of staff's and students' learning fits well with the different types of learning that Aspinwall and Pedlar (1997) suggest are the ones that indicate a learning organisation, i.e:

1 Learning *about* things
2 Learning to *do* things
3 Learning to *become ourselves, to achieve full potential*
4 Learning to *achieve things together* (adapted from Aspinwall and Pedlar, 1997, p.230).

Studies of teachers as learners (Day et al. 1987; Fullan and Hargreaves 1992; Stoll et al. 2003) all demonstrate the growth in confidence and self-esteem gained by the adults concerned. This in turn gives them the confidence to share with their own pupils or students each other's learning experiences, with the ultimate aim of each of them achieving their full potential. As Constable (1995, p.165) puts it: 'the attitudes to learning held by teachers are part of the learning environment for pupils'.

Support staff who are enthused by their own learning also report that their relationships with pupil learners can be transformed (see Foreman-Peck and Middlewood

2002), with some teaching assistants claiming greater understanding of the learning processes of those in their care, and focusing on strengths more than weaknesses.

Bowring-Carr and West-Burnham (1997) see this attitude of enthusiasm and being positive as being an essential part of the shift away from the teacher as superior and the learner as subordinate to one where learning is all-important – for everyone. The 'teacher as learner' will know the current position of the learner and 'build on strengths rather than attacking possible weaknesses' (p.162).

Ultimately the link between staff learning and the learning organisation in the organisation's capacity 'to make continuous improvement whilst adapting to change in the external environment' (Blandford 2000, p.5). As such, all employees will be able to set, plan and meet targets, because of the culture of learning that has developed.

Learning behaviour	Non-learning behaviour
Suggesting ideas	Discounting ideas
Repeating mistakes	Learning from mistakes
Admitting inadequacies	Blaming others/events
Being open about truth	Telling people what they want to hear
Looking at alternatives	Going for quick fixes
Taking responsibility	Expecting others to take responsibility

Figure 13.2 Learning and non-learning behaviour in organisations (adapted from Honey 1993)

The role of leaders and managers

If leaders and managers wish to enable staff learning to flourish, and the organisation to develop as a learning community, the following may be significant.

Be role models as learners

This should be on at least two levels. First, leaders and managers need to be personally committed to their own individual learning. If they are to lead their schools and colleges into future and unknown environments, they need the continuous development of themselves as self-aware people, constantly reassessing their own behaviour, emotions and reasoning in the light of new experiences, both their own and others'. Lifelong learning must be a reality for them personally.

Bezzina (2001, p.16) says that 'There are as many people who have truly retired at 25, as there are people still living life to the full at 70'. He implies that leaders and managers need to be in the second category, and as they become older, it is all the more important that they can transfer their wisdom and experience to those with the energy and excitement to make things happen (Schacter-Shalomi and Miller 1995).

Secondly, they display their own learning role by encouraging behaviours in the organisation which demonstrate learning and discourage non-learning, as Honey's model shows (Figure 13.2).

This encouragement and discouragement needs to be explicit and overt so that people understand that this is how they and their organisation learn and develop. A simple example is of the person who brings a problem to the leader or manager. Learning behaviour here is in the response: 'What are you proposing to do about this?' or 'What are the options for dealing with this?' The non-learning response is 'Okay, I'll deal with it for you'.

Support all employees as learners

This particular support has to be based upon the general support that the leader or manager provides for colleagues, one which is based on trust. Some key principles are expressed by Egan (1982, p.44):

Confidentiality	'If I tell this person about myself, she will not tell others'
Credibility	'Interpersonal trust is defined … as an expectancy held by an individual or group that the word, promise, verbal or written statement of another individual or group can be relied on'
Consideration in the use of power	The assumption here is that the helper is perceived as having power and as being the kind of person who will not misuse it
Understanding	The client says, 'If I tell this person about myself, he will make an effort to understand me'.

With these principles underpinning the relationship between the persons concerned, the task of the leader is to recognise that all members of staff are different and have different aspirations both personally and professionally. These differences need to be not only recognised but celebrated so that any achievement in learning and development by an individual can be reinforced. This reinforcement may be done informally through staffroom discussion or more formally, for example through certification rewards or public acknowledgement at meetings. Such practice also helps provide an environment within which staff feel that experimentation in learning is worthwhile, because occasional failure is tolerated as a 'learning experience'. One of the key principles for leaders in promoting staff learning is that the main limit to growth is the individual's own fear (Hopson and Scally 1981) and the leader's task is to create a context within which that fear is minimised.

Encourage the sharing of learning

Bruner (1996) refers to a definition of intelligence which sees it as 'distributed' in the individual's world and therefore it exists and is enhanced by the 'books one uses, the notes one habitually takes, the computer programs and data bases one relies upon, and perhaps, most important of all, the network of friends, colleagues or mentors on whom one leans for feedback, help, advice, even just for company' (p.77).

This need for educational employees to share and collaborate in order to develop is acknowledged at national levels, such as in the USA where the National Staff Development Council stresses for each of its standards that the context of 'adults grouped into learning communities' is crucial (Hirsch 2001). In Wales, where the entitlement of each individual to continuous professional development is now in statute, the need for sharing is also emphasised (Jones, 2003).

At institutional level, therefore, the task of the leader or manager is to facilitate this sharing and collaboration, both formally and informally. Some of the ways in which this can be done were described earlier.

Build an emphasis on learning into all management processes

The final section of this book deals with various processes which leaders and managers need to handle effectively – recruitment, selection, induction, appraisal, etc. The 'learning' school or college will stress learning at all these stages. At the recruitment stage, many schools and colleges stress the opportunities provided for staff development (e.g. by on-site programmes), so they can attract people who are committed to their own learning. At selection interviews, candidates can be asked about what they have learned over a recent period. In appraising performance, an emphasis on the individual's learning (and the pupil's or student's) since the last review can be made overt. Observations of a teacher or teaching assistant at work need to focus on learning. Bowring-Carr (1993, p.332), having described all the problems and difficulties associated with classroom observation, suggests that these can only be overcome through a long-term strategy to enable observation to 'be seen to be organic, a natural and routine part' of the way an educational organisation operates. He suggests this may be an aim for all the formal processes of school or college management.

Develop a culture of enquiry and reflection

Critical reflection cannot be practised in isolation. Day (1999) argues that schools and colleges need to be 'communities of reflective practice' and, for this to happen, opportunities need to be available for critical discussions so that shared wisdom and experience can thrive. The difficulty here lies in the pressures and expectations placed upon schools and colleges in most countries to deliver specific tangible results. These external pressures not only encourage passivity and conformity but decrease actual time for reflection and enquiry.

> By 'lack of reflection' is meant that the need for sheer survival and the anxiety naturally felt by everyone in the organisation that the machinery must be kept going at all costs together make it very easy indeed to forget why the enterprise was started in the first place. (Bowring-Carr and West-Burnham 1997, p.143)

In developing a culture in which performance and reflection can be led and managed, Vaill (1989) advocates the Chinese concept of Wu-wei – the art of non-action. This, he says, is about learning how to go with the flow, or follow the grain (of the wild river). This concept does not counsel passivity. It is a way to learn the art of judgement, knowing when to intervene and when to leave well alone. Too many managers, led on by the decisive, driving 'I'm in charge' model, intervene, offering solutions. Wu-Wei suggests stepping back, examining what is happening, gathering ideas, listening to others' perspectives, encouraging others to consider options, think about the situation and, only then, decide what action, if any, to take. The ideal is that, with leaders and managers operating in this way, all staff are encouraged to do the same and to reflect and return regularly to the 'how' and 'why' rather than the 'what'. Carnell's (2001) research in schools found that staff learning was developed through 'meta-learning dialogue', that is, where the more that people discovered about their own learning and the complex nature of learning itself, the more they needed to share this with others and thus move from the intuitive to the explicit in terms of normal staff practice.

Assess the effectiveness of staff learning

The need for leaders and managers to understand whether policies and practice in staff learning are being effective cannot be ignored, and this issue is one that has been found to be complex, precisely because it is about people. Although models for evaluation of the effectiveness of staff development programmes have been proposed (e.g. Stake et al. 1987; Middlewood 1997), and research carried out into the impact of continuous professional development on groups of staff or course members, it is the long-term impact of staff learning upon the school or college that is both crucial and harder to assess. The following are suggested as possible indicators of progress made towards establishing a more effective learning school or college over a period of time:

- Are meetings given over to debate about learning rather than operational issues?
- Are more staff using libraries and resources centres?
- Are more staff offering to lead discussions?
- Are staff acknowledging the role of other agents in the learning role, e.g. parents?
- Are staff willing to identify and acknowledge mistakes (their own and others') as learning experiences?
- Are the barriers to creativity in learning and teaching being recognised?
- Are the learning capabilities of *all* staff being recognised and acted upon?
- Are different learning styles for staff being recognised in their learning?
- Are all staff having opportunities to formalise their learning achievements, if they wish to do so, and what proportion are doing so?

Conclusion

Progress towards becoming a learning school or college is likely to be uneven and even turbulent. Disagreements are fundamental to a culture of critical reflection and debate. Hopkins et al. (1994) stress the importance of 'living with ambiguity' for staff as they progress in their own development and that of the organisation. What is certain is that staff learning 'cannot be an optional luxury' (Hargreaves 1997, p.101). It has to be made integral to the organisation's way of facing new challenges in a complex, rapidly changing world; that is the ultimate task for leaders and managers.

References

Aspinwall, K. and Pedlar, M. (1997), 'Schools as learning organisations', in Fidler, B., Russell, S. and Simkins, T. (eds), *Choices for Self Managing Schools*, London, Paul Chapman Publishing.

Balshaw, M. and Farrell, P. (2002), *Teaching Assistants*, London, David Fulton.

Barth, R. (1990), *Improving Schools from Within*, San Francisco, CA, Jossey-Bass.

Baud, D. (1995), 'Meeting the challenges', in Brew, A. (ed.), *Direction in Staff Development*, Buckingham, Open University Press.

Best, R. (2000), 'The training and support needs of deputy headteachers', *Professional Development Today*, 4 (1), 39–50.

Bezzina, C. (2001), 'A commitment to learning', *Managing Education Matters*, CCEAM, 3 (2),10, Hove, Education Publishing Co. Ltd.

Blandford, S. (2000), *Managing Professional Development in Schools*, London, Routledge.

Bowring-Carr, C. (1993), 'How shall we know quality in teaching and learning? Some problems associated with classroom observation', *Curriculum Journal*, 4 (3), 315–334.

Bowring-Carr, C. and West-Burnham, J. (1997), *Effective Learning in Schools*, London, Pitman.

Brighouse, T. (1991), *What Makes a Good School?* Stafford, Network Educational Press.

Brookfield, S. (1986), *Understanding and Facilitating Adult Learning*, Milton Keynes, Open University Press.

Bruner, J. (1996), *The Culture of Education*, London, Pitman.

Burton, T. (1994), 'The photocopy lady: the role of the reprographics supervisor', in Crawford, M., Kydd, L. and Parker, S. (eds), *Educational Management in Action: A Collection of Case Studies*, London, Paul Chapman Publishing.

Carnell, E. (2001), 'The value of meta-learning dialogue', *Professional Development Today*, 4 (2), 43–54.

Chisholm, L. and Vally, S. (1996), *The Culture of Learning and Teaching in Gauteng Schools*, Witterand Education Policy Unit.

Coleman, M. (2003), 'Developing a culture of learning and teaching', in Coleman, M., Graham-Jolly, M. and Middlewood, D. (eds), *Managing the Curriculum in South African Schools*, London, Commonwealth Secretariat.

Constable, H. (1995), 'Developing teachers as extended professionals', in Busher, H. and Saran, R. (eds), *Managing Teachers as Professionals in Schools*, London, Kogan Page.

Dale, M. (1994), 'Learning organisations', in Mabey, C. and Iles, P. (eds), *Managing Learning*, London, Routledge.

Dalin, P. (1994), *How Schools Improve*, London, Cassell.

Day, C. (1999), *Developing Teachers: The Challenges of Lifelong Learning*, London, Falmer Press.

Day, C., Whitaker, P. and Wrenn, D. (1987), *Appraisal and Professional Development in Primary Schools*, Milton Keynes, Open University Press.

Egan, G. (1982), *The Skilled Helper*, Monterey, CA, Brooks/Cole.

Ferguson, M. (1982), *The Aquarian Conspiracy*, London, Granada.

Foreman-Peck, L. and Middlewood, D. (2002), *Formative Evaluation of the Foundation Degree for Teaching Assistants*, Northampton, University College Northampton.

Fullan, M. and Hargreaves, A. (1992), *Teacher Development and Educational Change*, London, Falmer Press.

Gardner, H. (1983), *Frames of Mind: The Theory of Multiple Intelligences*, New York, Basic Books.

Glover, D. (1994), 'Introducing appraisal', in Crawford, M., Kydd, L. and Parker, S. (eds), *Educational Management in Action: A Collection of Case Studies*, London, Paul Chapman Publishing, pp.173–184.

Haq, M. (1998), *Human Development in South Asia*, Karachi, Oxford University Press.

Hargreaves, A. (1997), 'From reform to renewal: a new deal for a new age', in Hargreaves, A. and Evans, R. (eds), *Beyond Educational Reform*, Buckingham, Open University Press.

Harris, A. Busher, H. and Wise, C. (2001), 'Effective training for subject leaders', *Jour-

STAFF AND ORGANISATIONAL LEARNING

nal of In-Service Education, 27 (1), 83–94.

Hirsch, S. (2001), 'We're growing and changing', *Journal of Staff Development*, 22 (3), 10–17.

Honey, P. (1993), *Creating a Learning Organisation*, Maidenhead, Peter Honey Publications.

Honey, P. and Mumford, A. (1988), *Manual of Learning Style*, Maidenhead, Peter Honey Publications.

Hopkins, D., Ainscow, M. and West, M. (1994), *School Improvement in an Era of Change*, London, Cassell.

Hopson, B. and Scally, M. (1981), *Lifeskills Teaching*, London, McGraw-Hill.

Hughes, M. (2001), 'Teachers as role models for learning', in *Professional Development Today*, 4 (2), 7–12.

Jones, T. (2003), 'Continuous professional development in Wales', *Professional Development Today*, 6 (1), 35–42.

Khan, M. (2000), 'Teachers' professional development: a way of improving education in Pakistan', *International Studies in Educational Administration*, 28 (3), 57–67.

Law, S. and Glover, D. (2000), *Educational Leadership and Learning*, Buckingham, Open University Press.

Lumby, J. (2001), 'Framing teaching and learning in the twenty first century', in Middlewood, D. and Burton, N. (eds), *Managing the Curriculum*, London, Paul Chapman Publishing.

MacGilchrist, B., Myers, K. and Reed, J. (1997), *The Intelligent School*, London, Paul Chapman Publishing.

Middlewood, D. (1997), 'Managing staff development', in Bush, T. and Middlewood, D. (eds), *Managing People in Education*, London, Paul Chapman Publishing.

Middlewood, D. (1999), 'Some effects of multiple research projects on the host school staff', in Middlewood, D., Coleman, M. and Lumby, J., *Practitioner Research in Education: Making a Difference*, London, Paul Chapman Publishing.

Middlewood, D. (2001), 'The future of managing teacher performance and its appraisal', in Middlewood, D. and Cardno, C. (eds), *Managing Teacher Appraisal and Performance: A Comparative Approach*, London, RoutledgeFalmer.

Middlewood, D. (2003), 'Teacher professionalism and development', in Coleman, M., Graham-Jolly, M. and Middlewood, D. (eds), *Managing the Curriculum in South African Schools*, London, Commonwealth Secretariat.

Middlewood, D., Colman, M. and Lumby, J. (1998), *Practitioner Research in Education: Making a Difference*, London, Paul Chapman Publishing.

Ozga, J. (1995), 'Deskilling as a profession: professionalism, deprofessionalism and the new managerialism', in Busher, H. and Saran, R. (eds), *Managing Teachers as Professionals in Schools*, London Kogan Page.

Pell, A. (1998), 'Primary schooling in rural South Africa', in Moyles, J. and Hargreaves, L. (eds), *The Primary Curriculum: Learning from International Perspectives*, London, Routledge.

Reeves, C. (1994), *The Struggle to Teach*, Johannesburg, Maskew Miller Longman.

Revans, R. (1982), 'The origins and growth of action learning', Bromley, Chartwell-Bratt.

Schacter-Shalomi, Z. and Miller, R. (1995), *From Age-ing to Sage-ing*, London, Warner Books.

Stake, R., Shapson, S. and Russell, L. (1987), 'Evaluation of staff development programmes', in Wideen, M. and Andrews, I. (eds), *Staff Development for School Improvement*, Lewes, Falmer Press.

Stoll, L., Fink, D. and Earl, L. (2003), *It's About Learning (and It's About Time)*, London, RoutledgeFalmer.

Sugimine, H. (1998), 'Primary schooling in Japan', in Moyles, J. and Hargreaves, L. (eds), *The Primary Curriculum: Learning from International Perspectives*, London, Routledge.

Taylor, D. and Bishop, S. (1994), *Ready Made Activities for Developing Your Staff*, London, Pitman.

Terrell, I., Clinton, B. and Sheraton, K. (1998), 'Giving learning back to teachers', *Professional Development Today*, 1 (2), 13–22.

Vaill, P. (1989), *Managing as a Performing Art: New Idea for a World of Chaotic Change*, San Francisco, CA, Jossey-Bass.

Waters, M. (1998), 'Personal development for teachers – part 1', *Professional Development Today*, 1 (2), 29–38.

Author Index

Abrol, S. with Ribbins, P. 98, 101
Acker, S, 93
Afshar, H. 98
Al-Khalifa, E. 98
Allix, N.M. 11
Andrews, I. 145
Armstrong, M. 103, 104
Aspinwall, K. and Pedlar, M. 196

Badat, S. 53
Balshaw, M. and Farrell, P. 144, 194
Barnett, B. 163
Barth, R. 196
Bassett, S. 158, 178
Bassey, M. 177
Baud, D. 190
Baxter, G. 87
Beare, H., Caldwell, B. and Millikan, R. 52
Begley, P. 10, 98
Belbin, M. 110
Bell, L. 117
Bell, L. and Bush, T. 7, 8
Benn, S. 96
Best, R. 194
Betts, A. 16
Bezzina, C. 80, 198
Bines, H. and Boydell, D. 146
Bjerke, B. and Al-Meer, A. 81
Blandford, S. 102, 144, 197
Blaney, J. 128
Blauner, S. 78, 79
Blaunt, S. 79, 82
Bolam, R. 3, 22, 153
Bolam, R., Dunning, G. and Karstanje, P. 18
Bolam, R., McMahon, A., Pocklington, K. and
    Weindling, D. 164, 167, 168, 169
Bolman, L.G. and Deal, T.E. 5
Bolton, A. 67, 71
Bottery, M. 6, 12
Bowring-Carr, C. 199
Bowring-Carr, C. and West-Burnham, J. 197, 200
Bray, E. 98
Bridge, W. 55
Briggs, A. 5, 12, 20, 57, 62, 64, 65, 67, 68, 70, 71
Brighouse, T. 195
Brookfield, S. 82, 193

Brown, M., Boyle, B. and Boyle, T. 66
Brown, P. and Lauder, H. 172
Bruner, J. 199
Bubb, S., Hilbourn. R., James, C., Totteredell, M.
    and Bailey, M. 146
Burgess, S., Croxson, B., Gregg, P. and Propper,
    C. 25, 26
Burton, T. 194
Bush, T. 3, 16, 21, 22, 47, 50, 54, 55, 56, 63, 64,
    65, 66, 67, 68, 72, 97, 116
Bush, T. and Anderson, L. 23, 53,
Bush, T. and Chew, J. 163, 168
Bush, T. and Coleman, M. 164, 165, 167
Bush, T. and Glover, D. 161
Bush, T. and Jackson, D. 7, 12
Bush, T. and Qiang, H. 49
Bush, T., Coleman, M. and Glover, D. 131
Bush, T., Coleman, M. and Si, X. 5, 8, 126, 175
Bush, T., Coleman, M., Wall, D. and West-
    Burnham, J. 158, 162, 164, 165, 166
Bush, T., Glover, D. and Morrison, M. 116
Bush, T., Qiang, H. and Fang, J. 48, 63, 64
Busher, H. and Saran, R. 39

Caldwell, B. 184
Caldwell, B. and Spinks, J. 6, 48
Cambridge, J. 128
Campbell-Evans, G. 52
Cardno, C. 108, 109, 110, 114, 117
Cardno, C. and Piggott-Irvine, E. 175, 184
Carnell, E. 200
Chaudry-Lawton, R., Murphy, K. and Terry, A.
Chetty, D., Chisholm, L., Gardner, M., Mcgan,
    N. and Vinjevold, P. 110, 174
Chicago Public Schools Retention Unit 152
Child, J. 176
Chirichello, M. 11
Chisholm, L. and Vally, S. 190
Chong, K.C., Low, G.T. and Walker, A. 167
Clark, B.R. 65
Clayton, T. 32
Cockburn, A. 22
Crowther, F., Kaagan, S., Ferguson, M. and
    Hann, L. 28
Cole, O. 152
Coleman, M. 27, 65, 84, 96, 101, 190

Coleman, M. and Bush, T. 110, 117
Coleman, M., Low, G.T., Bush, T. and Chew, J. 165, 166
Coleman, M., Qiang, H. and Li, Y. 50
Commonwealth Secretariat 9
Commonwealth Secretariat and World Bank 142
Constable, H. 196
Court, M. 115, 116, 121
Crossley, M. and Broadfoot, P. 48
Crow, G. 157, 158, 167
Cuban, L. 4
Curtis, R. 34
Cutler, T. and Waine, B. 178

Dale, M. 191
Dalin, P. 190
Dalin, P. and Rust, V. 31
Daresh, J. 158, 163, 168
Daresh, J. and Playko, M. 158, 165
Davidson, M. and Cooper, C. 101
Davies, B. 159
Day, C. 149, 157, 192, 200
Day, C., Johnston, D. and Whitaker, P. 87
Day, C., Whitaker, P. and Wrenn, D. 189, 196
Deal, T. 54
Dean, C. 144
Debroux, P. 98
Deem, R. 63
Dellar, G. 6
Department of Education (DFE) 23, 108, 111
Department of Education and Science (DES) 36, 142
Department of Education and Skills (DfES) 32, 36, 38
Department for Education and Employment (DfEE) 82
Dimmock, C. 98
Dimmock, C. and Walker, A. 7, 48, 49, 78
Diocese of Sheffield 176
Downes, P. 134
Draper, I. 184
Draper, I. and Gwynne, R. 184
Draper, J. 149
Drucker, P. 27
Durcan, J. and Oates, D. 159
Dwight, C. 86

Eccles, R. 180
Egan, G. 198
Ehrich, L. 168
Elliott, G. 69
Elliott, G. and Crossley, M. 3
Elliott, G. and Hall, V. 16
Elliott, J. 174, 178, 181
Enderud, H. 68
Eraut, M., Alderton, J., Cole, G. and Senker, P. 18
Erculj, J. 82
Erikson, E. 84
Evans, L. 78, 86, 178
Everard, B. and Morris, G. 61
Evetts, J. 66

Farrel, D., Balshaw, M. and Polat, R. 35, 40, 81
Fenner, J. 35
Ferguson, M. 191
Fidler, B. 62
Fidler, B. and Atton, T. 39
Finn, R. 160
Fisher, C. 79
Fisher, C. and Yuan, A. 85, 87
Fitzgerald, T., Yangs, H. and Grootenbauer, P. 174
Fitz-Gibbon, C. 18
Foreman, K. 25
Foreman-Peck, L. and Middlewood, D. 36, 38, 40, 194, 196
Foskett, N. and Lumby, J. 20, 21, 22, 25, 55, 85, 96, 149, 181
Frase, L. 78
Freeman, A. 97
Fryer, M. 80
Fullan, M. 62, 87
Fullan, M. and Hargreaves, A. 50, 51, 196
Furukawa, H. 175

Gardiner, G. 99
Gardner, H. 192
Gentleman, A. 102
Gerry, C. 138
Glatter, R. 5, 7
Glatter, R. and Kydd, L. 7
Gleeson, D and Gunter, H. 177
Gleeson, D. and Husbands, C. 18, 19, 27
Glover, D. 193
Glover, D. and Bush, T. 167
Glover, D. and Law, S. 130
Gold, R. 93
Grace, G. and Lawn, M. 141
Gray, H. 96
Greenfield, T. 68
Gunter, H. 3, 11, 19

Hackett, P. 130
Hall, D. 146
Hall, R. and Rowland, C. 20
Hall, V. 69, 70, 71, 72, 125, 128, 180
Hallgarten, J. 149
Hallinger, P. and Heck, R. 112
Hampden-Turner, C. and Trompenaars, F. 175
Handy, C. 20, 21, 29, 77, 103
Haq, M. 194
Hardi, S. 134
Hardman, J. 128, 151
Hargreaves, A. 153, 201
Hargreaves, D. 42, 56, 57
Harper, H. 62, 66, 67, 69
Harris, A. 8, 9, 57
Harris, A. Busher, H. and Wise, C. 193
Harrison, G. 84
Hellawell, D. 184
Herzberg, F. 77
Hibert, K. 163
Hicks, G. and Tilby, J. 141, 150, 151
Hinton, P. 133
Hirsch, S. 199

Hobby, R. 176
Hobson, A. 164
Hofstede, G. 78, 84
Holloway, D. 145, 173
Honey, P. 197
Honey, P. and Mumford, A. 192
Hopkins, D., Ainscow, M. and West, M. 86, 87, 189, 201
Hopson, B. and Scally, M. 199
Howse, J. and MacPherson, R. 86
Hoyle, E. 51, 52, 54, 57, 67, 111
Hughes, M. 196
Humphreys, S. and Oxtoby, M. 178, 180
Hunt, J. 142, 143
Hutchings, M. Mentor, I. Ross. A. and Thomson, D. 82

Ifanti, A. 80, 126
Imants, J., Sleegers, P. and Witziers, B. 67
Ingvarson, L. 25, 82
Irvine, J. 103

James, C. and Colebourne, D. 24
Jantjes, E. 174
Jenkins, K. 101, 102
Jennings, K. and Lomas, L. 24, 175
Johnson, B. 118, 119
Johnson, D. 66
Johnson, M. 80, 81, 149
Jones, K. and Stammers, P. 146
Jones, T. 199

Kakabadse, A., Ludlow, R. and Vinnicombe, S. 82, 143
Katzenbach, J. and Smith, D. 107, 120
Kedney, B. and Brownlow, S. 33
Kerry, C. and Kerry, T. 31, 37, 41
Kerry, T. 37
Khan, M. 194
Kinlaw, D. 159
Kitan, M. and Van der Westhuizen, P. 144
Knowles, M. 82
Kolb, D. 159
Kremer-Hayon, L. and Goldstein, Z. 83

Lashway, L. 107
Lauglo, J. 5, 6
Law, S. and Glover, D. 130, 182, 192
Lee, B. 37
Leithwood, K. 11, 83, 114, 148, 153
Leithwood, K., Jantzi, D. and Steinbach, R. 19
Leung, M. L. and Bush, T. 158, 161, 162, 166, 168
Levačić, R., Glover, D., Bennett, N. and Crawford, M. 5
Lewin, K., Xu, H., Little, A. and Zheng, J. 64
Lewis, C. 81, 126
Local Government National Training Organisation (LGNTO) 32
Long, P. 173, 179
Longenecker, G. and Ludgwig, D. 179
Lorenz, S. 38, 136, 174

Luck, C. 164, 165, 167
Lumby, J. 3, 16, 36, 61, 62, 63, 65, 66, 67, 68, 69, 70, 71, 72, 152, 190
Lumby, J. and Briggs, A. 81
Lumby, J. and Li, Y. 87

MacBeath, J. 143
MacGilchrist, B., Myers, K. and Reed, J. 192
Mahony, P. and Hextall, I. 173, 177
Maslow, A. 77
McClelland, D.A. 88
McElroy, W. 94
McGregor, D. 77, 172
McPherson, J. 136, 137
McTavish, D. 3
Megginson, D. Clutterbuck, D. 101
Mercer, W. 153
Middlewood, D. 31, 34, 35, 36, 80, 85, 100, 113, 109, 137, 145, 173, 174, 175, 178, 180, 182, 183, 184, 190, 191, 196, 200
Middlewood, D. and Lumby, J. 17, 77, 93, 94, 97, 99, 113, 134, 135
Middlewood, D. and Parker, R. 41
Middlewood, D., Colman, M. and Lumby, J. 189
Miles, E. 137
Miller, T.W. and Miller, J.M. 11, 19
Mintzberg, H. 11
Mokgalane, E., Carrim, N., Gardiner, M. and Chisholm, L. 174
Morgan, C. 128, 131, 133, 137
Morgan, C., Hall, V. and Kackay, A. 133
Morgan, G. 47, 50, 56, 57, 58, 67
Morris, J. and Farrell, C. 26
Mortimore, P. and MacBeath, J. 148
Mortimore, P. and Mortimore, J. 79
Mortimore, P., Mortimore, J. and Thomas, H. 31, 35, 144
Moyles, J. and Suschitzky, W. 32, 40
Muijs, D. and Harris, A. 28
Mullins, L. 61, 62, 126, 129
Murphy, K. and Cleveland, J. 179
Mwanwenda, T. 78

National College for School Leadership (NCSL) 79, 116
National Commission for Education 148
National Foundation for Educational Research (NFER) 82
Naylor, D. 35
Newland, C. 8
Newman, J. and Clarke, J. 3
Newton, T. and Findlay, P. 173
Ngcabo, T. 52, 53, 103
Nias, J., Southworth, G. and Yeomans, R. 50, 51, 54, 112
Norris, K. 131, 133

O'Neill, J. 47, 48, 61, 69, 118
O'Neill, J., Middlewood, D. and Glover, D. 100
Odland, J. 22
Office for Standards in Education (OFSTED) 17, 112

Ozga, J. 81, 174, 192

Paine, L. and Ma, L. 66
Palmer, S. 38
Papps, I. 94
Parker, R. 86
Parker-Jenkins, R. 100
Parry, G. 179, 181
Pell, A. 192
Petzko, V., Clark, D., Valentine, G., Hackmann, D., Nori, J. and Lucas, S. 165
Plachy, R. 129
Playko, M. 166, 167
Pocklington, K. and Weindling, D. 165
Poster, C. and Poster, D. 178
Preedy, M. 177
Prosser, J. 57

Rai, A. 38, 40
Rajan, A. 158
Rajpu, J. and Walia, K. 181
Randle, K. and Brady, N. 69
Rea, D. 87
Reeves, C. 191
Reeves, F. 103
Revans, R. 190
Reynolds, D. 55
Reynolds, D. and Farrell, S. 81
Riches, C. 17, 18, 20, 76, 77, 133
Rikowski, G. 6
Riley, K. 88
Roberts, A. 158, 168
Robertson, M. 176
Rowe, J. 78
Rutherford, D. 109, 120
Ryall, A. and Goddard, G. 35, 40

Samier, E. 158, 168
Sapre, P. 3
Schacter-Shalomi, Z. and Miller, R. 198
Schein, E. 52, 54, 57, 142
School Management Task Force 144
Sebakwane-Mahlase, S. 181
Sehlare, B., Mentz, P. and Mentz, E. 146, 148
Senge, P. 178
Sergiovanni, T. 56
Shah, S. 98, 175
Sikes, P. 176, 177
Silverman, D. 69
Simkins, T. and Lumby, J. 33, 36
Slocombe, L. 104
Smith, R. 63, 70
Smith, W. 23
Smyth, J. and Shacklock, G. 174
South African School Act 53
Southworth, G. 71, 137, 164, 166, 168, 169
Spindler, J. and Biott, C. 27
Stake, R., Shapson, S. and Russell, L. 200

Stoll, L. 69
Stoll, L. and Fink, D. 86
Stoll, L. and Myers, K. 148
Stoll, L., Fink, D. and Earl, L. 35, 189, 196
Storey, J. and Sisson, K. 179
Strathern, M. 178
Sugimine, H. 191
Summers, A. 93

Taylor, D. 85
Taylor, D. and Bishop, S. 193
Taylor, J. 152
Terrell, I., Clinton, B. and Sheraton, K. 196
Thompson, M. 27, 84
Thomson, R. 129, 133, 144
Thrupp, M. 177
Thurlow, M. 23, 24, 126, 136, 174,
Thurlow, M. with Ramnarain, S. 184
Thurlow, M., Bush, T. and Coleman, M. 8
Tillotson, V. 97, 104
Todd, D. 36, 40
Tomlinson, H. 179, 181
Townley, B. 173
Tuckman, B. 115
Turner, C. 20, 55, 66
Turner, R. 70

Vaill, P. 200
Van Halen, B. 131

Walker, A. and Dimmock, C. 48, 96
Wallace, M. 107, 108, 109, 110, 111, 112, 115, 120
Wallace, M. and Hall, V. 51, 63, 65, 67, 119
Wamahiu, S. 104
Warwick, J. 97
Washington, K. 126, 176
Wasserberg, M. 4
Waters, M. 193
Webb, R. and Vulliamy, G. 12
Weindling, R. and Earley, P. 143
West, L. and Milan, M. 159, 160
West-Burnham, J. 174
Whitaker, P. 83
Wildy, H. and Louden, W. 65, 67
Williams, S., Macalpine, A. and McCall, C. 37, 136
Wilson, V., Schlapp, U. and Davidson, J. 32, 35
Wood, C. and Pohland, P. 173
Woods, P., Bennett, N., Harvey, J. and Wise, C. 12, 107
Woodward, W. 138
Wragg, E., Haynes, G., Wragg, C. and Chamberlin, R. 25, 179
Wragg, E., Wikeley, F., Wragg, C. and Haynes, G. 102

Yariv, E. 19
Young, B. and Brooks, M. 99

Subject Index

Added to the page number 'f' denotes a figure and 't' denotes a table.

absence from work 78
accountability dilemma for school principals 65
accountability pressures 111–12, 120
accountability for resources 173
adult learning 193
Africa
  achievement of gender equality 104
  approaches to learning and development 103
  cultural dimensions 52–3
  staff selection 55
  see also Bophuthatswana; Ethiopia; South Africa; Zambia
aggression cultures 49
aims of education 16
  and management 3
ambiguity models of organisational theory 68–9
ancillary workers
  boredom at work 79
  see also support staff
applicants, quality 132
appraisal *see* performance appraisal and review
appraisers 101–2
Asia
  examining teacher performance 175
  see also Bangladesh; China; East Asia; Hong Kong; India; Iran; Israel; Japan; Pakistan; Saudi Arabia; South Asia
assessment 17–18
  of the effectiveness of staff learning 200–1
  in the selection process 135–6
  see also evaluation; performance appraisal and review; threshold assessment
assessment centres 135
assessment exercises 135
assimilation into organisations 142–3
associate staff *see* support staff
associate teachers 36
attribution 177
attrition 150
Australia
  advantages of teamwork 118

site-based management in secondary schools 6
women's equality 93
autonomy, loss through teamwork 119
autonomy dilemma for school principals 65

'balkanized' culture 50–1
Bangladesh, educational improvement projects 190
Belbin's classification of roles 110
beliefs 47
  heroes and heroines as the embodiment of 52
  and organisational culture 50–1, 56–7
black staff, mentoring 101
Bophuthatswana, perceptions of the induction process 146–8
'boundary spanning' 71
Britain *see* UK
bureaucracy 66
  attitudes in different countries 8
  link with centralisation 5
business managerialism 3

Canada, human resource management (HRM) practices 98
career cycles 148–9
  motivation at different stages 83–4
career opportunities and retention 153–4
career structure and development for support staff 35–6
caretakers 39
cash incentives
  as recognition 87
  see also golden handcuffs; performance related pay (PRP)
Catholic primary schools
  composition of SMTs 109
  headteachers approach to leadership 120
centralisation
  influence on motivation and job satisfaction 80
  link with bureaucracy 5
  see also decentralisation
ceremonies 51–2
chairs of teams 110
change

link with leadership 4–5
moral imperative of educational
    organisations to lead 97
see also cultural change; organisational
    change
Chicago Teacher Retention Unit 151–2
China
    application of dimensions of societal culture
        49–50
    bureaucratic centralism 5, 8
    collegiality 66
    human resource management (HRM)
        practices 98
    mentoring 158
    organisational structure 63–4
    recruitment and selection 55, 126
    satisfaction factors 85
    teacher performance evaluation 175–6
    use of rewards and incentives 87
church schools 176
    see also Catholic primary schools
classroom assistants 32
    use of observation in the selection process
        136
    working relationship with teachers 40
    see also TAs
classroom observation 199
clerical staff, use of observation in the
    selection process 136
closure, schools due for 85–6
co-mentoring 158
co-ordination 62
co-ordinators of teams 110
co-principalships 115–16
coaching
    mentoring and x, 27, 158–61
    stages 159
coaching continuum 160t
collaboration, contradiction in SMTs between
    hierarchy and 115–16
'collective learning' 35
colleges
    and equal opportunities 94, 95–6, 104
        community context 98
    'people-centred' vii
    self-management *see* self-management
    see also further education colleges; learning
        colleges
collegiality 55, 66–7, 119
Colombia, educational improvement projects
    190
committees
    participation in 68
    pattern of 69
communication 104
'communities of reflective practice' 200
community-building 9
company workers 110
compensatory level of support for learning 41
completer finishers 110
conflict management 103
consideration societies 49

consulting 160
context for leadership and management viii,
    3–12, 120
    culture and 7–8, 48
    decentralisation and self-management 5–6
    differences within countries 8–9
    globalisation 6–7
    leading and managing people 9–12
contextualisation of staff learning 194
continuing professional support
    equal opportunities issues 100–1
    see also critical friendship; mentoring
control 62
    within teaching 119, 120
counselling 160
countries
    differences between 7–8
    differences within 8–9
    see also developed countries; developing
        countries
criteria for selection 134–5
critical friendship 157–8
critical reflection 200
cross-gender mentoring 101
cultural change 55–6, 58
    management structure as a tool 65
cultural consonance 55
cultural factors influencing motivation and job
    satisfaction 79
cultural globalisation 6
cultural 'labels' 47–8
cultural maintenance 56
culture
    and context 7–8
    effect on retention 153–4
    implications for motivation 84–5
    influence on performance management
        175–6, 178
    relationship between organisational
        structure and 69
    value of diversity of in the learning
        environment 96–7
    see also 'balkanized' culture; monocultures;
        national culture; organisational cultures;
        school culture; societal culture;
        subcultures; work cultures
culture of enquiry and reflection, development
    200
culture of learning, development in South
    Africa 23, 52–4, 190
'culture of self-management' 48
'culture of teamwork' 112
current holders of posts, involvement in
    selection process 134
Czech Republic, use of assistants to support
    Romany children 37

data collection on performance 180–2
    methods of collection 181–2
    sources of data 181
    types of data 180–1
Data Protection Act (1998) 127

decentralisation 5–6
  and globalisation 6–7
  see also centralisation
'decontextualized paradigms' 48
defensiveness, effect on team learning 114–15
departments
  and development of subcultures 51, 57
  and micropolitics 67
  for support staff 34
deputy headteachers
  and dissemination of school culture 54
  perceptions of their training 194
developed countries
  accountability for resources 173
  differences amongst schools 8
  equal opportunities 92–4
  induction 144
  marketisation of education 81
  retention of staff 149
  shift away from functionalist teaching and
    learning 182
  site-based training and development 194
  teachers as effective learners 190
developing countries
  differences between urban and rural schools
    8
  educational systems 7
  induction 144
  learning as a means to an end 191
  retention of staff 149
  staff development 190
  unqualified teachers 31
development coaching 159–60
development of leadership *see* leadership
  development
Diploma in Educational Administration (DEA)
  162–3
distributed leadership 9, 107, 111–12, 120
  link to teams 107–8
diversity in the learning environment 95–7
dress, equal opportunity issues 102
'Duty-oriented' job descriptions 129
'dynamic conservatism' 191

East Asia, status of teachers 81
economic globalisation 6
educational systems
  benefits of mentoring 167
  effect of economics 7
efficiency dilemma 65
Egypt, work culture 178
empowerment 28
England
  contemporary policy climate 11–12
  leadership in schools in challenging
    circumstances 8–9
  mentoring
    benefits for headteacher mentors 166–7
    for new principals 163–4
    of NQTs 162
  organisational structure 64–5
    influence of micropolitics 67

performance management 24–6
retention of teachers 21, 149
selection panels 131–2
use of cash rewards 87
enquiry, development of a culture of reflection
  and 200
environmental globalisation 6
equal opportunities ix, 92–104
  building into leadership and management
    99–104
    implications for leaders and managers
      103–4
    induction and continuing professional
      support 100–1
    performance management and appraisal
      101–2
    recruitment and selection 99–100
    staff learning and development 102–3
  definitions and theoretical perspectives 92–5
  implications for leadership and management
    97–9
    institution's context 98–9, 101
    leader's personal understanding 97
    societal context 98
  monitoring 93
  significance in educational organisations
    95–7
equity theories of motivation 77
Erikson, stages of human development 84
Ethiopia, educational improvement projects
  190
ethnic diversity in the learning environment
  96–7
ethnic minorities
  mentoring of 101
  use of assistants to support 37
ethos of trust 184
Europe
  approaches to learning and development
    103
  see also Czech Republic; Greece; Lithuania;
    Malta; Netherlands; Portugal; Russia;
    Slovenia; UK
evaluation 17–18
  of teams 112–13
  see also assessment; performance appraisal
    and review
evaluators 110
examinations *see* public examinations
'exit interviews' 129
extension level of support for learning 41

factionalism 119
feedback 180–1, 183
  360 degree 181, 184
foundation degrees for TAs 36, 38
functionalist teaching and learning 192
  shift away from 182
funding constraints and modifications to
  hierarchy 62
further education colleges 5
  changing patterns of teaching and

management 70
collegiality 66
conflict between organisational aims and
    individual aspirations 16
development of several cultures 69
implementation of equal opportunities 97
and managerial efficiency 3
micropolitics 67
middle managers 5, 20, 62, 70, 71
organisational structure 64–5
    hierarchy 62–3, 66
role distinctions between academic and
    other staff 33
structural ambiguity 68–9
and subjective models of organisational
    theory 68
support staff 33
    undervaluing 36–7
temporary and part-time staff 152

gender
    achievement of equality in Africa 104
    and mentoring 101, 168
    and motivation 84
    and organisational structure 65
    societal context 98
'generativity versus stagnation' 84
globalisation 6–7, 48
goal theories of motivation 77
goals of education *see* purpose of education
golden handcuffs 150–1
governing bodies 57
governments, standards agenda 20, 111
governors 131
grant-maintained schools 131
Greece
    centralist control 80
    learning as a means to an end 191
    recruitment and selection 126
Greenland secondary school 53
group norms 51
group-oriented cultures 49

'hard variant' of human resource management
    16
Heads of Premises 34
headteachers
    benefits of mentoring 164–5
        for mentors 166–7
    and bureaucracy 66
    gender influence 65
    influence on organisational culture 54
    and peer-mentoring 158
    and performance management 18–19, 24
    and shared leadership 111, 120
    women as 84
    see also deputy headteachers; principals
heroes and heroines 52, 54
Herzberg's 'two factor' theory 77
hierarchy
    contradiction in SMTs between collaboration
        and 115–16

and organisational structures 62–4, 66
hierarchy of needs, Maslow's 77
high achievers 88
high schools
    micropolitics 67
    see also secondary schools
higher education structures 63
higher level teaching assistants (HLTAs) 34, 36,
    38
holistic cultures 49
Hong Kong, student mentoring 161–2, 166
Hong Kong Baptist University, mentoring
    161–2, 168
human development, stages of 84
human resource development, contradiction
    between performance and 18
human resource management (HRM)
    'hard variant' 16
    societal context 98
    of support staff 39
    and transformational leadership 19
Human Rights Act (1998) 92–3

ideological manipulation and control 56–7
implementors 110
in-tray exercises 135
incentive theories of motivation 21, 25
incentives
    external control over 81–2
    see also cash incentives; rewards
India, collection of data on performance 181
individual action plans 184
individual aspirations, conflict between
    organisational aims and 16
individuality in motivation 83–5
    and different cultures 84–5
    and gender 84
    and stages of career 83–4
induction x, 141–8, 154
    effectiveness 146–8
    entitlement 144
    equal opportunity issues 100–1
    importance 145–6
    links between retention and 141–2
    management 144–5
    paradigms of teacher 145
    as part of a continuous process 146
    purposes 142–3
    for support staff 36
induction programmes 145
innovators 110
institutional level
    importance of leadership 82–3
    motivational strategies 83–8
'institutionalised' mentoring 168
institutions
    importance of context in establishing a
        culture of equal opportunities 98–9
    training and development 194
    see also colleges; schools; universities
instruments for assessing candidates 135–6
intelligence 199

internal promotions 151
international schools
    inequalities in pay and conditions of service
        151
    recruitment and selection 128
interpersonal conflict due to teamwork 119
interpretative level of support for learning 41
interviews 135–6
    building an emphasis on learning into 199
    shortcomings 133
    see also 'exit interviews'
intrinsic theories of motivation 21
Iran, societal context for equal opportunities
    98
Islam, assessment of teacher performance 175
isolation 79
Israel
    ineffective teachers in primary schools 19
    school managers and teachers' attitude to
        work 83
    teachers' career structures 82

Japan
    attitudes to performance and appraisal 175,
        178
    learning as a means to an end 191
    societal context for equal opportunities 98
    status of teachers 81
jiaoyanzu 64, 66
job descriptions 69, 129–30, 132
job dissatisfaction 78–9
    link between absence or withdrawal from
        work and 78
    pay as a cause of 81
job satisfaction ix, 78
    factors influencing 79, 80–2

Kolb's learning cycle 159
KwaZulu-Natal
    aims of schools 53
    collegiality 66
    external control of school structures 64
    selection of secondary school principals 136
    SMTs 109, 113

labour market 127
lay personnel
    influences on policy 57
    involvement in recruitment and selection
        131–2, 137
leaderless group discussions 135
Leaders in Education programme 163
leadership
    and culture 54–8
    definition 4
    distinction between management and 3, 4–5
    successful see successful leadership
    see also distributed leadership; shared
        leadership; transactional leadership;
        transformational leadership
leadership development 12, 27
    influence of globalisation 7

mentoring as a strategy 165
and professional coaching 160
learning
    ethnic differences in approaches 103
    levels of support 41
    new context 182–3
    sharing 199
    types and levels 191–2
    see also adult learning; 'collective learning';
        culture of learning; organisational
        learning; staff learning and development;
        teacher learning; team learning
learning behaviour in organisations 197f
learning colleges 190–2, 199
    progress towards 201
learning cycle, Kolb's 159
learning organisations x, 190, 191
    link between staff learning and 195–7
learning schools 190–2, 199
    progress towards 201
learning support assistants (LSAs) 34, 35
lecturers, working relationships with support
        staff 37–8
legislation
    for equal opportunities 92–3
    for recruitment and selection 127
lifelong learning 197–8
limited relationship cultures 49
Lithuania, recruitment and selection 134
long hours working culture 80
LSAs (learning support assistants) 34, 35
lunchtime supervisors 35
    see also midday supervisors

McGregor's 'X' and 'Y' theory 77
Madrasas 175
Malta, centralist control 80
management 3
    distinction between leadership and 3, 4–5
    see also self-management
management by objectives (MBO) 173
management roles 69–72
    linking structure and 72–3
    role conflict and ambiguity 71–2
management schemes 193
management styles 96
managerial globalisation 6
'managerialism' 3
marketisation of education 81
Maslow's hierarchy of needs 77
matching 137
MBO (management by objectives) 173
'meaninglessness' 78–9, 81
meetings 110, 119
men, management styles 96
mentees, benefits of mentoring 164–6
mentoring x, 27
    benefits 164–7
    coaching and 158–61
    counselling as an element 160
    equal opportunity issues 101
    examples 161–4

features of successful 169
limitations 167–8
meaning 157–8
in the New Visions programme 160–1
training 166
mentors, benefits of mentoring 166–7
'meta-learning dialogue' 200
micropolitics 67
and school culture 57
midday supervisors
enhancement of self-esteem 37
specific skills 40
see also lunchtime supervisors
middle managers 57
development 12
and the development of subcultures 51
in further education colleges 5, 20, 62, 70,
71
induction 144
involvement in personnel and training 132
in universities 70
mission statements 16
monitors 110
monocultures 51, 56, 57
moral purpose of education 95
moral support as an advantage of teamwork
118
morale 78–9, 150
as an advantage of teamwork 118
motivation ix, 20–1, 76–88, 150
clarification of term 76–8
factors influencing 26–7, 79
of high achievers 88
and leadership at institutional level 82–3
limits to influence of leaders 80–2
relative impact of influencers 82, 83f
strategies at institutional level 83–8
employee ownership of work 87–8
individuality in motivation see
individuality in motivation
opportunities for professional
development 85–6
provision of strategic direction 86
recognition 78, 86–7
theories 21, 77–8
movers 149
multiple intelligences 192
mutual adaptation 114

National College for School Leadership see
NCSL
national cultures 8, 48, 49, 52
see also societal cultures
national curriculum 5, 80
NCSL 3, 5, 7, 12, 108, 120
development programmes 116–17, 160–1
needs theories of motivation 77
negotiation 103–4
Netherlands, and micropolitics 67
new college hierarchy 62
'new learning paradigm' 182–3
New Visions programme 4, 160–1, 167

New Zealand
co-principalship 115–16
comparison of teachers' effectiveness 177
development of polytechnics 86
sources of data on performance 181
teachers' career structures 82
teamwork 108, 109, 110
training and development 114–15
newly qualified teachers see NQTs
non-contact time for teachers viii
non-learning behaviour in organisations 197f
norms 58
development of shared 51
NQTs
induction programmes 141–2
mentoring of 162
benefits 165, 166

observation
as an assessment technique 136
building an emphasis on learning into 199
office managers 34
Office for Standards in Education (Ofsted)
inspection framework 17, 18, 112–13
oral presentations 135
organisational aims, conflict between
individual aspirations and 16
organisational change 58
organisational cultures ix, 7–8, 47–59
central features 50–2
definition 47–8
distinction between societal culture and 7–8,
49
'fitting' of new employees 130
leadership and 54–8
limitations 56–8
people and 58–9
understanding 143
organisational factors influencing motivation
and job satisfaction 79
organisational learning x, 189–201
role of leaders and managers 197–201
in developing a culture of enquiry and
reflection 200
role models as learners 197–8
in supporting employees as learners 198–9
to assess the effectiveness of staff learning
200–1
to build an emphasis on learning into
management processes 199
to encourage the sharing of learning 199
significance of a focus on 189–90
organisational mentoring 157
organisational structures and roles ix, 61–73
determinants 64–5
and hierarchy 62–4, 66
leadership and management roles 69–72
linking role and 72–3
nature and purpose 61–2
objectives 61–2
and organisational theory 65–9
organisations

assimilation into 142–3
see also institutions; learning organisations
outcomes, measurement 177–8
ownership of initiatives 87–8

Pacific Rim societies, status of teachers 81
pairing in mentoring 168
Pakistan
    assessment of teacher performance 175
    societal context for equal opportunities 98
    training of teachers 194
paraprofessionals viii, 31
    in Portugal 37
    see also support staff
parents
    inclusion on selection panels 131–2, 134
    role in the learning process 183
part-time staff
    induction 144
    procedures for recruitment and selection 100
    retention 152
particularistic approaches to staff selection 55
patriarchal leadership in China 50
pay
    as a cause of dissatisfaction 81
    see also performance related pay (PRP)
peer coaching 160, 161t
peer-mentoring model 158
people
    and culture 58–9
    leading and managing 9–12, 19–22
    as a resource vii
'people-centred' schools and colleges vii
people/performance debate 20
performance viii, 16–28
    achievement of competent 143
    contradiction between human resource
        development and 18
    data collection *see* data collection on
        performance
    focus on vii-viii
    improving 26–8
    managing for *see* performance management
    as a measure of the effectiveness of selection
        137
performance appraisal and review x, 17–18,
    172–84
    building an emphasis on learning into 199
    equal opportunity issues 101–2
    problems 177–9
    of support staff 36
    see also assessment; evaluation
performance coaching 159
performance management 17–19
    at individual site level 179–80
    critique 18
    in England and Wales 24–6
    equal opportunity issues 101–2
    future 182–4
        changing scenario 182–3
        principles for effectiveness 184
    headteacher support 18–19

importance of context 175–6
purposes 172–5
    background 172–3
    perceptions of 173–4
    in South African schools 23–4
        mistrust of purposes of appraisal and 174
        sources of data 181
    teacher attitudes 19
    and transactional leadership 19
performance management schemes x, 24, 25,
    28, 176–7, 179, 183
    data collection *see* data collection on
        performance
    development at individual site level 180
    discussion between manager and employee
        182
    implementation 193
    nationally imposed 174–5
performance related pay (PRP) 25–6, 81–2,
    178–9
performance of staff *see* staff performance
performance threshold scheme 25–6, 82
person specifications 129, 130, 132
personal development 192–3
personnel involved in recruitment and
    selection 131
    training 131–2
physical disability, support of staff with 101
political globalisation 6
polytechnics, development in New Zealand 86
Portugal, paraprofessionals 37
positive discrimination 94, 95
powerlessness 79
praise 153
prescribed curriculum 80
primary schools
    balance between teamwork and hierarchy
        115
    collegiality 66–7
    composition of SMTs 109
    role overload 71
'the principal as visionary' 10
principals 111
    dilemmas of restructuring 65
    influence on organisational culture 54
    mentoring
        benefits for mentors 166
        in England and Wales 163–4
        in Singapore 162–3
        in the USA 165–6
    and peer-mentoring 158
    see also co-principalships; headteachers
professional development 22, 27, 192–3
    equal opportunity issues 102–3
    international significance 22
    as a means of motivating staff 85–6
    as a means of retention 152–3
    of support staff 34–5
    see also coaching; induction; mentoring;
        training
professional portfolios for teachers 184
professional socialisation 157

professional/lay roles in the selection process
137
see also lay personnel
promotions, internal 151
PRP (performance related pay) 25–6, 81–2,
178–9
'psychological androgyny' 96
public examinations 111, 190
targets vii, viii
pupil involvement in the selection process 134
pupil learning, link between staff and 196
purpose of education
definition 16
and management 3
see also moral purpose of education

qualitative data 180
The Quality of Teachers' Working Lives 82–3
quantitative data 180
questioning in interviews 136
quota systems for employment 94

racism 93–4
receptionists, use of observation in the
selection process 136
recognition 178
as a motivator 78, 86–7
and retention 153
recruitment and selection ix-x, 125–38
building an emphasis on learning into 199
effect of cultural variables 55
effective 128–9
effective management of selection 134–7
equal opportunities 99–100
factors affecting 126–8
factors affecting selection management
132–3
leading and managing in difficult contexts
138
monitoring the effectiveness of processes
137
personnel involved in appointing 131, 134
training 131–2
stages 129–30
strategic context 125–6
to achieve cultural consonance 55
written policies 128–9
reflection
development of a culture of enquiry and 200
effect of focusing on performance 177–8
relationships
between role holders 69
and successful leadership 9
religious belief, influence on reviewing
performance 176
reprographics supervisors 194
'resistance groups', sub-units as 57
resource investigators 110
resources
accountability 173
people as vii, 39
responsibilities 78

restructuring 65, 67
influence of responsiveness on 62–3
'Results-oriented' job descriptions 129
retention x, 21, 141, 148–54
at a national level 149–50
during staff shortages 142, 150–2
importance 148
links between induction and 141–2
long-term strategies 152–4
of temporary and part-time staff 152
rewards 87, 178–9
for team efforts 184
see also cash rewards; incentives
rituals 47, 58
expression of culture through 51–2
overreliance on 57–8
role ambiguity 71, 72
role clarity 71
role conflict 71
role models 95, 98–9
role overload 71
role play simulations 135
role strain 71
role theory ix, 69
role-focused learning 194
'role-making' 70, 72
'role-taking' 70, 72
roles
changing nature 184
effect of self-management of schools and
colleges 39
linking structure and 61
played by team members 109–10
see also management roles
Romany children, use of assistants to support
37
Russia
employee ownership of work 87
satisfaction factors 85

same-gender mentoring 101, 168
satisfaction theories of motivation 21
Saudi Arabia, status of teaching 81
school culture
micro-political perspective 57
role of headteachers in defining 54
and symbols 51–2
School Management Task Force 144, 163
school-based research-centred professional
development programmes 85
schools
benefits of mentoring 167
in challenging circumstances 8–9
changing role expectations 70–1
due for closure 85–6
effect of size on number and type of teams
110
and equal opportunities 94, 95–6, 97, 104
community context 98–9
and micropolitics 67
'people-centred' vii
self-management *see* self-management of

schools and colleges
  see also church schools; grant-maintained
    schools; international schools; learning
    schools; primary schools; secondary
    schools
Scotland
  further education 3
  teachers' career plans 149
secondary school management teams 63, 65
secondary schools
  collegiality 66
  micropolitics 67
  organisational structure 65
secretaries 39
'secure human relationships' 88
segregated societies, societal context for equal
    opportunities 98
selection, recruitment and see recruitment and
    selection
selection panels 131–2, 133
selectors
  fallibility 132–3
  quality 132
self-estrangement 79
self-management 5–6, 31
  effect on roles 39
  lay influences on policy 57
  and recruitment and selection 131
  see also 'culture of self-management'
self-oriented cultures 49
SEN co-ordinators (SENCOs) 34
senior leadership teams see SLTs
senior management teams see SMTs
senior managers, development of 12
Seychelles and bureaucratic centralism 5, 8
shapers 110
shared leadership 107, 120
  and pressures of accountability 111
  see also teams
shared norms and meanings 51
shortages of staff see staff shortages
Singapore
  mentoring for aspiring principals 162–3
  teachers' career structures 82
site-based training and development 194, 196
Slovenia, teachers' career structures 82
SLTs 108, 110
  impact of Working Together for Success
    (WTfS) 117
SMTs 51
  composition 108–10
  in further education colleges 62
  synergy in 118
  see also secondary school management
    teams
social factors
  influencing equal opportunities 98
  influencing motivation and job satisfaction
    79
socialisation 142–3, 157
  see also mentoring
societal culture 7–8, 48–50, 58–9

'dimensions' 49
  distinction between organizational culture
    and 7–8, 49
society, status of educational staff 81
South Africa
  collegiality 66
  culture of learning 23, 52–4, 190
  and equal opportunities 93, 98
  identification and celebration of sporting
    heroes 52
  institutionalised differences in schools 8
  learning as a means to an end 191, 192
  organisational structures 63, 66
    external control 64
  performance management in schools 23–4
    mistrust of purposes of appraisal and 174
    sources of data 181
  rationale for teamwork 108
  recruitment and selection 126–7, 134
  SMTs 108–9, 111–12, 113–14
  staffing problems 78
  see also KwaZulu-Natal
South African Schools Act (1996) 53
South America, bureaucracy in 8
South Asia, training for serving teachers 194
specialists 110
staff
  empowerment 28
  status in society 81
  valuing viii
  see also lecturers; support staff; teachers
staff learning and development 192–3
  effectiveness 193–5
    assessment 200–1
  investment 9
  link between the learning organisation and
    195–7
  methods of learning 194–5
  see also professional development; teacher
    learning
staff motivation see motivation
staff shortages
  and recruitment and selection 125, 138
  retention during 142, 150–2
standards agenda of governments 20, 111
starters 149
status of educational staff in society 81
stayers 149
stereotyping, avoidance of 84
stoppers 149
structural ambiguity 68–9
structures, organisational see organisational
    structures
student involvement in the selection process
    134
student learning, link between staff and 196
student mentoring in Hong Kong 161–2
sub-units 51, 57
  and cultural change 56
  and micropolitics 67
  as 'resistance groups' 57
  see also departments

subcultures 51, 57, 69
  and change 56
subjective models of organisational theory 68
successful leadership
  dimensions 8–9
  nature 10–12
supply teachers 152
support staff viii, 31–42
  career structure and development 35–6
  classification 32–3
  designated leaders and managers 34
  effectiveness in leadership and management
    38–41
    general entitlement 39
    need for holistic view 40–1
    recognition of special issues 40
  enhanced status 70
  induction 144
  internal promotion 151
  role viii, 32, 40, 41
  training and development 34–5
    effect on relationships with pupil learners
      196–7
  undervaluing 35, 36–7, 81
  working relationships 37–8
  see also ancillary workers; classroom
    assistants; TAs
symbols 47, 58
  and misrepresentation 57
  and school culture 51–2
synergy in teamwork 112, 118

target-setting in education 16, 24, 28, 190
TAs 32
  responsibility for 34
  and training 194, 197
  working relationship with teachers 37–8, 40
  see also classroom assistants
'Teach First' 138
teacher induction, paradigms 145
teacher learning, as an advantage of teamwork
  118
Teacher Retention Unit (Chicago) 151–2
teachers
  attitudes to performance management 19
  career stages 148
  cultural attitudes to 175
  empowerment 28
  external pressures 20
  ineffective 19
  as learners 196, 197
  non-contact time viii
  reduction in workload 36, 38
  role 32
  status 81
  views on performance assessment in the
    future 183
  views on performance related pay (PRP) 26
  working relationships with support staff
    37–8
  see also associate teachers; headteachers;
    NQTs; supply teachers; unqualified

teachers
teachers' professional portfolios 184
teaching
  as an individual activity 118
  framework of control 119, 120
  shift away from functionalist 182
teaching assistants see TAs
team appraisal 184
team learning 114–15
team members, 'interdependence' 112
team training and development 114–15
team workers 110
teams ix, 107–21
  composition of leadership and management
    108–10
  development of effective 111–14
  development and learning 114–15
  hierarchy 63
  rationale 107–8
teamwork 107
  advantages 117–18, 120
  disadvantages 118–19, 120
  factors leading to successful 120
teamwork in action 115–17
technology
  and co-operation in working relationships
    38
  developments 7
temporary staff
  induction 144
  recruitment and selection 100
  retention 152
testing of children vii, 78–9, 111, 190
threshold assessment 25–6, 82
title, status conferred via 81
training
  for mentoring 166
  for recruitment and selection 131–2
  for school principals in Singapore 162–3
  and staff learning 192, 193
  of support staff 34–5
transactional leadership 11, 19–20, 27
  and performance management 19
transformational leadership 11–12, 19–20, 27,
  111
  effect of government policies 111
  link with human resource management 19
trust, ethos of 184
Tuckman's model of team development 115
turnover 150
'two factor' theory, Herzberg's 77

UK
  approach to education 5
  importance of support staff 31–2
  recruitment and selection 134
  working culture 80
  see also England; Scotland; Wales
undervaluing of support staff 35, 36–7, 81
union representation in the selection process
  134
universalistic approaches to staff selection 55

universities, middle managers 70
'unlearning' 193
unqualified teachers 31
USA
  employee ownership of work 87
  and equal opportunities 93
  mentoring for school leaders 163
    middle school principals 165–6
  micropolitics in high schools 67
  organisational restructuring 65
  performance management 173
    challenges to appraisal outcomes 179
    collection of data 181
  recruitment and selection 134
  and the sharing of learning 199
  support staff 31
  teacher retention 21

values
  heroes and heroines as the embodiment
    52
  and leadership 4, 8–9
  and organisational culture 47–8, 50–1, 56–7,
    58
vision
  development 10
  effect of bureaucratic centralism 5
  implementation 10–11
  and leadership 4, 5, 8–9, 41
  and transformational leadership 11
'vision derived goals' 10
vocational post-compulsory sector of education
  145
Vryburg high school 53

Wales
  mentoring for new principals 163–4, 169
  performance management 24–6
  selection panels 131–2
  and the sharing of learning 199
  use of cash rewards 87
weighting of criteria for selection 134–5
withdrawal from work, link with job
    dissatisfaction 78
women
  and equality in Australia 93
  as headteachers 84
  management styles 96
  quota systems for employment 94
work, employee ownership of 87–8
work cultures 178
  in the UK 80
Workforce Remodelling programme viii
working parties 66
  participation in 68
  patterns 69
Working Together for Success (WTfS) 116–17
workload
  effect of teamwork 119
  reduction in teachers' 36, 38
written policies on recruitment and selection
  128–9
written reports 135
Wu-wei 200

'X' and 'Y' theory, McGregor's 77

Zambia, importance of 'secure human
  relationships' 88